sions. Our messages alter our communication environment; presently, they are becoming increasingly coarse. Selfish cynicism manifest in and propagated by much of today's public communication leaves us less inclined to consider the repercussions of our expressions on our community is depleted, and community is degraded.

Unlike the puritanical sort who condemn and decry the manifestations of Hollywood vulgarity (e.g., breasts, butts, whole bodies, profanity, antiauthoritarian themes), of greater interest about coarseness in public communication are the culture's attitudes that facilitate it. Market logic, when unencumbered by what some might characterize as the quaint sentimentalities of yesteryear, liberates us to cynically communicate whatever and however we want. If we go broke doing it, then its adherents argue that the market has spoken disapprovingly. If we become fabulously rich, on the other hand, the market has nodded its approval. Whether the former was an artistic masterpiece depicting motherly love or the former is a teenage sex-and-drug television program is entirely immaterial to this logic.

Coarseness is our culture's acquiescence to vulgar, aggressive, and unreasonable messages. We acquiesce because we dismiss our own individual judgment as merely subjective, and instead abide by the mythology that the only truth about humans is that we are motivated solely by "rational self-interest." In this post-1960s era of giving voice, practicing tolerance, and embracing diversity our willingness and desire to criticize has been quieted. Who, particularly in academia, wants to be criticized for condemning alternative and unorthodox modes of communication when doing so can be construed as silencing minorities or the underprivileged? Positively, abstaining from criticizing coarse public expression has contributed to unprecedented access by the underrepresented to various means of public expression. Just the same, it has allowed for unprecedented levels of stupidity, nonsense, and noise—and not necessarily by those interests that have recently acquired access.

This book says that it is okay to criticize public expression primarily because much of it is stupid and distracting, and we suggest that a large quantity of this stupidity is either intentional or knowingly permitted. Bill Bennett isn't wrong for criticizing "baby-daddy" paternity tests on *The Maury Show*. There is nothing wrong with Michael Medved applying pressure to the vulgar products of Hollywood. It's even okay for liberals to argue that violence in children's programming is unacceptable, and that linking cartoon leprechauns to cereal brands is unethical. Doing so doesn't concede that all instances of nudity, profanity, violence, and stupidity are unacceptable in public expression. Where many of these critics often go wrong is in failing to recognize their own hypocrisy when they promote free-market ideology as the corrective for society's ills, because the attitude that gave rise to the books, radio programs, and television shows they use when promoting their puffery is no longer contained in the marketplace of branded products. Pecuniary logic is more than existent in realms such as entertainment, politics, and art; it is ubiquitous to the point of simply being the way things are done.

This way of doing things, what we term "market logic," has insinuated its way into all areas of public expression. Modern communication is communication performed to accomplish goals, to complete tasks. Communication, *good* communication, we are taught today is *measured* in market terms. Good is what earns. It's what attracts audience. Good communication gets click-through traffic. Good communication gains compliance, gets votes, attention, sales, mindshare, and so forth. As of this writing, Pope Benedict XIV has 2,195 Twitter followers. Howard Stern has 561,753. Our culture today views other communication outcomes such as achieving truth, harmony, beauty, discovery, illumination, friendship, and love as superfluous and flakey—kumbaya stuff. Today's communication is deemed good or bad by virtue of its ability to achieve desired ends as determined by those seeking the ends. That's it. And when the standards for determining quality communication are reduced solely to efficacy, the old-fashioned notion of responsibility becomes a nonentity, relegated to the concerns of suckers and do-gooders. Thus, Jon Kyl lies in the Senate because it helps achieve his goal of linking anti–Planned Parenthood antipathy to the Democrats' budget position. South Carolina Representative Joe Wilson yells "You lie!" during President Obama's State of the Union address in order, we suggest, to reinforced the idea that home viewer rage is justified and widespread, shared even by members of Congress. Paramount Studios produce tacky films because doing so makes money. Time Warner produces violent and misogynistic rap music because it makes money. It's all effective. But after it is expressed, is the world left unchanged? No.

When computers "interact," other than delivering data back and forth, nothing changes. They don't affect one another's moods. Provided there are no viruses attached, computer-generated messages don't affect how subsequent messages are accepted or interpreted by other computers. Certainly they don't affect unattached computers. They send and receive messages back and forth in predictable and controlled ways. Comparing humans to computers, though commonplace, is an unacceptably simplistic and dehumanizing model for understanding how humans communicate. Humans live in a semantic environment, in a web of meaning, with meanings that change with each message expressed. Hans Georg Gadamer explains that humans interpret messages in what he terms the "hermeneutic circle," a process of moving back and forth from the part to the whole, comparing message with context. Computers don't have context. Humans do, and it isn't static. The contexts within which we communicate are dynamic and are altered by what we contribute to them, particularly when publicly expressed or consumed. As such, others unseen and never to be met can and are affected by our expres-

On April 8, 2011 Arizona Senator Jon Kyl said on the floor of the U.S. Senate, "If you want an abortion, you go to Planned Parenthood, and that's well over 90 percent of what Planned Parenthood does." After being heavily criticized for this grossly inaccurate statement, as the accurate percentage is three[16] (or zero with respect to the use of federal dollars on abortion since federal law outlaws such use), Senator Kyl's office responded to questions from CNN's T. J. Holmes, explaining that "his remark was not intended to be a factual statement, but rather to illustrate that Planned Parenthood, an organization that receives millions of dollars in taxpayer funding, does subsidize abortions."[17] Evidently, during the tense budget negotiations of March and April 2011, Kyl was promoting a reduction to or an altogether end to federal funding for Planned Parenthood. What does Kyl's strategic and intentional use of a public falsehood have to do with Hollywood's excesses? What does it have to do with public coarseness? Everything.

Princeton philosopher Harry Frankfurt would term Kyl's statement "bullshit."[18] Peter Sloterdijk calls is "cynicism."[19] Moralists would call it a lie. Marketers, on the other hand, would likely call it brilliant execution. Jules Henry in his book *Culture against Man* explains that the culture of marketing has become the overall mindset governing how our culture reasons. Advertising talk, or "puffery," which is fraught with absurdly misleading content (though it is at times taken literally) is talk that has no literal meaning. It functions to reinforce a brand's image, impart an edgy quality, or make ad consumption fun and rewarding. Is Snapple really "made from the best stuff on earth?" Is Ragu "America's favorite pasta sauce?" Does Avis really "try harder?" None of these statements are crafted to be believable, but they reinforce an impression about the product. What does this mean that this manner of communicating is being adopted by elected deliberators in the U.S. Senate, and not just in conversation, but on the record, on the floor of the Senate? Or when a Mitt Romney campaign operative explains of political advertising:

> First of all, ads are propaganda by definition. We are in the persuasion business, the propaganda business. . . . Ads are agitprop. . . . Ads are about hyperbole, they are about editing. It's ludicrous for them to say that an ad is taking something out of context. . . . All ads do that. They are manipulative pieces of persuasive art.[20]

Or when Donald Trump advises the continued rhetorical use of the "birther" argument because, as he advised, "People love this issue."[21] This "pecuniary logic," as Henry puts it, is central to Kyl's, the Romney campaign's and Trump's public statements: it's okay because it works, and veracity matters less than function. And that Kyl defense, that his comment wasn't intended to be factual, suggests that this manner of thinking is commonplace, that

ducing proselytizing pictures, without an eye toward margin and profit, they'll be in violation of their corporate charters and may be held liable by their stockholders. Medved, we suspect, is well aware of this. This knowledge is quite likely why he doesn't produce movies, despite his purported ability to portend film market trends. Medved, like Breitbart, Glenn Beck, Sean Hannity, and their ilk, isn't much different from late-night infomercial hucksters pitching get-rich-selling-real-estate systems who make their money selling the get-rich product and not real estate. Medved makes his money by selling his complaints about the very system about which he complains without contributing anything to fix it.

While this book may get catalogued with others critiquing the sorry state of our culture, it is quite different from what readers might find shelved nearby. While we deal with the degradation of public communication, much to the chagrin of Robert Bork at no point will we point our fingers at collectivistic 1960s hippies, primarily because that argument is a bad one. Entertainment companies aren't run by hippies. They are run by capitalists who are responsive to corporate boards, seeking to make money, keep their jobs, and retire with large bonuses—hardly the Woodstock sort. The "Big Six" entertainment companies are run by ambitious and successful capitalists. Time Warner's CEO Jeffrey Bewkes has a Stanford MBA and is on the advisory board for the Yale School of Management.[10] Viacom's CEO Phillippe Dauman is a Yale graduate and a lawyer who helped Sumner Redstone complete a hostile takeover of that company.[11] News Corporation, owner of Fox Entertainment Group, has well-known conservative Rupert Murdoch as its CEO and chairman. Walt Disney Corporation's CEO Robert Iger has been in the entertainment management since 1973 and was ranked as Forbes' third for executive pay in 2011.[12] Sony's CEO Sir Howard Stringer is an Oxford graduate, knight, and decorated Vietnam veteran who worked his way up through CBS's management.[13] Brian Roberts, CEO of Comcast, is a Wharton School of Business graduate[14] and, perhaps more importantly, the son of Comcast's cofounder Ralph Roberts.[15] The notion that any member of this crew is anything less than a full-throated advocate of capitalism is the product of ignorance, willful or otherwise.

Has Hollywood become more crass? Without even looking for empirical support for or against this claim, we accept that it has, though we offer the caveat that past Hollywood eras and pre-Hollywood entertainment has always been racy, albeit in more veiled ways. Yet, people who fixate on and lament these problems alone, we suggest, are capitalizing on a *symptom* simply for short-term political gain. Still, while politicians and other public voices make gains by attacking Hollywood, they often undermine any progress they ostensibly hope to make when equating the symptoms with the cause of the problem by participating in and championing the very system that gave rise to the undesirable behavior.

Indeed, taking such predictable stances against entertainment has become a tried and true political maneuver of the political right ever since the emergence of democracy forced the rich and ruling classes to find ways to distract the masses from material inequity. Quite different from the aforementioned trend, this book makes the argument that entertainment products that draw the most right-wing ire are perhaps the best manifestations of contemporary conservative ideology. Like producing jet engines, lunchboxes, and paper plates, the liberty to produce entertainment that others want is, from a conservative standpoint, sacrosanct, while determinations of value (or lack thereof), beyond ratings and earnings, are deemed merely subjective. American consumers know what they want, proponents of contemporary conservatism argue, and government should be kept small enough to ensure that the innovation that spawns from free markets remains unabated.

In his 1992 book titled *Hollywood vs. America* conservative radio talk show host and film critic Michael Medved argues that the drop in film receipts and movie approval is due, in part, to intensifying "dissatisfaction with the content of the popular culture, rather than the temporary impact of financial hard times."[6] This argument is absurd for a whole list of reasons, but the two most important reasons is that he himself perpetuates the ideology that gives rise to the very motion picture products he laments. In his later work titled *The Five Big Lies about American Business* Medved states, "There's nothing especially honorable about a novelist or painter starving in a garret, or relying on government grants, rather than selling his work at a handsome profit to those who value it."[7] So, if people will pay for smut but ignore moralistic yarns, we can conclude, based upon Medved's criticism, that the smut has value? Medved is a full participant in the same system that gives rise to the cultural products that he laments—contemporary conservatism and market logic. He has the gall to turn around and point his finger at one segment of the capitalist system and say "Shame!"—the very segment from which he makes his own money, and often by maligning it. Sure, *Sister Act* made plenty of money and surprised people, as Medved notes, but if this film was evidence of a groundswell of desire for pro-Judeo-Christian storylines, for instance, then where are the subsequent successes of moral-themed film? Since then, there have been shocking successes like *The Passion of the Christ* and overwhelming turkeys like *Evan Almighty*. There is no trend here, except perhaps what can be found with former child star Kirk Cameron's *Fireproof*, which, like reality television, relied on a tiny budget in order to ensure a higher margin on the few tickets it sold.[8] If we can borrow from Medved and other strict capitalist apologists, these successes and failures can be explained by the simple fact that people prefer *good* movies—*Fireproof*, like *The Passion of the Christ*, is an exception because it was able to rely on free marketing through Evangelical groups, despite the fact that it attracted very negative reviews.[9] As soon as movie production companies start pro-

Introduction: Atlas Slouched

Civilization is the process of setting man free from man.

—Ayn Rand, 1944, *Readers Digest*[1]

Attacks on America's entertainment industry, against everything from publishing, Vaudeville, to Hollywood and the music industry, have become so commonplace that they are as ubiquitous as the content they denounce. In the late nineteenth-century U.S. Postal Inspector and founder of the New York Society for the Suppression of Vice Anthony Comstock was condemning and destroying, among other things, books for being "lewd and lascivious."[2] Soon after, progressives were condemning early film houses as "recruiting stations of vice."[3] In 1947 the chairman of the House Un-American Activities Committee declared Hollywood a "Red propaganda center."[4] Nearly thirty years ago, *Murphy Brown* became a convenient target of Vice President Dan Quayle for daring to have a fictional baby without a fictional husband. In 1995 then-Senator and aspiring presidential hopeful Bob Dole condemned the film industry for producing "nightmares of depravity." More recently, Andrew Breitbart has written a recurring *Washington Times* column with a Hollywood focus and has begun a news website titled BigHollywood.com, both of which decry the lack of artists and quality right-leaning product. Big Hollywood, he explains,

> is not a "celebrity" gabfest or a gossip outpost—it is a continuous politics and culture posting board for those who think something has gone drastically wrong and that Hollywood should return to its patriotic roots.[5]

Contents

Published by Fairleigh Dickinson University Press
Co-published with The Rowman & Littlefield Publishing Group, Inc.
4501 Forbes Boulevard, Suite 200, Lanham, Maryland 20706
www.rowman.com

10 Thornbury Road, Plymouth PL6 7PP, United Kingdom

British Library Cataloguing in Publication Information Available

Library of Congress Cataloging-in-Publication Data
Dalton, Philip.
Coarseness in U.S. public communication / Philip Dalton and Eric Kramer.
p. cm.—(The Fairleigh Dickinson University Press series in communication studies ; 7)
"Co-published with The Rowman & Littlefield Publishing Group."
Includes bibliographical references and index.
ISBN 978-1-61147-503-6 (cloth : alk. paper)—ISBN 978-1-61147-504-3 (electronic)
1. Communication—Political aspects—United States. 2. Communication—Social aspects—United States. 3. Vulgarity—Social aspects—United States. 4. Communication and culture—United States. 5. Mass media and culture—United States. 6. Mass media—Social aspects—United States. 7. United States—Civilization—21st century. I. Kramer, Eric Mark. II. Title.
P95.82.U6D35 2012
302.20973—dc23
2012020150

Printed in the United States of America

Coarseness in U.S. Public Communication

Philip Dalton and Eric Kramer

FAIRLEIGH DICKINSON UNIVERSITY PRESS
Madison • Teaneck

The Fairleigh Dickinson University Press Series In Communication Studies

General Editor: Gary Radford, Department of Communication Studies, Fairleigh Dickinson University, Madison, New Jersey.

The Fairleigh Dickinson University Press Series in Communication Studies publishes scholarly works in communication theory, practice, history, and culture.

Recent Publications in Communication Studies

Philip Dalton and Eric Kramer, *Coarseness in U.S. Public Communication* (2012)

Creede, Catherine, Beth Fisher-Yoshida, and Placida Gallegos (eds.), *The Reflective, Facilitative, and Interpretive Practices of the Coordinated Management of Meaning* (2012)

Aritz, Jolanta and Robyn C. Walker, *Discourse Perspectives on Organizational Communication* (2011)

Groom, S. Alyssa and Fritz, J. M. H, *Communication Ethics and Crisis: Negotiating Differences in Public and Private Spheres* (2011)

MacDougall. R. C., *Digination: Identity, Organization, and Public Life* (2011)

Eicher-Catt, Deborah and Isaac E. Catt (eds.), *Communicology: The New Science of Embodied Discourse* (2010)

Cassino, Dan and Yesamin Besen-Cassino, *Consuming Politics: Jon Stewart, Branding, and the Youth Vote in America* (2009)

On the Web at http://www.fdu.edu/fdupress

Coarseness in U.S. Public Communication

criticism, opinions, and products is the same attitude that packages nudity with violent film themes. It isn't reasonable to be critically selective when arguing that people deserve others to be communicatively responsible. Society either deserves responsible public communication or it doesn't. And if it does, then it isn't just in the realm of entertainment. Our obligation to be responsible to one another also applies to political talk, marketing messages, news-gathering and dissemination, among many areas. Then again, maybe we are being too generous in assuming that these critics are trying to promote reason at all.

Chapter 1 lays out the argument of the book. We begin by explaining in depth what this attitude toward public communication is all about, comparing its instrumental qualities to its expressive potential. In short, market logic has us communicating instrumentally, modeling computers, seeking efficacy and efficiency, all at the expense of both the relationships of which we are aware and the neglected binds we have with strangers. In a world in which the intrinsic value of the other is dismissed in exchange for his/her demonstrable, empirical, and measureable value to *me* (i.e., money), the self becomes paramount. The boundaries of one's ego become determined solely by the ego's resources, and when one's resources are boundless, so is the ego. The financial resources of Donald Trump, Rupert Murdoch, and David Koch bless them with few worldly limits. Their willingness to abide by conventional standards for public comportment is reflected in their promotion of free-market ideology, which frees them from any responsibility for the messages they introduce into the communication environment with their nearly unlimited ability and resources for broadcasting those messages. The freedom to question Obama's birth certificate; to air programs with entertainment has-beens relevant only to the reality TV postcelebrity circuit; propagate partisan, adversarial news talk; and to gin up astro-turfed protest is the price to pay, they might argue, in order to keep the marketplace free to foster the innovation that makes America great.

Tremendously wealthy capitalists are the heroes of the day. They are *players* whose allegiances have gone global, which is to say they have allegiance to no nation at all. After all, what are the benefits of national identity if one can somehow transcend the arbitrary and fickle preferences of a local population (precisely what the WTO is trying to help facilitate)? These egos are greater than ever. These individuals are more important than anyone and everyone else. For them, the rules don't apply. Rupert Murdoch, a once-citizen of Australia who became an American for reasons of media ownership compliance reasons, appealed directly to the FCC to have media ownership rules adjusted for him alone. His wish was granted. [22] Egos like these are exaggerated—hypertrophic.

Chapter 2 considers what the implications of the near-universality of market logic and instrumental communication are on the public sphere. This question is dealt with early in the book because, we suspect, many people equate criticisms of coarseness with classism and ethnic bias, as the enforcement and perpetuation of conventions often works to silence people with less power and access. As the avenues to public communication are more numerous and wide, many more voices gain access to the airwaves, radio and television, and publication. The Internet, though still not universally used, gives anyone with online computer access or a public library a megaphone with which to say or blog whatever s/he wants and to build an audience. These voices, some readers may fear, that communicate through different or opposing conventions, or that have gained access by breaking communicative conventions, may be appearing coarse to us. This *must* be addressed because we fear falling into the trap Herbert Gans describes of applying high culture standards in our criticism; we are, after all, two middle-aged Caucasian men. Nevertheless, it must be okay to criticize and we believe we lay out in this chapter a nuanced and inclusive rationale for doing it. In fact, we warn that a failure to do so surrenders the public sphere to noise and cacophony perpetrated by the privileged.

There is a tension, we maintain, between the democratic necessity of public contestation or oppositional argument and the stability of the communication environment. On the one hand, any governing system approximating a democracy *must* have disruption, contentiousness, and opposition: not just argument but unrest! If political systems ever tend toward stable states, their stability is almost a sure sign that someone *isn't* being heard. The many people who hearken back to the peaceful and prosperous 1950s probably weren't Southern blacks whose voices were systematically quieted. Yet, those who'd argue that the 1960s were combative would likely recognize, in hindsight, the necessity of the conflicts during that period (e.g., civil rights movement, Vietnam protests). Social movements may not always look so good when they are taking place, but the collective ability and willingness to partake is a testament to a democracy's ability to solve its problems and remain legitimate.

That alternative voices should be heard must not be understood to mean that *anything* should be said or tolerated. In fact, critics' silence helps open the floodgates of public communication to everyone and everything, and can help function to render those with important arguments un-listened-to. Numerous voices communicating at the same time, competing, for instance, with endless Internet offerings ranging from cute kitty pictures with adorable quotations (lolcats) to amateur vomit fetish video, keeps audiences small and helps change the subject quickly.

"Silencing" opposition by cluttering the public sphere facilitates Jurgen Habermas's refeudalization.[23] Among the ways fabulously wealthy elites stand to gain from a coarse public sphere is if the noise and stupidity of it all undermines the public's ability to sustain conversations and to coalesce a critical and active mass. Here, we outline three observations. First, public coarseness begets public coarseness. Given our description of the communication environment, messages have the effect of influencing the environment by normalizing themselves by virtue of their presence. Second, we argue that coarseness disrupts public conversational continuity. We change subjects from national debt, to creating Medicare vouchers, to complaining about pink toenail paint on a boy in a J. Crew catalogue.[24] The voracious appetite of the twenty-four-hour news cycle necessitates new information—not an informed citizenry and the result is that no topic can "run its course," so to say. Shocking news is conveyed just long enough for us to be dismayed. Third, we introduce the contention that privileged, mainstream, public communicators have co-opted the rhetoric of contestation.

The general and theoretical discussion of coarseness in chapter 2 is followed by chapter 3's closer examination of coarseness in the context of politics. News of politics may be the first place that readers become aware of coarseness. Norman Rockwell paintings never seem to convey the strife often seen in country's best democratic moments. Politics is a messy matter, and such pacific images of it create unrealistic expectations. Still, there's an important distinction to be made between political discord and what we describe as the strategic performance of stupidity and tumult for purposes of generating political confusion.

After Representative Gabrielle Giffords was shot in the head by Jared Loughner people on both sides of the political aisle engaged in something like a debate—to the extent that a debate can be executed today—regarding the role of extreme antigovernment rhetoric. Democrats claimed that Republican talk contributed to the shooting,[25] while conservatives dismissed the claim, believing instead that Loughner was a madman.[26] We wonder why a madman would target a representative. He could have shot at clouds, books, or kittens. Instead, he shot a politician in the head. Why did he have a gun in the first place? If his behavior was truly the random acts of a madman, the odds that his bullet would be planted in the head of a U.S. representative are astronomical. As such, we maintain that the communication environment cultivated these outcomes, and that those who contribute to anger and intolerance toward opponents are culpable in this assassination attempt. This communication evidences market logic and its attendant instrumental communication that seeks to effect political outcomes without consideration for the long-term consequences of what people say.

This chapter examines three components of our communication system: politicians, our media, and the voters themselves. The careful observer can find evidence of both the player mentality and the consequences of market logic in and through all three. Our politicians, for instance, are blatantly influenced by the rich, deny assistance to the lower classes on principle, discard principle in order to deliver for business, and do it all while marketing themselves as just like you and me. Delaware candidate for U.S. Senate Christine O'Donnell isn't a witch. She tells us, "I'm you." Her performance was no less cynical and contrived as Andover, Yale, and Harvard graduate George W. Bush's 1999 purchase of his ranch in Crawford, Texas just before running for president.[27] Eager politicians don't shoulder all of the blame; the media is equally complicit in the coarsening of politics. Facing numerous changes to the realities of the media marketplace, most notably Reagan's 1987 repeal of the Fairness Doctrine, the news media has had to adapt to profit motive and fragmented audiences caused by growing channels and competitive multimedia. The changes have redefined what constitutes news and has degraded the role of the media in informing the citizenry. Finally, this section considers the role of voters in the coarsening of political communication. Specifically, when political communication becomes increasingly personal, oppositional without issues, and volatile, voters become more than victims to the system, but also participants in it. We describe how politically savvy citizens participate as guerillas in cynical media performances of disruption and rage. And while many readers may applaud such citizen activism as a sign of political health, we note that these performances aren't done to advance or articulate arguments, but to control and confuse public discussion.

Confusion in public discussion is, to the extent that coarseness is propagated intentionally, one of its most insidious consequences. Whereas conservatives once lamented the deterioration of the public forum, we maintain that the assumptions underlying contemporary conservatism aligns it with many of the forces contributing to its deterioration. Chapter 4 lays out our argument that public coarseness (e.g., absurdity, vulgarity, fragmentation, anger) works to the advantage of elites. While in chapter 1 we explain that coarseness functions to disrupt the continuity of public discussion, chapter 4 goes into greater depth, showing how thoroughly embedded the mainstream regime of coarseness is. We proceed from the assumption that the status quo is difficult to alter within our democratic system, that a critical mass is much more difficult to muster, if the subject is constantly changed. Moreover, if the normative means with which to critique public communication are abandoned (critical thinking and focused reason), public efforts to counter the status quo in politics get dismissed as self-serving campaigning.

Chapter 4 considers four topics related to the state of public reasoning in the United States today. First, we look at the history of reason, describing its central role in helping Western society emerge from the Dark Ages, thus establishing the foundation for the democratic freedoms and responsibilities we enjoy today. Second, we evidence the collapse of reason in contemporary political discourse. Public arguments made today, particularly by today's political "mind guard"[28] of America's economic elite, rely on the suspension of criticism and historical ignorance, as well as acquiescence and indifference. Too often our politicians and their surrogates make little sense, and in the case of Jon Kyl, their statements need not even be true. Third, we describe the parallels between public communication described in this section and the "pecuniary logic" of Jules Henry. Veracity as we once knew it is being supplanted by truth as determined by what we more broadly term "market logic," that what sells, what works, what gains audience is "true," or true-right-now. Finally, we outline our position that this kind of coarse reasoning, this constant heated, disrupted, contentious, and unreasoned discourse is laying the groundwork for the new regime of "pharaonic rule," a manner of governance that concedes authority to leaders because of some presumed God-like or extra-human quality that is reinforced by modern public communication techniques and acquiescent yes-men who publicly perform confidence and deference to the contradictory and ill-supported dictates of their leader.

Art is a canary in every culture's coalmine. One might conclude that a culture that produces beautiful things isn't likely to be coarse. Likewise, a culture busy producing cheap and ugly things, and that loses the ability to appreciate beautiful artwork, is coarser by comparison. Quite in keeping with market logic, this chapter maintains that art has been almost exclusively redefined as value—money. We see this definition of art playing out in the recurring Iowa debate over whether the state legislature should force the University of Iowa to sell its Jackson Pollack painting *Mural*. Republicans in the Iowa state legislature, namely State Representative and Character Counts! Executive Director Scott Raecker, argue that the painting's value warrants breaking Iowa's promise to the late Peggy Guggenheim not to sell it. Their proposal was to sell the painting, valued roughly at $140 million, and redirect that money toward scholarships. It is estimated that an endowment funded by the sale could annually fund as many as one thousand scholarships. In response to this, University of Iowa art and art history professor Christopher Roy stated, "It would be a disgrace to a civilized place such as Iowa. Whoever did such a thing would go down in history as one of the most disgraceful people in the history of the state."[29] We fear, given the prevalence of market logic, Roy will eventually lose this battle in an age of cities and states selling off their public assets: buildings, skyways, and street parking.[30] In fulfillment of Ayn Rand's vision of civilization (noted in the quotation opening the introduction), public assets are being sold and privatized, thus freeing *rich* men and women from their obligations to their fellow men and women. Note that the most recent proposal to sell the painting emerged without any exigent need for revenue. Nor was there any mention of the potential loss to the state. The painting, to Raecker, is quite simply a honey-pot of untapped cash.

Raecker displays a complete lack of appreciation for beauty, skill, or insight, which we argue in chapter 5 comes with little surprise. We live in a day and age in which there is little appreciation for anything more than convenience, money, and efficiency. Today, we operate under the assumption that *anyone* can make art. And while it may seem elitist to make such a remark, even famous street artist Banksy has recently stated his position that everyone *can't* make art. Some of what poses as art today devalues the skill, ability, time, and effort needed to make something new and beautiful. We argue, however, that a society that fails to appreciate skill writ large loses its ability to empathize. We've devalued gratitude. The *process* of work has become vastly underappreciated because our culture approaches process simply as something to be reduced; the time and expense it takes to make something with quality and beauty is to be defeated. What we make is reduced solely to its function and then mass produced. Unions are under attack simply because of their cost. Four unskilled laborers are cheaper than one well-trained and highly skilled specialist. The beauty, for instance, of the handmade Pierre Le Bourgeois flintlock gun made for Louis the XIII with inlay and crowned monogram of the king is replaced today by the pure functionality of the all-black 25mm magazine-fed XM25 airburst laser sited smartgun grenade launcher that explodes ordnance above the heads of the enemy. The XM25 is built by ATK, which prides itself on driving "efficiencies through continuous improvement in our processes and procedures."[31] As we look at art, we find that after World War II, art, pop art in particular, has increasingly become self-referential, critical, ideological self-parody. As a consequence, little more than saleable value is taken seriously. What sells is good. Selling *Mural* is good.

What institutions, if any, ever kept coarse public expression in check? Certainly, one can't deny the role of morality and its proponents (e.g., religion) providing a kind of dialectical counterforce. Religion, we might expect, ought to keep the forces of greed, egoism, and selfishness in balance. Chapter 6 considers religion in the present moment and finds that it shows signs of evolving to accommodate market logic realities. Recently, secular Mormon entertainer and political commentator Glenn Beck offered America a revised definition of "social justice,"

Here's my definition of social justice: Forced redistribution of wealth with a hostility toward individual property rights, under the guise of charity and/or justice.[32]

Beck's point is to argue that the only legitimate means of remedying suffering is through a church, not the government. He goes on to explain that Obama and others cunningly appeal to American morality in order to pass legislation that redistributes wealth. The problem with his argument is that redistributing wealth through government *does* help alleviate social-justice issues inasmuch as it puts food in the mouths of people who can't afford it. Nevertheless, leaving it to religion leaves the individual giver as the agent; ultimately s/he gets to choose how much (if anything), to whom, how, and for what purpose money will be given, as well as what will be received in exchange (e.g., deference to God, attendance at church). We don't believe Beck's maligning of social-justice imperatives is indicative of attitudes held by most traditional and mainline Protestant churches, but these churches are, for the most part, shrinking. Catholics in the United States are holding steady because of Catholic immigration from Central and South America, but many other more traditional churches are finding their numbers falling while their overhead costs are growing. Competing against them is an entirely new model of religion—postdenominational mega-churches. These are growth-oriented churches, many of which are run by MBAs. With one or two pastors for congregations of more than 2,500, these churches have high margin, and are thus very profitable. They offend nearly no one by displaying little or no Christian symbolism, rarely mentioning the Bible, and talking very little of sin and obligation. Combining public messages condemning the contemporary use of "social justice" by Christian politicians with the ethos of the postdenominational mega-church and you effectively remove society's strongest barriers to unabated market logic.

In chapter 6, we argue that postdenominational Christianity reflects the altered metaphysical assumptions regarding humanity's relationship with God. Medieval paintings, mosaics, and tapestries quite often show Christ in the center and larger than the others depicted. Others populating creation are arranged around Him, depicting spatially their relationship to Him. Flanked by angels, Christ often finds the people of the earth smaller and at or beneath his feet. Hierarchically, people are beneath Christ. Heaven's perfection is to be modeled on earth. We tailor our behaviors after His desires. Today, we contend, this relationship has flipped. People are drawn to the likes of Joel Osteen because of his "name it and claim it" theology. We no longer exist for God, but God exists for us. Poor? Put your faith in "increase," and claim wealth! Claim that promotion! Marriage failing? Go to the mega-church and join their marriage-counseling group. Alcoholic? Join their twelve-step program. You may even be able to have your tires changed. Church and God serve me, not the other way around. And worse, others become a measurable commodity just like plate collections. The Holy Spirit expresses His approval through the growth of the flock; increasing church attendance, for instance, is both an end and a sign of God's approval. Likewise, I wouldn't have wealth if it wasn't with God's sanction. Therefore, one can conclude that *how* attendance is increased or *how* wealth is generated is immaterial.

Thus, even religion, we find, has acquiesced to our late-modern market logic ethos. While Protestants believe in varying combinations of the *solas* (e.g., *sola scriptura, sola fide, sola gratia*) no mainline Protestant faith has succumbed to abandoning Christ as the center of the faith and the belief that a Christ-like life is demonstration of God's grace. Considering the increasing amount of emphasis Protestants place upon the individual, relative to Roman Catholicism, in the worship of Christ, this is a feat. It would take considerable changes in the culture, changes that position the ego firmly in the center of the cosmos, before an E. W. Kenyon "Word of Faith" church could find the soil within which to take solid root. Today's rapidly growing postdenominational churches are manifestations of the very worst combinations of late-modern Christian theologies. The deemphasis on learned and trained clergy and the underscoring of individual communication with God, individual priesthood, channeling the Holy Spirit through feelings, combined with the potential antinomian consequences of the *Sola Fide* doctrine come to full expression in churches like Osteen's.

Quite often the first target of criticism in arguments like ours is entertainment. "Family values" criticism of entertainment content is widespread, often maintaining, for instance, that television and music are corrupting influences on our children. While we don't have reason to disagree with this, our argument is considerably different. In chapter 7 we begin by accepting the contention that many of our culture's entertainment products are coarse, and then proceed from there. We direct the bulk of our argument instead toward the defenses of entertainment products. The people who produce and distribute entertainment rarely defend the content on its merits, and instead retreat to a procedural position that they have a right to produce it and that we have a right to choose it, or not. With this argument, entertainment CEOs fail to clash with their critics. From an argumentative standpoint this is a nonresponse. An evasion. From a rhetorical standpoint, we believe the way the argument is employed is rich with meaning.

We term the "we can do it, you can choose it" defense of entertainment content the "entertainment market-as-democracy meme." The entertainment marketplace functions like a democracy, we are told. Ostensibly, this means that "the people" or "consumers" get what the majority wants. The meme is an effective rhetorical instrument because of our culture's attitude toward most anything that is accused of limiting democracy and choice. An "elite" found condemning a television show, for example, is dismissed for his/her arrogance; his/her opinion is merely subjective. "Who are you to tell all of us what we can or cannot watch?" We actually appreciate the sentiment, yet the reality is that people *are* in the position of determining what we can and cannot watch every single day. What are the values governing their decisions?

The entertainment market-as-democracy meme, while being rhetorically powerful, has important flaws that betray its cynical purpose: to condition the public to reject any actual exercise of power over the industry. The meme is predicated on the inherent value, even wisdom, of majority preference, something most conservatives and elites reject out of hand in the political arena. The meme also ignores the reality that the majority *doesn't* rule in the entertainment marketplace. Some television shows, even widely popular ones, are cancelled or never aired because they are too politically provocative. A show need only be more profitable than another, not more watched. Some audiences, "voters," are more important than others. For example, televised golf gets awful ratings, but it has the virtue of being watched by wealthy audiences with expendable income. The meme also promotes a version of democracy that applauds self-interested voting, an idea quite often opposed by conservatives as anathema to the true intent of democracy. This democratic marketplace rhetoric puts its faith in regulatory power of the invisible hand of the marketplace, absolving entertainment producers of public-interest obligations. It also shifts blame for coarse products from the producers to the consumers.

The book sums with an argument about our culture's cynicism, defined according to Peter Sloterdijk's definition of the term.[33] Sloterdijk's notion of cynicism manifests among elites as an attitude toward truth that treats it as inconsequential. These elites, or players, have, Sloterdijk explains, an "enlightened false consciousness," a product of modern ideological criticism. Material wealth is real while every other way of sizing up reality is manufactured, inconsistent, and contradictory. Cynically, elites promote an ideology of hedonism or self-interest. Our communication environment, shaped by the elites who shape our superstructure, fosters the cultural attitude that the only truth about human behavior is that we are motivated by selfishness. Selfishness is a natural law, and altruism is a chimera. We are taught that acting in our "rational self-interest" is pragmatic and that the aggregate behaviors of our citizens and consumers generate reason. This is both produced by and helps reproduce the hypertrophic individualism that we identify as the root cause for the coarseness evidenced throughout this book. We end by warning that we are entering a Third Sophistic period characterized by communication that views lying and deception as strategic and wise. Truth in this period is determined less by evidence and reason than by aggregate approval. This, we maintain, is resulting in troubling consequences for both our democratic system and in the material quality of life for the people living in it.

NOTES

1. Ayn Rand, "The Only Path to Tomorrow," *Readers Digest*, January 1944, 88–90.

2. Wayne Edison Fuller, *Morality and the Mail in Nineteenth-Century America* (Champaign: University of Illinois Press, 2003), 175.

3. Karen Ward Mahar, *Women Filmmakers in Early Hollywood* (Baltimore, MD: Johns Hopkins University Press, 2006), 67.

4. Nora Sayre, "Assaulting Hollywood," *World Policy Journal* 12 (Winter 1995–1996): 51.

5. Andrew Breitbart, "Breitbart: A Million Stories to Tell," *Washington Times*, January 5, 2009, www.washingtontimes.com/news/2009/jan/05/a-million-stories-to-tell/.

6. Michael Medved, *Hollywood vs. America* (New York: Harper, 1993), xviii.

7. Michael Medved, *The Five Big Lies about American Business: Combating Smears against the Free Market Economy* (New York: Random House, 2009), 28.

8. James Russell, "Evangelical Audiences and 'Hollywood' Film: Promoting *Fireproof* (2008)," *Journal of American Studies* 44 (2010): 391–407.

9. Russell, "Evangelical Audiences," 391–407.

10. "Jeffrey L. Bewkes," Time Warner Corporation, www.timewarner.com/our-company/management/senior-corporate-executives/jeffrey-l-bewkes/.

11. Peter Lattman, "Sumner Redstone's Longtime Lawyer is Viacom's New CEO," *Wall Street Journal*, September 5, 2006, blogs.wsj.com/law/2006/09/05/sumner-redstones-longtime-lawyer-is-viacoms-new-ceo/.

12. "Robert A. Iger," *Forbes*. people.forbes.com/profile/robert-a-iger/79382.

13. Katherine Griffiths, "Sir Howard Stringer, U.S. Head of Sony: Sony's Knight Buys Tinseltown Dream," *Independent*, September 18, 2004, www.independent.co.uk/news/business/news/sir-howard-stringer-us-head-of-sony-sonys-knight-buys-tinseltown-dream-546718.html.

14. "Brian L. Roberts," The Comcast Corporation, www.comcast.com/corporate/about/pressroom/corporateoverview/corporateexecutives/brianroberts.html.

15. Parija Bhatnagar, "Comcast's Roberts: Hungry for More," CNNMoney, February 11, 2004, money.cnn.com/2004/02/11/news/companies/comcast_roberts/index.htm.

16. "Planned Parenthood at a Glance," Planned Parenthood, accessed April 18, 2011, www.plannedparenthood.org/about-us/who-we-are/planned-parenthood-glance-5552.htm.

17. Steve Benen, "Not Intended to Be a Factual Statement," *Washington Monthly*, www.washingtonmonthly.com/archives/individual/2011_04/028869.php.

18. Harry Frankfurt, *On Bullshit* (Princeton, NJ: Princeton University Press, 2005).

19. Peter Sloterdijk, *Critique of Cynical Reason* (Minneapolis: University of Minnesota Press, 1987).

20. Thomas Edsall, "The Reinvention of Political Morality," *New York Times*, December 5, 2011, campaignstops.blogs.nytimes.com/2011/12/05/the-reinvention-of-political-morality/?hp.

21. Evan McMorris-Santoro, "Trump Warns Cantor Not to Give up Birther Fight: 'People Love This Issue.'" TPM, tpmdc.talkingpointsmemo.com/2011/04/the-donald-warns-republicans-not-to-give-up-the-birther-fight.php.

22. Jayson Blair, "FCC to Waive Rules for Acquisition by Murdoch," *New York Times*, July 21, 2001.

23. Jurgen Habermas, *The Structural Transformation of the Public Sphere*, trans. Thomas Burger and Frederick Lawrence (Cambridge: MIT Press, 1991).

24. Susan Donaldson James, "J. Crew Ad with Boy's Pink Toenails Creates Stir," ABC News, April 13, 2011, abcnews.go.com/Health/crew-ad-boy-painting-toenails-pink-stirs-transgender/story?id=13358903.

25. David Gewirtz, "Heated Rhetoric, Social Networks, and Armed Psychos: A Deadly Combination?" ZDNew Government, www.zdnet.com/blog/government/heated-rhetoric-social-networks-and-armed-pyschos-a-deadly-combination/9845.

26. See, for instance, Charles Krauthammer on *The O'Reilly Factor* January 11, 2011, www.foxnews.com/on-air/oreilly/transcript/charles-krauthammer-analyzes-jared-loughner.

27. Bill Minutaglio, "Bush Buys Land near Crawford: Town Expects Changes after 1,500-Acre Deal," *Dallas Morning News*, August 10, 1999.

28. Irving Janis, *Groupthink* (Orlando, FL: Houghton Mifflin, 1972).

29. Allie Johnson, "Bill Would Force UI to Sell $140 Million Pollack Painting," *Daily Iowan* February 10, 2011.

30. Emily Thornton, "Roads to Riches," *Businessweek*, May 7, 2007, www.businessweek.com/magazine/content/07_19/b4033001.htm.

31. "Our Values," ATK, www.atk.com/Values/values_ourvalues.asp.

32. Glenn Beck, "What is Social Justice," FOX News, www.foxnews.com/story/0,2933,589832,00.html.

33. Peter Sloterdijk, *Critique of Cynical Reason*, trans. by Michael Eldred (Minneapolis: University of Minnesota Press, 1988).

Chapter One

Noise, Fragmentation, and Absurdity in U.S. Public Communication

Community leaders, figures in our community need to say "look, we can't stand for this." This is a situation where—people don't—they really need to realize that the rhetoric and firing people up and, you know, even things, for example, we're on Sarah Palin's targeted list. But the thing is that the way that she has it depicted has the crosshairs of a gunsight over our district. And when people do that, they've gotta realize there's consequences to that action.

—Rep. Gabrielle Giffords, March 25, 2010, *The Daily Rundown*[1]

The truth of the matter is that there has been, I think, a coarsening of our political dialogue that I've been running against since I got into politics.

—President Barack Obama, September 13, 2009, *60 Minutes*[2]

Conservatives have been arguing for quite a while that the public sphere is being tainted by smut, filth, violence, and vulgarity. Lamenting our low public standards at the highest levels, in 1998 Bill Bennett wrote in *The Death of Outrage*:

Bill Clinton's presidency is also defining public morality down. Civilized society must give public affirmation to principles and standards, categorical norms, notions of right and wrong. Even though public figures often fall short of these standards—and we know and we expect some will—it is nevertheless crucial that we pay tribute to them.[3]

Six years later on the floor of the U.S. Senate, Vice President Dick Cheney advised Democratic Senator Patrick Leahy, "Fuck yourself." Cheney, who was doubling that day in his role as Senate president, uttered these words on the same day that the Republican-led Senate passed the Defense of Decency Act by a vote of ninety-nine to one.[4]

This book could be about the fact that a vice president would say such a thing in a formal and public environment. It could also be about the role of the Senate in "defending" decency. Those phenomena aren't, in our opinions, very important or interesting. More interesting about the *Washington Post* that covered the story about Cheney, from our standpoint, is that it made its way into a newspaper at all. We don't know enough to say whether senators and other public officials use vulgarity when they think microphones are off and away, but we suppose that they do. Still, devoting column inches on the fourth page of your paper to reveal that a vulgarity was uttered in a semiprivate exchange has meaning in and of itself. In what kind of culture has "Fuck yourself!" become news?

Paul Farhi of the *Washington Post* noted in a column that in 1936 President Franklin Delano Roosevelt collapsed on his way on stage to accept the Democratic nomination when his leg braces snapped. Nobody reported it. That's quite a bit of restraint by today's standards. Sixty years later, Farhi noted, "153 dailies, 7 TV networks, 9 wire services and two comedy shows" covered Senator and Republican presidential nominee Bob Dole's fall from a stage during a campaign stop in 1996.[5] Whereas journalists once refused to snap photographs of presidents smoking, today's photographers, journalists, and editors seem quite pleased to catch an image of a president doing something less than flattering. Someone captured video of George W. Bush picking his nose at a Rangers game. David Letterman regularly showed video of Bush spitting on the White House lawn. Pictures of President Obama smoking in college while wearing a Panama-style hat circulated quickly in the media. *Time* magazine posted the Obama pictures in their online photo feature titled "Obama: The College Years."[6] Andrea Mitchell of MSNBC reported on the *Time* photos.[7] Now the pictures are ubiquitous on the Internet, with many people speculating about the contents of the cigarette.

We believe that the change in media and journalism over this period of time reflects a phenomenon that is much more significant and goes well beyond the media's freer use of rough language and pervasiveness of violent and sex-themed entertainment. This phenomenon manifests in the realms of deceptive advertising, misleading business practices, equivocating political talk, unfair competition, lack of appreciation for skill, ability, and quality, and comportment. Its consequences are cynicism: a prevalent public attitude that measures all things according to the self. We believe there is a coarsening of the public sphere writ large. As we proceed we will make reference to both public communication and public discourse. The former includes all sorts of public expression, and subsumes the latter. The latter, more precisely, involves public discussion for purposes of decision making. Furthermore, we believe that this cynicism manifests as an overall abandonment of concern for community impact for public expressions. No one can argue that showing a picture of President Obama smoking as a young man or a report of a vice president swearing are adequate evidence, by themselves, of public coarsening. We will, however, make the case that when one looks at public communication in general a significant change in what is deemed publicly acceptable is seen.

This book, however, is focused less on evidencing the coarsening of public discourse, and is devoted more to understanding the nature and significance of that coarsening. More precisely, we want to know *what* is going on, what *motivates* the changes we are seeing, and what these changes *mean*. In this book, we argue that, in essence, Bill Bennett didn't identify a problem with America when he complained about President Clinton's honesty and sexual habits. Instead, Bennett was a manifestation of the problem he, perhaps strategically, misdiagnosed in his book on the demise of public outrage. His contributions to the Clinton-Lewinsky discussion helped perpetuate a public discussion of a man's private sexual activity, while misplacing the blame on the so-called excesses of the 1960s liberal grass smokers. Moreover, it encouraged a visceral and public response to matters deemed by the likes of Bennett to be inappropriate. The irony here is that feminist efforts to make private matters legitimate grist for the critical mill have helped open the door for conservatives to make hay out of their adversaries' private lives.

COARSENESS

Coarseness is defined for our purposes as communication that reflects the public's use of and acquiescence to vulgar, aggressive, and unreasonable messages. The coarsening of public communication is most apparent in messages that are confrontational, emotional, shocking, titillating, misleading, and inaccurate, but these manifestations are just the surface of the larger phenomenon. Individual public messages that people find inappropriate are symptoms of something larger. It is easy to lose sight of the true problem if we fixate on the traces of coarseness.

The kinds of public messages we address in this book reflect a largely unexamined attitude toward the self, the Other, the public, the public sphere, toward a community ethic that regulates the public messages that people produce and direct toward each other. Desmond Morris insists that humans are biologically predisposed to being altruistic, but that present-day urban environments train this out of us.[8] Lewis Mumford argued that the "sprawling isolation" of our modern environments "proved an even more effective method of keeping a population under control."[9] But whereas Mumford believed that centralizing mass communication's control in the hands of a select few effectively surrendered control, Harvard law school fellow David Weinberger offers an alternative perspective on modern communication that informs this book. Bypassing the spatial demands of paper, Weinberger argues in *Everything Is Miscellaneous* that our digital era has erased the need to accommodate information to all but personal organizational schemes. Today, he argues, we are experiencing:

> a startling change in our culture's belief that truth means accuracy, effectiveness requires adherence to clear lines of command and control, and knowledge is power.[10]

Coupled with Morris's concerns about urban alienation, Weinberger's observations are more disconcerting. Not only do our modern physical, political, and economic environments foster radical individualism, but even our information infrastructure is undermining the notion of authority. *Nobody is wrong.*

Throughout this book, we describe the predominant contemporary attitude toward communication as ends-oriented communication. Here, we draw a careful distinction between interaction intended to maintain social relationships (expressive communication) and communication intended to perform tasks (instrumental communication). Whereas any message can be said to do both, different messages are oriented differently toward the Other. A parent thinks when watching his teenage child talk on the phone for hours on a school night that it is possible for absolutely nothing to be accomplished despite hours devoted to talk. Of course, the teenager would disagree; perhaps a friendship was further cemented or caring was indirectly expressed. In the case of the phone call, the teenager and the friend are being-with; they've become a "We" rather than a "you and I." Concern for time is abandoned; it becomes inconsequential. Contrast this with the adult who schedules a fifteen-minute call to Mother on her birthday. While the call reflects a desire to maintain the relationship, the amount of time devoted is arbitrary and it cannot sustain being-with. The time spent isn't governed by the content of the conversation, how Mom feels, what she has to say, or even how much the child loves her. The call is an item on a list of things to do; an obligation satisfied minimally. The example of the teen is relatively more expressive. The adult, on the other hand, functions in this scenario much more instrumentally. Communication is performed to accomplish an objective, a function, an operation in the daily administration of mechanical time.

The difference between instrumental communication and expressive communication is very similar to approaching communication as a means or end, respectively. Increasingly, we believe, the messages that people criticize for their vulgarity evidence a transparent desire to accomplish one's own ends. More importantly, this approach to communicating reflects a flawed modern conception of interaction that separates message, sender, and receiver. Once separation is achieved, the receiver becomes an object to be acted upon. A U.S. representative telling a constituent at a town hall meeting, "I wouldn't dignify you by peeing on your leg"[11] ; a professional tennis player at the U.S. Open telling a line judge, "I swear to God I'll fucking take the ball and shove it down your fucking throat"[12] ; a musician interrupting a reward-recipient's acceptance speech to announce his feelings that another artist, ostensibly more deserving, "had one of the best videos of all time!"[13] ; bumper stickers reading, "If you can read this, you are too close, ASSHOLE!"; energy drinks named *Bawls*; rubber testicles dangling from a pickup's tow hitch; and so forth, accomplish the ends of the messenger. In some cases, messengers are just relieving tension. In others, messengers are branding themselves as edgy, even threatening. The pickup's driver finds the offense of others entertaining. In each of these instances, their own ends are paramount. This is evident either in the content of the expression or in the decision to express the content at all.

HYPERTROPHIC INDIVIDUALISM

The point of this book isn't to blame the mass media for reducing our defenses against our more puerile desires for coarse forms of entertainment, though we don't deny that it plays some role. Blaming mass media is much too easy, and it misses much of what is going on throughout, behind, and beyond the media. Blame stems more from the vulgarization of Adam Smith's ideas than it does with modernization of Guglielmo Marconi's inventions. Our thesis throughout this book is that capitalism, as it manifests in the United States today, has helped foster and encourage a gross form of individualism, what we term "hypertrophic individualism." Individualism is a sense of self that is separate from the collective. It becomes hypertrophic, or exaggerated, when the individual sees himself or herself as entirely abstracted from any obligation to the Other. This is the downside of liberation and progress in the sense promoted by the liberal tradition. Progress is always a movement away from something and liberation from the group means being freed from obligations. But those same bonds of obligation sustain the very same individual who wants to abandon them in the name of self-efficacy and self-determination. It is ultimately naïve and, in fact, demonstrably false to believe that any one of us can have a modern lifestyle without thousands of others making it possible.

Hypertrophic individualism is a delusion, meaning that it is not an accurate appraisal of reality. Humans need emotional and physical support. We remain highly social animals. But the desire for control, the will-to-power distilled into a social fragment, the individual, is an immature childhood fantasy. The more this fantasy is pursued and promoted, the greater our alienation becomes. The relationships that we develop based on our own fickle terms deny the needs of the Other. The genuine Other, the authentic Other is not a TV channel that can be consumed on a whim and then switched off. Still, in a world of hypertrophic individualism the world is a field of play occupied by objects with whom we interact for the purpose of meeting our individual needs.

Hypertrophic individualism is an understanding of the self characterized by the assumption that the individual is the measure of all things; thus obligation has no intrinsic positive aspect. That which has no relevance to me or to my ends doesn't matter. One possessing this attitude believes s/he can transcend the dated and old-fashioned attitudes that have people perceiving themselves as bound to others, tradition, community, employer, employee, team, family, or honor, for instance. Or, one can remain "blinded" by these seemingly outmoded and "unproductive" ways of relating to others and understanding self. The former, in its extreme form, is what we term a "player." A player possesses a mentality that views the world and its contents as completely abstracted from self. The world is a resource base available for manipulation at will—a field of lifeless building blocks with which to make whatever one wishes. This includes the formation of networks of others. People are reduced to a single term, a single narrow and abstract function such as "labor" or "consumer." The player defines others in accord with his/ her own interests as they are narrowly conceived. He views him/herself as transcending quaint collective obligations, and instead pursues profit at any and all costs. Thus, as George Homans contends, all human relationships are assessed based upon a purely selfish cost/benefit analysis. [14] This is the transfer of a simple economic model to human existence. Everything is reduced to rewards or punishments.

Human socialization is thus reduced to conditioning, training, rather than mentoring toward what chivalry called the "gentle heart," or to what the classicists (e.g., Joseph Campbell) called wisdom and virtue. [15] According to social exchange theory no one does anything unless there is a net gain for their ego-interest. So if a marriage, a business partnership, or a friendship seems to involve more "costs" than "benefits," then it is rational to abandon it. According to this worldview, sacrifice, true altruism is a fiction. Even Christ's sacrifice can be seen as a net gain for him personally as his sacrifice is the price paid to rewrite a covenant with man that will repopulate the heavens with the souls of his worshippers. He attains eternal hero status, historically profound esteem, adoration and worship, divine status and glory. Minimally he defeats sin. In this worldview any true altruism is a failure to secure personal advantage and is irrational—a mistake. To be a hero is stupid, or it is a mistake in calculation.

In this world of zero-sum calculus, the hypertrophic individual is "abstracted" from the world in which s/he lives. This means that his/her attitude toward the world, its institutions, and its inhabitants are determined by personal, ego interest. They have value or consequence only insofar as they are exploitable by the individual to support personal desire. Real allegiance to anything beyond personal interest is a misstep. Everything exists only as an operation that can yield measureable results toward a desired end. We see this, for instance, in the globalization of world markets, the collapse of trade barriers, corporate relocation to international tax havens, the abandonment of international obligations and institutions. Relocating a corporation's headquarters to an island nation P.O. box in order to avoid taxes is good business, but bad citizenship (except according to Randian logic; the ideology that if each individual pursues his or her selfish interests all will magically end well). Fleeing the IRS reflects a complete lack of allegiance to the nation in which much of its raw materials, labor, and lucrative markets are found. The CEO of this imaginary corporation may be hailed for her brilliant and bold money-saving move. Such a move reflects cultural values that have begun to manifest at the level of the work-a-day individual. Our culture encourages individuals to maximize their personal power. If in need, we are taught to think, no one else will respond to your call of distress; you shouldn't respond either. Experts advise women in case of assault to not yell "help" or "rape" because no one will respond. Instead yell "fire" because they will respond to a threat to their own property.[16] Rugged individualism is characterized by the thought that community is for sissies, or harmless losers. Under such an ideology we risk plunging into a Hobbesian darkness of all-against-all.

This perspective helps us understand what happened at Enron, for instance. In 2000, Enron was caught up in a scandal that involved manipulating the California energy markets. Enron lobbied then-Senator Phil Gramm to deregulate the California energy market. After the California Deregulation Plan was passed and power provision became competitive, Enron orchestrated a bogus collapse in available energy by enticing power companies to shut down power plants to perform unnecessary maintenance during times of high demand. This artificially drove up power prices, further enriching Enron. It resulted in thirty-eight blackouts. The utter disregard for the Other is demonstrated in the recorded Enron phone calls that were released evidencing the company's efforts to shut down the power plants. These calls give voice, literally, to the ideology that only stupid people play nice.

Kevin: So the rumor's true? They're [expletive] takin' all the money back from you guys? All the money you guys stole from those poor grand-mothers in California?

Bob: Yeah, Grandma Millie, man. But she's the one who couldn't figure out how to [expletive] vote on the butterfly ballot.

Kevin: Yeah, now she wants her [expletive] money back for all the power you've charged for [expletive] $250 a megawatt hour.

Bob: You know—you know—you know, Grandma Millie, she's the one that Al Gore's fightin' for, you know?[17]

In the end, the personification of the hypertrophic ego, Arnold Schwarzeneg-ger, California's so-called "Governator," rode to office on the back of this fraud.

Nothing about the profits Enron earned from this scheme was the product of free markets. The only freedom exhibited was in Enron's abuse of an underregulated marketplace. Law is a poor measure of good behavior. Ethi-cal and/or moral imperatives extend far beyond the dictates of law. Morality, unlike law, kicks in when you stop yourself from behaving badly. And whereas some might lament that people aren't ethical or moral enough in their manner of communication, not even the law stands as a solid boundary against acts that harm people. In some cases, Enron rewrote the law. In other cases, they reinterpreted the law. In the style of the player who transcends the rules, the law itself becomes a mere tool for pursuing self-interest. Due to profound hubris and overconfidence, they finally ended up getting caught violating the law. The realm between reinterpreting and breaking the law is that of the player. The player does not abide by petty laws. S/he manipulates their application and even their creation. The player sees him/herself as a superman, the rare posthuman who thrives above not merely the law but also the unwritten norms and mores that sustain community values. Up until the law was breached, it would have been difficult to define Enron's corporate citizenship as good, though it was legal. Few would disagree that corpora-tions do not do good by society solely by the extent to which they pay their employees' salaries. Still, criticizing corporate citizenship these days is often disregarded as liberal, progressive, bleeding-heart socialism, especially by those politically aligned with Bill Bennett. The law alone is the standard that Enron, countless corporations, and, increasingly, individuals use as a stan-dard for public propriety. But with the separation of the subject and the object and the subsequent denial of credibility and validity to subjectivity as compared with objectivity, what is moral becomes separated from what is legal and the law is case-object. While what is good is relegated to imprecise subjective judgment, the objective "external" law takes precedent. This ultimately leads to a widespread cynicism by all the subjects who see an act as wrong but can do nothing because the act is protected by the law. Initially, law transcends individual subjects. It assures that no man is above it. But as more and more law descends from divine origins into ignoble and personally motivated debates, it comes to represent and even manifests "interests." Thus, the meaning of law changes in the modern world as something very different from virtue and morality. What is legal has nothing to do with what is moral. This disconnect reduces law to a political phenomenon determined by the power of interests in competition. Law itself becomes the product of a kind of political Darwinism. And so emerges a mainstream contempt for law, as federal and state "regulation" is perceived by many to be the machinations of a bunch of lawyer/politicians out of touch with real people and real morality. Deliberative bodies sink in the public opinion polls. Reagan's quotation that "government isn't the solution to the problem. Government is the problem" becomes a popular governing mantra as those fighting for "the people" are seen as either hopelessly naïve or as pathetically soft-headed, which is to say, irrational.

If the same anything-goes ethic is applied to communication, much of which is influenced by the marketplace, we believe that a society ends up with the types of phenomena we focus on in this book. Television shows dedicated to displaying barely dressed young people drinking pureed animal penises, children's cartoons with countless acts of violence, news video of professional athletes assaulting spectators, college football players punching each other after games, zoomed and enhanced YouTube videos of people jumping from the top floors of the World Trade Center, and similarly offensive offerings become commonplace. The defense? If authority determines that these media products or messages don't harm somebody in a measurable way, then they aren't punishable. The inept logic follows, then, that they aren't bad. But the recognition that a distance is "far" based on common experience is still meaningful even without the application of a ruler. Nevertheless, in our culture today we cannot identify an attitude or manner of being that is "bad" when we have no scale with which to measure "how bad" things are; thus, we are silenced by an ideology of quantification before we even begin to address the quality of life we lead.

The messages and media products we critique are, in the minds of some, good because they reflect diversity and marketplace innovation. The defense reflects many of the elements of the Enron culture; primarily, if something is legal then it is acceptable. Moreover, if it works and outperforms its competitor in a measureable way (i.e., revenue), it is good (at least by comparison with the subjective gripes of others). Government rarely acts to regulate if somebody isn't measurably harmed, and very few speech acts are deemed by law to be harmful. Thus, today's logic suggests that if a message *can* be crafted, it should be. If it draws an audience, it is good.

THE FREE MARKET OF COMMUNICATION

This book describes and critiques the economic philosophy of "free markets." People who follow the news, and particularly those who listen to political talk radio, are familiar with this term. The free market or marketplace, as it applies to our communication environment, stems from two innovative thinkers: Adam Smith and John Stuart Mill. Of Mill's *On Liberty* (1859), David Spitz says:

> *The Communist Manifesto* apart . . . certainly no tract has been more significant as a statement of the liberal position on the importance of freedom for the discovery of truth and for the full development of individuality. Far more than the restrictive defenses of liberty set forth by in Milton's *Areopagitica* (1644) and Locke's *Letter* (1689–92), it is the classic argument for freedom of thought and expression and the right of privacy.[18]

Of course, we also have to acknowledge the Enlightenment philosophers who inspired Jefferson's first ten amendments to the U.S. Constitution (the Bills of Rights), the Federalist Papers, as well as the constitution itself. Mill is essential because he applies the free-market concept to "ideas" before information was seen as an asset. Today, Mill's notion is used to justify all sorts of speech and information; while Mill was stressing the democratic principle of free exchange of ideas leading to the principle of let-the-idea-win, today we've warped this into measures of ratings, sales, votes, hits, and clicks determining the best message. Best in the pecuniary sense means the content that makes the most money, which is then for economists conflated with rationality.

The notion of a free marketplace as governed by some metaphysical force originates with Adam Smith who outlined his philosophy of capitalism in the *Wealth of Nations.* In it, he introduces what he called the "invisible hand."

> By directing that industry in such a manner as its produce may be of the greatest value, he intends only his own gain, and he is in this, as in many other cases, led by an invisible hand to promote an end which was no part of his intention. Nor is it always the worse for the society that it was no part of it. By pursuing his own interest he frequently promotes that of the society more effectually than when he really intends to promote it.[19]

The invisible hand directs us, according to Smith, to do that which is in the best interest of the public even when it isn't the intention of the individual actor. The individual enacts the invisible hand by acting in his/her self-interest. So, choosing to buy the cheapest rice, for instance, is one of many acts of rice purchasing that collectively reward the producer for his/her method of production, marketing, and delivery. With the systematic distortion of Mill's notion of the free marketplace of ideas comes the choice of which channel to watch or which website to select. Likewise, buying *anything* is an act participating in the will of this invisible hand and every purchase advances the hand's will, thus helping us all. Taken to its logical end, this applies equally to food purchases and selecting shock radio content over classical music. This was the problem for Lord Reith and the BBC in the 1960s. When the noncommercial BBC finally did some audience ratings research they found that a majority of people were listening to pirate radio playing rock-and-roll instead of radio documentaries and Shakespeare. Reith was a paternalist who believed that radio, and later TV, was too powerful to be given over to base entertainment. He wanted to use broadcasting to elevate the citizenry and so he put forth three channels: BBC 1, 2, and 3, each with graduated high-brow content. He thought that people initially drawn to the base content of BBC 1 would tire of it and discover BBC 2, and so on. The ratings data shocked Lord Reith; people were choosing pirate broadcasters operating out of the English Channel, Radio Luxemburg, and Armed Forces Radio at Lakenheath over news documentaries, lectures by luminaries and professors, and classical art.

Smith's invisible hand and free markets are tightly related. The will of the invisible hand can only do its work if it isn't obstructed. Except, of course, this never happens. Publically funded advertising for U.S. products and services are seen all over the world. Taxpayers subsidize trade junkets, farms, tax breaks for "business expenses," and so on. Still, the free-market advocate professes a concern about whether the proper production of rice, for instance, is truly being encouraged if the rice that one purchases is subsidized by the government of the country in which it was produced. Is laziness or lack of industry being perpetuated by tariffs that keep my competitor's rice artificially more expensive? Following this logic, government efforts to assist or protect markets harms the marketplace and the people who rely on it. Thus, one can conclude that government should stay out of the marketplace; the market should be left free of government intervention. It should butt out. The example of Reith and the BBC just helps to bolster this perception that meddling with the invisible hand produces an inferior product.

This free-market mantra, ostensibly carrying with it all of the entailments of the invisible hand, is repeated again and again in contemporary politics. In his November 14, 2008 radio address following the onset of the U.S. economic and banking collapse, President George W. Bush said:

The benefits of free-market capitalism have been proven across time, geography, and culture. Around the world, free-market capitalism has allowed once-impoverished nations to develop large and prosperous economies. And here at home, free-market capitalism is what transformed America from a rugged frontier to the greatest economic power in history. Just as important as maintaining free markets within countries is maintaining the free movement of goods and services between countries. There are many ways for nations to demonstrate their commitment to open markets. The United States Congress can take the lead by approving free trade agreements with Colombia, Panama, and South Korea before adjourning for the year.

Governments should stand back and let the markets run their course. This is more clearly articulated by libertarian-leaning GOP congressman Ron Paul responding to the same economic issue as President Bush:

Well, the first thing is, is if you're really concerned about the consumer you would have to defend the free market and no federal regulations whether it has to do with toys or financial instruments. What you have to have are basic rules, especially by the states that you can't commit fraud, you can't sell bad products and you have to be liable, but the consumer becomes king in a free market.[20]

And as the free market appeared to contribute to the massive worldwide banking failure, conservatives still came to its defense. Conservative talk-radio host Laura Ingraham said in response to the collapse:

Conservative free-market principles apply in the good times and the bad times. Conservative free-market principles will get us out of this if we allow them to.[21]

Speaking more generally, conservative talk-radio host Rush Limbaugh sums up the free-market economy this way:

The whole concept of the United States, the capitalist system, is the free market—and the free market is fueled by freedom! Freedom leads to ingenuity, invention, entrepreneurism, and what is the pursuit? The pursuit is profit. The profit derives from success.[22]

The point here isn't to say that adherents to free-market ideology are wrong. Instead, it is to demonstrate that the public's acquiescence to this ideology functions, in effect, to opt the public out of any oversight role, thus giving large market operations, such as corporations, the run of the house. The irony is that players in the marketplace *don't* follow these rules. Free-market ideology, as it manifests today, gives corporations carte blanche to do what they want with whatever resources are available—public or private. Even in the case of the worldwide banking collapse, a problem that so clearly could have been prevented by government oversight, free-market advocates both direct-ly and indirectly turned their blame *toward* regulation (arguing that govern-ment somehow caused it in order to cover the role played by reduced regula-tion following the repeal of the Glass-Steagall act) while relying on govern-ment for bailout money—effectively guaranteeing a win-win situation for nearly every millionaire and billionaire involved. When we use the word "mantra" to describe the function of the free-market term in public discourse, we intentionally use it for its mystical overtones. The notion of an infallible and benevolent "invisible hand" channeled through our purchasing decisions is an economic metaphysic not based on any concrete understanding of hu-man reality. And, the knee-jerk speed with which people invoke "free mar-kets" without careful consideration of the situation to which it is being ap-plied further reflects the extent to which both the free markets and the invis-ible hand have become God-like: people behave as though a lapse of absolute faith in free markets will somehow resort in the wrath of God's hand!

The notion of survival of the fittest as applied by Francis Galton, Karl Peirson, and Herbert Spencer is extremely coarse if "coarse" includes an indifference to human dignity—a law of the universe that just does its thing without concern for individuals. How this all applies to coarse communica-tion in the contemporary United States stems from the historical point at which our law came to shift to liberalize the so-called "marketplace of ide-as." Supreme Court Justice Oliver Wendell Holmes wasn't a cause of today's situation, but his words reflect an important legal turn. In Abrams vs. The United States (1919), Holmes wrote:

> When men have realized that time has upset many fighting faiths, they may come to believe even more than they believe the very foundations of their own conduct that the ultimate good desired is better reached by free trade in ide-as . . . that the best test of truth is the power of the thought to get itself accepted in the competition of the market, and that truth is the only ground upon which their wishes safely can be carried out. That at any rate is the theory of our Constitution. [23]

American history is often described as a march toward liberty, as more and more people are extended basic rights and protections. First, land-owning white males, then white males, then black men, then women. Throughout that march, both the *de jure* and *de facto* authority of the government to quiet speech has been increasingly curtailed. The justification for these rights goes beyond the idea that a right to expression is God-given; according to the marketplace of ideas, the proliferation of expressions helps everyone. The U.S. government struggled with the meaning of and challenges to the many freedoms ensured by our Constitution. Could a person say *whatever* s/he wanted *wherever* s/he wanted? It is a little known fact to many, but the radical freedom of expression taken for granted today wasn't quite as open and celebrated several generations earlier. Women were banned from speaking in many situations. Blacks weren't allowed to speak wherever they wanted. Sexual themes weren't tolerated in public, or in the mails. Even certain *political* themes weren't tolerated. And though the "marketplace of ideas" phrase may not have originated with Oliver Wendell Holmes, he is credited with introducing the idea. When Holmes helped start freeing the marketplace from local or federal government regulation, he likely hoped, as Mill believed, that *reason* and *logical consistency* would be transcendent regulators. With the coarsening of discourse one of the major problems is that the public sphere is becoming increasingly irrational with bombast and hyperbole and contradiction. Rules of logic have been cast aside for emotional appeals—if it bleeds it leads. This is not being prudish; coarsening has to do, in part, with dumbing down discourse (our ultimate concern). Sarah Palin, Glenn Beck, Michael Savage, Ann Coulter, the attack on science and global warming—these are all examples.

We are not arguing for the elimination of competition but instead the reintroduction of *true* competition. Ben Bagdikian put it most succinctly when he concluded that, "Mass advertising is the engine that drives much of the media into giantism, toward monopoly, toward socially insignificant editorial content, and raises barriers to new media entrepreneurs."[24] "Socially insignificant editorial content" is a sign of mass jadedness. This is one of the most problematic consequences of mass media monopoly and its singular motivation. Only a handful of companies control all that we see and hear in the media. Bagdikian noted two gaps emerging that are now canyons. The first is a decreasing interest in news programming by major media corporations and their audiences. Newspapers are going out of business. The audience most interested has aged past fifty-five now.[25] As a result younger generations are increasingly disinterested and ill-informed. News does not sell advertising targeted to the most lucrative market segments—children and young adult. Second, also tied to advertising revenue, media increasingly fit their content to serve the geographic boundaries of the 210 major markets in the country and not the nineteen thousand plus municipalities. Expensive mass marketing favors the chain retailer who buys space or time for sales messages that cover vast areas, making it impossible for the mom and pop retail operation to compete. The small, family entrepreneur is forced to either buy advertising time and space that reaches audiences far beyond their neighborhood or to not advertise at all. Also, local candidates running for office do not run from market areas. They do not, as Bagdikian puts it, "represent shopping malls."[26] Local political action is largely drowned out by media that cater to large markets that cover dozens and often hundreds of municipalities such as counties, school districts, and state and federal legislative districts. What is pumped is the sensational corruption of a local politician or their sexual improprieties as those do not pertain to the district yet are of prurient interest to all within the media market. The political relevance of such stories is minimal to nothing. Like cheap shows that gather amateur video of funny pet antics or sports accidents, the content has no local relevance. It is purely sensational. Decisions of what to run in the media are increasingly commercial rather than journalistic or based on community needs to know. Content has shifted from what the community needs to what disinterested (alienated) viewers and advertisers want. This goes to the heart of democracy as no citizen can vote intelligently without knowledge of the issues and candidates. We subsequently see a steady decline in voting participation. But it goes deeper than that. It goes to an increasing escapism, an attempt to escape from relevance and cognitive effort. As news budgets are cut there is a growing reliance on "official" corporate and government news sources so that those being covered are writing the news, a problem that has plagued financial news coverage so that no one saw Enron or Bernie Madoff coming or even the massive failure in the banking and home-lending industry that threatened the entire world's financial system.

Cuts to news budgets have also led to a profound lack of context for the facts reported. In 2004 Bagdikian wrote, "The large media conglomerates do not want greater political and social diversity because it would dilute their audiences and thereby reduce the fees they can demand for the commercials that produce their unprecedented profit levels."[27] Repeated efforts to regulate and limit the size of monopolies in all media including cable television and now in Internet providers have failed. Today huge media conglomerates function as if they "own" every channel of communication in the nation. They already do own the vast majority of production companies. And in fact, beginning in the late 1990s the federal government started to auction off broadcast channels, thereby undercutting its only leverage for regulatory oversight that operated in the nation since 1934. The rationale for the fundamental change in the public's ownership of the electronic spectrum was based on the Reagan-era argument that with cable television scarcity of channels was eliminated. But the point is not a scarcity of channels but a scarcity of owners. Now one owner can own hundreds of radio stations across the country, eliminating regional differences and purveying a single message: replicating a single model that is profitable. This leads to a single retail as well as cultural and political monoculture.[28] Not to mention that Limbaugh's show is simply given away for free in "barter deals" to small and medium market radio stations.[29] Lack of competition in shoes or automobiles leads to various economic problems, including a propensity for stagnation in innovation and the quality of the product. But if we all were forced to wear the same low-quality shoes and drive the same low-quality car, that would not affect our political discourse. Media, especially news content, is fundamentally a different product from other products. A single, low-quality source of news impoverishes the public sphere and damages the quality of our thinking and political decision making. The typical economic model that may be applied to other products does not apply to information, especially in a democracy. Selling information as entertainment content based on mass market and mass audience appeal impacts the quality of information. A fundamental cause of the coarsening of our public sphere is the rush to create the cheapest, lowest quality information that the market will bear. Thus we see a proliferation in reality TV and a replacing of news content with vitriolic pundits. After several editions of his classic *The Media Monopoly*, in which, over a decade Bagdikian traced the decline in the number of media owners in the United States from a couple of dozen down to just five, he tries at the very end of the last edition to sound an optimistic note.

> The raw power of major corporations joined with the media conglomerates has aroused increasing protest on the Internet and in the alternative print and broadcast media. More young people—once the age group attributed the lowest percentage of voting among those eligible—have become activists, mobilizing protests, petitions, and votes. [30]

Unfortunately, ownership of Internet sources and providers has become the target of the same old-fashioned media conglomerates and it too is being totally commercialized, raising the issue of net neutrality and privacy from Net-provider consumer analysis.

After the rise of the Internet several authors are sounding the alarm, an alarm Bagdikian was not equipped to recognize. As Weinberger explained the fragmentation of mediated uses and gratifications, combined with a lack of fundamental education among many of its users, "everything is miscellaneous." Likewise, Lawrence Lessig, an early expert and author about the Internet writes in 2008 that many, including himself, were naïve about the potential of the Internet to create diversity and freedom.

> Many of us felt we had seen something beautiful in the Net, felt that something needed to be protected, felt there were powerful interest that felt differently about all this, and thus felt we needed to make clear just how important it was to protect the Net of the present into the future. This cheerleading tended to obscure certain increasingly obvious facts of the Internet. Put most succinctly, there was a growing and increasingly dangerous lot of stuff on the Net. The first notice of this crud pointed to pornography. In response, civil libertarians launched a vigorous campaign to defend the rights of porn on the Net. But as the crud got deeper and more vicious, the urge to defend it began to wane. Spam became an increasingly annoying burden. Viruses, and worse, became positively harmful. Like a family on a beach holiday not wanting to confront the fact that "yes, that is a sewage line running into the water just upstream from the house we have rented," many of us simply turned a blind eye to this increasingly uncomfortable fact: The Net was not in Kansas anymore. [31]

The panacea of the Internet is fading. Pandering not to an ideological tendency but to individualism itself has led to an informatic system designed to enhance individualism, to help the individual avoid diversity of ideas and take refuge in narrow-casting of entire channels dedicated to a particular interest or ideological predispositions. The netizen need not expose him/ herself to diverse opinions or ideas. S/he can retreat into her information sphere, assume a virtual identity and ignore diversity. In 2008 Mark Bauerlein published *The Dumbest Generation: How the Digital Age Stupefies Young Americans and Jeopardizes Our Future.* Rick Shenkman (2008) published *Just How Stupid Are We.* Likewise, Maggie Jackson in 2008 published the book *Distracted: The Erosion of Attention and the Coming Dark Age* in which she explores how babies first learn how to focus their awareness to solve problems, how to pay attention over time, how to sift through stimuli and identify and categorize what is important and what is not. Jackson surveys the landscape where increasing numbers of young people and adults complain of being unable to do the most fundamental of cognitive functions and traces much of it to the noise created in our world by information overload, much of it spiraling upward in sensationalism (in both content and form such as HD and 3-D signals) as signals compete in a cacophony of commercialism for even the most fleeting of attention. Things become increasingly incoherent in what she calls an "attention-deficient culture."[32]

Communication coarseness to content means rudeness, incivility, vulgarity, and the like. But in this book we are presuming a more fundamental aspect to the reality of coarseness, one that presumes that, à la Lewis Mumford and later Marshal McLuhan, the medium is also a message. Perhaps, people are spoiled to have total control of their media. They have endless Internet channels and switch constantly, aimlessly browsing and grazing. We risk lacking the patience necessary for logical/analytical reflection. Not the best idea but the best webpage colors and bling draw attention. Books are all very similar in their presentation but webpages are not. Coarseness does not simply apply to the content of messages but to the quality of the media environment overall. The very ability to concentrate is being eroded by a rough, loud, incoherent, semantic field. Ads run alongside news messages even on news providers' pages. The notion of "headline" is further abbreviated by Google and Yahoo webpages that list ten or fewer news teases. This is the extension of televisual incoherence and constant distraction. On American commercial TV, one is watching a poignant news story about a civil war in Africa one second, and the next second (literally) one is watching a commercial full of happy faces and bouncy music selling a Disney vacation package. On the Internet messages stream side-by-side on the same screen. Consciousness itself is becoming increasingly fragmented and incoherent and all content is losing its sense of significance. The only logic, the only criteria for guidance that Smith's invisible hand has for us is how, in a market with comparatively limited choices (comparing Smith's world with today's), economic Darwinism would yield the best products and services. The bling world is winning out. Form is winning over substance.

In fifth century BC, Isocrates said we think in words. Today we must add images. And insofar as this is true, which many scientists have demonstrated that it is, then vulgar words and images mean vulgar thinking. Our minds reflect the environment to which they are exposed. Irrational, contradictory, sensational images and words lead to that sort of thinking/world. The fact that prevalent and public mechanisms for censoring them are now limited is not the focus of this book. Instead, we want to know *why* in an environment that guarantees the virtual ability to say whatever one wants and even have it broadcast to millions, or even billions of people, our communication can be so easily characterized as coarse. Walter Lippmann wrote that the freedom to express is not a guarantee of good government:

> For in the absence of debate unrestricted utterance leads to the degradation of opinion. By a kind of Gresham's law the more rational is overcome by the less rational, and the opinions that will prevail will be those which are held most ardently by those with the most passionate will. For that reason the freedom to speak can never be maintained by objecting to interference with the liberty of the press, of printing, of broadcasting, of the screen. It can be maintained only by promoting debate. [33]

Lippmann, it seems, had in mind the value of public argument as necessary to an informed public. But as Habermas notes this presumes an educated public and an arena guaranteed by the transcending power of government to protect the weak voice from the strong so that the public sphere is open and free. Nevertheless, the point of citing Lippman here is to reinforce the idea that the guarantee of free expression and the exercise of free expression is not a guarantee of *worthwhile* expression.

Looking through a free-market or marketplace of ideas lens, a person comes to an altogether different conclusion than Lippmann. The best ideas win; by virtue of their having "won" an expression must be good. According to this logic, Howard Stern must be one of the most virtuous people around. In 2005, following his enormous contract with Sirius Radio, Stern was the second-highest paid entertainer in the world, having earned $302 million that year[34] and recently signed a new five-year, $400 million contract.[35] Say what you want about Howard Stern; he may be the everyman working-class hero. He may advance the interests of homosexuals and labor unions with his commentary. Whatever the reader's position, we doubt anyone would want to defend the position that his 2005 cultural contributions were the second-most valuable in the world or that his efforts in 2011 were worth 1,607 times the average U.S. worker's income.[36]

COMMUNICATION ENVIRONMENT

The free market is an attractive mechanism for assessing public discourse for a few reasons; it is dispassionate, measureable, and ostensibly objective. Should classical music or sitcoms dominate evening television? The free-market oracle tells us with precision which is most valuable. Classical music loses, as sitcoms draw larger audiences for which advertisers pay more money. One airing of a popular American situation comedy episode such as *Seinfeld* reaches more people than all the people combined that have ever attended a play written by Shakespeare. Football displaced baseball on the major networks because of this simple profit-oriented metric. Reality television appears to be besting scripted television at the moment because it is more affordably produced, despite the fact that scripted television still dominates the ratings. Standing a chance against such a parsimonious, efficient, and intuitive mechanism is difficult, especially when anyone who challenges it appears to be subjective. It is a single motive.

On what philosophical ground do we stand as we level our criticism? On one level, we appeal simply to human dignity. Do people laugh better or harder at Chris Rock than they did at Jack Benny? Is Lisa Lampenelli funnier than Lucille Ball? In all likelihood, they are equally as funny. Watching Benny or Ball now won't bring the same laughs because our standards for what is funny have changed, but we imagine that our parents and grandparents laughed as mightily at these comedians as we do at our greats of today. Somehow, however, Ball, Benny, Red Skelton, Steve Allen, and many others managed to make people laugh without being vulgar. Sure, they were irreverent, but they weren't vulgar. Their irreverence was covertly political, and less shocking.

Beyond gut-level appreciation for human dignity, we approach coarseness from the perspective of democratic theory. Put simply, we proceed from the assumption that democracy necessitates deliberation and contestation. We don't prescribe any form of deliberation, such as Lippman's argument, but we do believe that two things are necessary. First, people need to feel safe to express themselves whether their messages are mainstream or counterpublic contestation (precisely what these concepts mean is discussed in greater depth in chapter 2). Right now, we'd say that there is an abundance of expressive freedom for most people, though that admittedly varies with a number of things including race, ethnicity, class, sexuality, and other factors. More problems come from the absence of the second item: an ethic of listening. Listening, we maintain, involves *engaging* others.

If the reader interprets our argument to mean that the public sphere is completely bereft of valuable expression, then our contention is misunderstood. Our argument isn't about the quantity of valuable content that is available to those willing to listen. Instead, we are arguing that the ethic of listening has been deteriorated by the preponderance of coarse and senseless public expressions. We believe that the messages introduced to the public communication environment shape that environment and the attitudes with which people engage it. Thus, there is no *direct* or *empirical* harm caused by coarse public expressions. Instead, statements, like those attributed to Bill Bennett above, function to further legitimize or normalize public talk of the president's sex life. Now, this is a precarious line for us to walk because we don't think the president's sex life should be off limits. Still, vivid description of oral sex in the Oval Office do more than introduce the topic of marital infidelity to the public forum. In fact, we think the Starr Report's lurid descriptions of genital manipulation functioned by being titillating—certainly distracting from any prolonged discussion of national debt, voting rights, foreign aid, or whatever else. This approach to critiquing public communication and public discourse is shared by those who understand our messages as constituting an environment, and the interaction of our messages on our culture as like the study of human cultural ecology or, as we refer to it throughout the book, our "communication environment."

We ask the reader to disabuse him/herself of the idea that there is a natural and uniform human response to uniform situations and stimuli. Instead, we are held aloft in a net of symbolism. Depending on the net on which we stand for our vantage point, the net is often confused for solid ground. And we darn the net as we go; without knowing it we build our own ground. The grammar, the rules of that process can be either logic or illogic. Our ground, as certain of it as we may be, is not the ground our parents stood upon. We live in a different environment, and the means and manner of communication in these different environments vary. Ernst Cassirer wrote of our symbolic world:

> Man cannot escape from his own achievement. He cannot but adopt the conditions of his own life. No longer in a merely physical universe, man lives in a symbolic universe. Language, myth, art, and religion are parts of this universe. They are the varied threads which weave the symbolic net, the tangled web of human experience.[37]

We live in a symbolic milieu, and the reality we synthesize is a function of the symbols and meanings that we and others construct and employ. Our symbols and their meanings change with our history, yet logic can act to guide us through contingencies. Our natural attitude accepts the world as a given, but that attitude is shaped and influenced by the communication environment in which people are immersed. Edmund Husserl, a philosopher/mathematician who wrote some of the most important texts on logic in the twentieth century, asks us to assume an unnatural attitude or perspective, to try to question the presumptions we take for granted and expose them to logic. Thus, a lot can be learned about how we engage our world by examining the philosophical and moral assumptions implicit in our messages. The first step in a critical approach is to question the self-righteousness of self-righteousness, which, if too arrogant, makes us deaf to other voices, other realities, other perspectives.

What the reader encounters in the following chapters is an assessment of our communication environment. What does our communication say about ourselves, others, our values, and our relationship to the world we inhabit? What do different varieties of messages introduce to the environment in which our children are being raised? Albert Bandura's Social Learning Theory and George Gerbner's Cultivation Theory both suggest that how we learn to behave is a function of what and who we observe. Causal evidence linking violent programming directly to violent behavior is underwhelming, but the two often correlate. The connection is intuitive, anyway; if a person is surrounded by violence, violence is the perceived norm. If the tenor of political discourse becomes increasingly combative or stupid, we maintain that combativeness and stupidity become the perceived norm. If a churchgoer is immersed in self-serving theology, selfishness becomes the perceived norm. If an entertainment-seeker keeps encountering vulgarity, vulgarity becomes the norm. And so on.

We contend that critical thinking is a redundant phrase. We also contend that good listening, *real* listening, is always critical listening. Critical listening is short-circuited, we believe, by diversions: sensational words and images. Reagan could divert criticism with humor. Others could divert criticism with various fallacies such as "they did it too only worse." Another way to depoliticize a population is to give them ever more sensational images; bigger and badder hits in football and cage fighting, ever more sexy storylines and fashion, ever more "pop" in "extreme" sports and videos, ever more exposure of intimate and embarrassing situations à la Jerry Springer and reality TV in general; bigger and louder music, hypertrophic body manipulation from the obsession with thinness, to muscle development and breast augmentation for purely aesthetic appeal. Violence, actual and symbolic, proliferates and is exaggerated from children's games to turning the family pet into a killing monster and hypertrophic drug abuse (both legal and illegal). Even artists today seek to destroy the definition of art.

A significant problem with hypertrophism is that it has no sense of reasonable limits. Thus it ultimately becomes suicidal. This is the age of "X." Suicidal extremism from music that makes you deaf, to art that makes you blind, to games that kill you, the ego craves sensation and attention. Suicidal extremism, from hydrogen bombs to disfiguring "cosmetic" surgery, is the logical conclusion to unfettered ego-hypertrophy. The age of ideology is also the age of exploration for its own sake and for the sake of amassing fortune, it is also the age of extreme individualism and extreme massification. As Jean Gebser says:

> The current situation manifests on the one hand as an egocentric individualism exaggerated to extremes and desirous of possessing everything, while on the other it manifests an equally extreme collectivism that promises the total fulfillment of man's being. In the latter instance we find the utter abnegation of the individual valued merely as an object in the human aggregate; in the former a hyper-valuation of the individual who, despite his limitations, is permitted everything. This deficient, that is destructive, antithesis divides the world into two warring camps, not just politically and ideologically, but in all areas of human endeavor. [38]

Thus, we have what David Reismann called *The Lonely Crowd* (1969) and Vance Packard called *A Nation of Strangers* (1972) and *Status Seekers* (1961), and the existential crisis that characterizes the environment within which the social sciences emerged largely over the concern for modern alienation and anomie. Thus, we have Sigmund Freud writing *Civilization and Its Discontents* (1930) while Husserl is writing about the problem of meaning followed by Carl Jung writing *Modern Man in Search of a Soul* (1933) and Viktor Frankl writing *Man's Search for Meaning* (1959). The modern urban aggregate does not have the organic sense that characterizes the womb-like sense of the ancient tribe. The modern ego emerges with needs that include attention, consumption, and therapy. The demand for attention is often suicidal and it leads to coarseness. The cacophony of an aggregate of individuals stridently pursuing personal ambitions and identity is not harmonious on a collective level. The din is also self-reinforcing creating an environment where everything and everyone is miscellaneous. When everyone has a TV channel, a *you* tube, a *my* space, a *face* book, personal webpage, and so on, then who is watching? The cohesion that mass media once enabled is increasingly fragmented as individuals strive to have an identity, to gain celebrity status. The original environment, which gave birth to the modern ego, was one still dominated by human-scale communities. But today with nationalism and beyond to globalism, only through extremism—from weapons of mass destruction versus merely "conventional weapons," to death rock and a "wall of sound" versus ballads, to superstardom versus singing together in a family parlor, to hypertrophic bodybuilding exhibitionism to playing together, to competitions for everything from eating to cooking—can the individual in the modern global population rise above the din. In the process individuals become self-objectifying . . . an exhibit in an increasingly visiocentric world. [39] To be is to be on the cover of a magazine or on a talk show. The strongest form of individualism is the celebrity. With fragmentation and hypertrophic perspectivism vision becomes di-vision. Only in this milieu can a person be a "nobody"—the raw material of the hypertrophic player's world.

The messages in our public sphere that help shape our communication environment encourage and reinforce hypertrophic individualism. Messages both implicitly and explicitly champion the idea that not only are needs and desires of the individual paramount, but they *simultaneously delegitimize the ethos of collective orientation and action*. This is the coarsening of public communication; it reflects strict egoism, whether it seeks to display the self publicly, push ideas, or accrue audience. It suits the needs of the individual; it is ends-oriented. In this world everyone gets a trophy to put on their mantle, particularly if they can afford it. The deficiency of this perspective leads to self-contradiction. If everyone is special, then no one is. The traces that our messages leave behind are often of little consequence to those producing them. Worse, by design some are intended for this very purpose. Like mountain-top removal or hardwood clear-cutting, much contemporary public discourse culls value from the environment with no mind for environmental impacts that resonate long after the extraction of value is through.

Messages to the contrary do exist and are found to be compelling by many, but we've found them to be less prominent as the free market has found such ideas relatively less popular and profitable. In a sense, the free market of public communication helps ensure that lack of popularity begets a lack of popularity. Meanwhile, Paris Hilton is continually hounded by the media for being famous, thus perpetuating her fame. And if Elisabeth Noelle-Neumann's Spiral of Silence theory is right, the perception that one's idea or belief is uncommon will lead a person to silence him/herself, thus compounding the silence.

While the abstraction of equality may be occurring in our present atomized condition, the notion that the marginalized have equal *power* is what we question. The amorphous notion of equality does not guarantee power over anything but one's self. People with equality are allowed to sit where they want on a bus, visit a gay bar, quit a job, or vote. People with power sold the bus, sell liquor to the gay bar, hire, and influence the choices on the ballot. These are the players, and they are hardly threatened by individual acts of speaking out, as such actions just further reinforce the ethic of individual pursuit, thus buttressing our pervasive butt-out ideology.

Instead of our argument being construed as a modern and Habermas-inspired effort to freeze or repeal the growth of arational expressions in the public sphere, we seek to contribute to an effort to identify expressions that help degrade a communication environment that might otherwise be conducive to dialogue. The messages and contexts we examine in this book have little to do with the voice of the marginalized, but instead reveal the co-opting of alternative means of expression for the purpose of perpetuating what might be called "individualocracy." More voices, more choices, more channels, more messages means more fragmentation, further ensuring the perpetual control of resources by those who already have them, justified by a philosophy that regards market choice over coordinated political action. The present arrangement is a harmonious and yet insidious balancing of the interests in Madisonian democracy; the minority (property-owning class) is protected from the tyranny of the majority (lower classes) at the same time that minorities, however defined, are claiming unprecedented access to the public sphere.

NOTES

1. "Dangerous Backlash," *The Daily Rundown*, MSNBC, March 25, 2010.
2. "Obama on *60 Minutes*," *60 Minutes*, CBS, September 13, 2009, www.cbsnews.com/video/watch/?id=5305734n.
3. See William Bennett, *The Death of Outrage: Bill Clinton and the Assault on American Ideals*. (Florence, MA: Free Press, 1999), 9.
4. See Helen Dewar and Dana Milbank, "Cheney Dismisses Critic with Obscenity," *Washington Post*, June 25, 2004.
5. See Paul Farhi, "How Low Can TV Go? Stay Tuned to Find Out," *Vancouver Sun*, March 14, 2000.
6. See "Obama: The College Years," *Time*, accessed January 31, 2011, www.time.com.
7. As cited in Jason Linkins, "Obama Smoking Picture: Andrea Mitchell Investigates," *Huffington Post*, www.huffingtonpost.com, December 17, 2008.
8. See Desmond Morris, *The Human Zoo* (New York: Kodansha, 1996).
9. See Lewis Mumford, *The City in History* (New York: MJF Books, 1989), 512.
10. See David Weinberger, *Everything is Miscellaneous* (New York: Times Books, 2007), 229.
11. See "Pete Stark Won't Pee on Your Leg," Politico, September 15, 2009, www.politico.com.
12. See Lawrence Donegan, "Serena Williams is Fined $10,500 for U.S. Open Line Judge Tirade," *Guardian*, September 9, 2009, www.guardian.co.uk/sport/2009/sep/13/serena-williams-tirade-us-open.
13. See Nekesa Mumbi Moody, "West Gives VMAs Rude Awakening," *Washington Post*, September 14, 2009.
14. See George Homans, "Social Behavior as Exchange," *American Journal of Sociology* 63 (1958): 597–606.
15. See Joseph Campbell, *The Power of Myth* (New York: Doubleday, 1988).
16. See Lee Williams, "DIY Self-Defense Is Teen's Goal," *Oregonian*, August 8, 2006, www.oregonlive.com/living/oregonian/index.ssf? /base/living/115499853367770.xml&coll=7.
17. See Richard Oppel Jr., "Word for Word/Energy Hogs; Enron Traders on Grandma Millie and Making Out Like Bandits," *New York Times*, June 13, 2004.
18. See David Spitz, preface to *On Liberty*, by John Stuart Mill (New York: Norton, 1975), vii.
19. See Adam Smith, *The Wealth of Nations* (New York: Penguin, 1999), 32.
20. See Ron Paul, "Rep. Ron Paul Is Interviewed on FOX Business Network," June 17, 2009.
21. See Jennifer Harper, "Talk Radio Voices Bailout Anguish; Listeners Seek Calm from Hosts," *Washington Times*, September 30, 2008.
22. See Rush Limbaugh, "Rush Limbaugh," www.en.wikiquote.org.

23. Oliver Wendell Holmes, "U.S. Supreme Court: Abrams vs. U.S., 250 U.S. 616 (1919)," Findlaw.com, caselaw.lp.findlaw.com.

24. See Ben Bagdikian, *The Media Monopoly* (Boston: Beacon, 1987), 230.

25. See Eric Alterman, "Out of Print: The Death and Life of the American Newspaper," *New Yorker*, March 31, 2008.

26. See Bagdikian, *The Media Monopoly*, 221.

27. See Ben Bagdikian, *The New Media Monopoly* (Boston: Beacon, 2004), 260.

28. See Eric Kramer, *The Emerging Monoculture: Assimilation and the Model Minority* (Santa Barbara, CA: Praeger, 2003)

29. See Bill Mann, "Limbaugh's Dirty Little Secret of Radio 'Success,'" *Huffington Post*, www.huffingtonpost.com, April 12, 2009.

30. See Bagdikian, *The New Media Monopoly*, 265.

31. See Lawrence Lessig, "Forward," in *The Future of the Internet and How to Stop It*, by Jonathan Zittrain (New Haven, CT: Yale University Press, 2008), 7–8.

32. See Maggie Jackson, *Distracted: The Erosion of Attention and the Coming Dark Age* (Amherst, NY: Prometheus, 2008), 29.

33. See Walter Lippmann, *The Public Philosophy* (New Brunswick, NJ: Transaction Publishers, 2009), 129.

34. See Phyllis Furman, "Cruise-ing to Top of Forbes's Celeb 100," *Daily News*, June 16, 2006.

35. See Georg Szalai, "Analyst: Howard Stern-Sirius XM Contract Worth $400 Million," *Hollywood Reporter*, December 9, 2010, www.hollywoodreporter.com.

36. Dividing $400,000,000 by the five years he has signed to work at Sirius XM, divided by $49,777 or the average U.S. worker's salary according to U.S. Census Bureau's press release titled "Income, Poverty and Health Insurance Coverage in the United States: 2009," www.census.gov.

37. See Ernst Cassirer, *An Essay on Man: An Introduction to a Philosophy of Human Culture* (Hamburg: Meiner Verlag, 2006), 30.

38. See Jean Gebser *The Ever-Present Origin*, trans. Noel Barstad and Algis Mickunas (Athens: Ohio University Press, 1985), 3.

39. See Eric Kramer, "Videocentrism," in *Proceedings for the Twenty-Fifth Annual Husserl Circle*, delivered at the Twenty-Fifth Annual Husserl Circle Conference (Chicago: DePaul University Press, 1993), 106–18 and his "Visiocentrism," *The Journal of the Bulgarian Journalist Association*, trans. L. Raicheva 36 (1994): 37–40.

Chapter Two

Coarseness in the Public Sphere

We do need to re-establish the lost connection between ethics and politics, but this cannot be done by sacrificing the gains of the democratic revolution.

—Chantal Mouffe, 1993, *The Return of the Political*[1]

Let's assume that the bourgeoisie public sphere that Habermas describes in *The Transformation of the Public Sphere* was as civil as he implies. By contrast, in contexts in which counterpublics, often silenced both by public sphere norms and coercion, find the need to disrupt the ostensibly tranquil status quo, their disruption is warranted and valuable. If the reader accepts the latter, then the notion that coarse communication would be condemned becomes problematized, particularly if it originates from a counterpublic source. Read this way, it appears that we are condemning the discourse of the politically impoverished, e.g., racial, ethnic, gender minorities and the economic underclass. We deem it necessary to address this matter early in the book because the reader must understand where we are coming from before encountering the bulk of our criticism.

The following carves out a position that we believe gives us ground for criticizing contemporary public communication: recognizing it as harmful to public debate, the resolution of controversy, and our capacity to listen to each other as equals with worthwhile things to say. The alternative is to avoid criticizing contemporary public messages for fear of being wrongly construed as intolerant of free expression or curmudgeonly. We maintain that a failure to criticize the content of our communication environment actually risks greater harmful consequences for the politically impoverished than does remaining silent. Harm can come to those seeking to employ the liberating potential of public expression from an ethic that accepts any and all public

45

expressions as either equally valuable or harmless. We explain below our concern that the last thing the disenfranchised need is for the public sphere to be muddied and atomized, rendering our public discussion noisy, fragmented, and absurd.

Our perspective is grounded in phenomenology, which presumes the validity of human experience *as* experienced. To the extent that people know coarseness when they experience it tells us that there is such a thing; coarseness is a valid phenomenon. A loose definition of public coarseness involves public expressions that disrupt "tranquility," real or perceived. However, to the extent that Americans also embrace democracy and the unrest that this occasionally engenders, we know that there must be a distinction between coarse communication and what Nancy Fraser terms "contestation."[2] Thus, disruptive communication is important and necessary, and often *appears* to be coarse because it upsets public tranquility (among many other things). The two overlap, certainly. Any democracy must accommodate coarseness. Still, that's no reason to remain agnostic about everything communicated publicly. The value here lies more in the concern with a public sphere constituted almost exclusively by nonsense and emotional appeal than it does necessarily with promoting formal rational debate as an elixir.

To have a healthy democracy, the appearance of coarseness cannot be cause for silencing others. Yet, we ask the reader to consider how healthy a democracy can be if the public sphere is inundated with coarseness. The ruling regime of reason, according to most writers about public sphere theory, is what any period refers to as the mainstream mode of discourse. How does a counterpublic break through the din to disrupt the status quo if so much public discourse is modeled after it? In 1963, a black Southern Baptist minister marched on Washington, DC—no doubt risking the life he'd later sacrifice to the cause—and delivered his *I Have a Dream* speech, challenging America to fulfill its promise of guaranteed unalienable rights. Fifty-three years later on the anniversary of King's speech, talk-radio host Glenn Beck arrived in Washington, DC to hold a self-billed nonpolitical rally about honor, faith, God, charity, and fear about the coming struggle for the country. Beck's speech took the form of a disruptive protest, yet explicitly promoted little more than prayer to a crowd overwhelmingly composed of Caucasians. What is *real* disruption in the present context?

Beck's Washington, DC speech is interesting on a number of levels, but we propose that his rally functioned to put a positive face on a rather coarse "astro-turfed" Tea Party "movement" that disrupted town hall events and participated in public rhetorics of anger, insurrection, and rebellion. While the DC event may have strategically put a polish on a rather tarnished movement for centrist voters who'd only begun to pay attention to upcoming 2010 congressional races, it couldn't withdraw the "contributions" that the Tea Party had made to the communication environment up to that point.

The notion of the "communication environment" asks the reader to consider the implications of rhetoric outside of the individual controversies from which it emerges. Whereas either a mainstream or counterpublic campaign may have achieved its desired goal, we ask what the words, thoughts, strategies, and images used during the campaign contribute to the larger culture. If how we communicate reflects, reinforces, and shapes a society's attitudes about ourselves and what we are in relation to others, then we are responsible for what and how we communicate even after the outcome of a controversy is determined. Our semantic or communication environment is shaped by what we say and do. In his explanation of philosophical hermeneutics Hans-Georg Gadamer explains that people always look at the world from a standpoint. That is, we are always prejudiced; it is impossible to be objective. Yet, as modern humans we've been made to believe we *can* be objective. Thus, if we think we are objective when it's impossible to be, the perspective, standpoint, or attitude that we *do* have is outside of our awareness—we don't even know that it is there shaping the world to which we attend and assign meaning. We cannot transcend our prejudices (be objective) because our prejudices are necessary "conditions whereby we experience something—whereby what we encounter says something to us."[3] The key to our argument is Gadamer's assertion that prejudices and meanings can be shaped by our language—though he's clear that thought isn't absolutely determined by language. Still, language, he explains, "provides an initial schematization for all of our possibilities of knowing."[4] Our concerns emerge from these assumptions; if our attitudes and the objects of our awareness are influenced by the communication environment in which we are immersed, then an environment of public coarseness will beget a coarser, cynical, and atomized society.

If the reader accepts that each time we talk, to greater and lesser extents depending on the circumstances, what we choose to say and how we choose to say it alters our communication environment, the next matter to consider is what the consequences are of the use of unconventional and disruptive strategies, techniques, methods, words, images, and so forth in public discussions or controversies. What attitude toward others or toward listening do our messages encourage? We describe three consequences of coarse communication; we argue that (1) coarseness normalizes coarseness, (2) coarseness contributes to a noisy public sphere, thus crowding the voices of the politically impoverished, and (3) coarseness is a consequence of elite's expropriation of the rhetoric of contestation, weakening the rhetorical force of counterpublics.

These three phenomena tend often to be generally addressed in concerns about growing political disaffection—what Kendall Phillips terms the "decline narrative."[5] Typically, this is understood as cynicism, political ignorance, poorly formed attitudes, or a refusal to vote. We contribute a facet to the decline narrative, the idea that people stop listening. Political philosopher James Bohman explains that in a democracy there must be "uptake."[6] Benjamin Barber asserts that the health of political communication is determined by how much reflection it nurtures.[7] People must be able and willing to listen to ideas and to ruminate over them. Susan Herbst prescribes middle- and high-school instruction in what she terms "hard listening" in order to restore political civility.[8] Concerns over public sphere voice, access, and contestation are well-addressed by disruptive discourse if there is a stable public sphere to disrupt. However, when the floodgates are opened, we question whether the effect of countless voices is any different than censorship. There's one important difference with censorship; that being allowed to participate can in our present setting foster the impression that one has had an actual chance at affecting the system.

In the context of a social controversy rhetorical scholars Kathryn Olson and G. Thomas Goodnight explain that "oppositional argument" necessitates that the advocate upset social conventions and provoke discussion.[9] Anyone in-the-know advising someone to get attention through all of today's noise will instruct them to do or say something that stands out. Want to make a point about gun rights? Hold a convention in the town of a recent high-school massacre.[10] Want to advocate for the ethical use of cows? Use a billboard exploiting Rudy Giuliani's prostate cancer, linking milk to the disease.[11] Career waning? Release a sex tape.[12] This, we maintain, creates a noisy public space that normalizes visceral appeals. And what happens when oppositional argument becomes the norm of public discourse? Worse, what happens when that tact is adopted by the mainstream? George W. Bush has been dubbed by some the first postmodern president because of, among other things, his disregard for the facts.[13] Should rich, white, conservative millionaires be subjected to the hegemonic forces that seek to maintain bourgeoisie deliberative mechanisms (we ask with tongue in cheek)? What if every interest adopts the standpoint and rhetorical strategies of a counterpublic? Before the *Citizens United* ruling, were corporations needlessly silenced by a bloated and tyrannical government? Will Rand Paul be successful in restoring from our overreaching government the God-given right of business owners to discriminate based on race?[14] When will billionaires stop being punished for their successes by oppressive progressive taxes? When will bereaving rich families stop being assaulted by death taxes?

Combining the glut of public communication, a lack of listening (or uptake), right-wing oppositional absurdity, with an attitude (particularly academic) discouraging the critique of counterpublic expression, and you have our present situation. It's Noelle-Neumann's Spiral of Silence stood on its head; when no public expressions are criticized or condemned, the world gets noisy,[15] which enables conversation to become increasingly groundless and absurd. This chapter discusses these matters, explaining what we mean by the changing communication environment and giving theoretical justification for the critique of public expression.

THE COMMUNICATION ENVIRONMENT

The communication environment is the public context of our talk; it is both the time and space in which we talk and the reality we constitute, challenge, and/or reinforce with our messages. Our messages are both a product of and shape our own attitudes and the attitudes of others. We talk differently at home than we do at work, for instance, because these places are different. They necessitate different ways of speaking. At the same time, how we talk designates what kind of space we are in. To illustrate our point, Southern black Baptists *do* church in a manner that is extremely different from relatively more high church Roman Catholics. Still, we'd be wrong to walk away from either thinking they were doing the same things in different ways. Their manner of worship reflects their theology or attitudes about God, self, world, and others. Baptists, for instance, place a great deal of emphasis on salvation through the sacrament of baptism. Once saved, there is cause for jubilation and outward expressions of joy. All are equal in the eyes of God, thus there is no preferred manner of behavior. Grace is bestowed equally. The Baptist service is a celebration. Roman Catholics, on the other hand, worship in a very different manner. The mass is formulaic and incantatory—held less to celebrate grace as it is to commune with God who *is* present. Adherence to form is necessary in order to uphold and perpetuate timeless and holy ritual. The Roman Catholic mass is formal dinner with your father. Likewise how we communicate publicly reinforces, endorses, and challenges how we talk, how we think, and what we think about—it shapes our attitudes.

We believe that our communication environment has changed considerably over the last two generations, and has thus altered our attitudes. This warrants close examination. We propose that the range of normal public messages has been profoundly broadened to the point of having few if any limits, having two important effects. Positively, it has enabled various different communities of people, or publics, to participate in public controversy more easily. Enough cannot be said about the value of this development. This has allowed nonwhite, nonmale, nonstraight, nonrich people to our democratic table, so to speak. And the history of this access does not involve these publics being *invited* to the discussion. They *took* their place; they fought for it. For these reasons, their manner of communication is, as a necessity, disruptive and shocking. These groups demanded that they be heard. Their struggles are an important complexity with implications for our argument that we deal with below. Negatively, the fear of quieting marginal voices by criticizing public expressions often discredits and chills efforts to criticize how and what people say. We've lost our will to condemn harmful messages. We are not lamenting our society's inability to censor messages. Instead, our concern is with the inability to have a serious conversation about the tone, content, veracity, and verbiage of our messages without being labeled an elitist.

Let's consider an example of the rhetoric surrounding the public discussion of appropriate rhetoric. The following example is interesting for two reasons. First, it shows the "elitist" trope at work, condemning criticism of public expressions. Second, it is being used by a defender of the Tea Party— a group that can hardly be described as marginal. Prior to the 2010 congressional elections, Tunku Varadarajan defends the Tea Party in *The Daily Beast*:[16]

> What bothers me, however, is that although ideological differences are at the bottom of the Tea Party assaults, the critique is almost purely aesthetic: The Tea Partiers, it is said, are crude, sloganeering, lemming-like, heartland Bible-Beltists who don't understand policy or David Brooks' subtleties.

Varadarajan is responding to an actual *substantive* criticism of the Tea Party leveled by *New York Times* columnist David Brooks. Varadarajan's goal, it seems, is to reduce the criticism to an assessment to *aesthetic* matters—doing precisely what we describe above. Criticism of coarse public communication is dismissed as a subjective, elitist rant. These remarks are a response to Brook's piece in the *New York Times* titled "The Tea Party Teens."[17] In it, he criticizes Tea Party ideology:

> The tea party movement is a large, fractious confederation of Americans who are defined by what they are against. They are against the concentrated power of the educated class. They believe big government, big business, big media and the affluent professionals are merging to form self-serving oligarchy— with bloated government, unsustainable deficits, high taxes and intrusive regulation. The tea party movement is mostly famous for its flamboyant fringe.

In an instance in which Brooks substantively criticizes the Tea Party, he is accused of being a classist or an elitist. Varadarajan's rhetoric is one that capitalizes on the appeal of anti-elitism. Americans appear conditioned, at the ready to dismiss criticism of any kind as an elitist move to quiet the marginalized (ironically, in this instance, the voices of billionaire libertarians). In the present context, subjection to such criticism functions to legitimize the content of the criticized. Varadarajan adds:

> David Brooks is not alone in his disdain: On right and left, "educated" people have given vent to their contempt for the Tea Party crowd, leading me to conclude that there must, surely, be considerable significance in a movement that has had scorn poured on it by such varied names as David Frum, who is

also, like Brooks, a friend of mine; Michael Goldfarb, a former spokesman for the McCain presidential campaign; Paul Krugman; Chris Matthews; and Keith Olbermann.

Brooks's argument pointed out that, less than ideology, the Tea Party was defined by what they opposed. As such, there was little with which to take issue. The issues aren't, he seems to imply, ideologically consistent. Varadarajan's response was to say that taking exception to Tea Party opposition to the "educated class" constitutes elitism. Varadarajan doesn't examine the criticism of Brooks, Frum, Goldfard, Krugman, Matthews, or Olbermann. Instead, he simply notes that the existence of such broad resistance lends the movement support and legitimacy.

What we see here is a contemporary hermeneutic horizon that functions *in light of* American developments throughout the 1960s, and the experiences of that sedimented history have affected the coding and meaning of today's public protest and advocacy. We are disciplined to *not* criticize because it smacks of elitism and we fear that our silence enables public absurdity. The doors to public discussion have been opened wide enough to accommodate today's hypertrophic ego, delivering to the powerful another rhetorical technique necessary to accomplish its ends. As the boundaries of absurdity, stupidity, and vulgarity are pushed further, they meet less and less resistance; it becomes normalized, and thus boring, leading to yet coarser expression.

Our argument has implications for "public sphere theory." Public sphere theory is an area of social, democratic, and philosophical writing that looks closely at Western democracies to explain how democracy manifests and to what ideals it should aspire in today's complex and modern settings. The following section addresses public sphere theory in order to situate our argument within it. At first glance, that our argument encourages the evaluation of public communication appropriateness may cause question of its consistency with commonly accepted facets of public sphere theory. We believe, however, that we present a nuanced argument that explains how our communication environment limits the pursuits of democratic dialogue while fostering the impression that it is more open and democratic than ever before.

THE PUBLIC SPHERE

The following is an effort to explain some of the theoretical questions that academic readers are likely to have. Yet, to keep it readable it is tailored to the curious reader. The goal is to explain precisely where in the area of public sphere theory our argument is situated. This necessitates explaining public sphere theory as it pertains to our thesis, and presenting and explaining our argument that oppositional public tactics have been expropriated by those with hegemonic authority and power in our democracy. We consider in what ways mainstream authority in our country uses oppositional tactics in order to effect what Habermas's terms "refeudalization." Refeudalization is the jumping-off point for our argument.

In the traditional liberal sense, good argument has a liberating ability. Appeals to reason and the use of evidence, it is believed by some, constitute what enables people to push back against authority, bureaucracy, ideologies, mythologies, biases, superstitions, and assumptions. By contrast, where nonsense reigns, tyrants, opinion leaders, and passions lead. Lippmann, John Dewey, and Jurgen Habermas all agreed that a reasonable public was important or necessary for democracy, though they differed on whether it was achievable. Dewey argued for its necessity. Habermas became a champion of reasoned and open public discourse. This ideal, he believes, is necessary to ensure that the public balances out the power exercised by the state.

Habermas's arguments are criticized for presupposing the existence of a universal standard for rational argument. His critics contend that his work helps perpetuate the notions of ahistorical, noncontingent, and universal forms of argumentation and truth; that there is one truth, and a proper way to arrive at it. It is widely accepted, particularly in academia, that faith in these universals, particularly as they are practiced in Western societies, is hegemonic—thus, norms function to marginalize and silence others.

Habermas argues for the necessity of a vibrant public sphere in successful democracies. The public sphere, he explains, is a "place" in which debate is enacted. Several people gather together and argue as equals. He defines it as follows:

> The bourgeois public sphere may be conceived above all as the sphere of private people come together as a public; they soon claimed the public sphere regulated from above against the public authorities themselves, to engage them in a debate over the general rules governing relations in the basically privatized but publicly relevant sphere of commodity exchange and social labor. The medium of this political confrontation was peculiar and without historical precedent: people's public use of their reason. [18]

Ideally, nobody pulls rank or is censored. All are invited. Where or if this description of the public sphere has ever existed is an important question. Habermas maintained that it was the existence of an educated bourgeoisie public that provided necessary counterweight to the state. As Western governments evolved, they developed from being states that legitimized themselves into states that gained their legitimacy from their public or publics—from the governed.

The public sphere is a concern of Habermas's because he warns that the relationship between the public sphere and the state is being turned. Whereas the state, beginning in the late seventeenth and eighteenth centuries, ideally sought its legitimacy from the public, today, he warns, we risk the state *manufacturing* the assent of the public. He terms this process "refeudalization." Mass communication has produced an environment in which those possessing abundant resources, influence on the production of knowledge, and control over the means of communication can orchestrate and generate public discussion.

To counter refeudalization, Habermas argues that we need to devote our energies to maintaining a healthy public sphere. In his description of the "ideal speech situation," Habermas prescribes the following: that every subject with the competence to speak be allowed to participate in discussion, that everyone be allowed to question any assertion, that everyone be allowed to make an assertion, and that no person be disallowed from participating.

Most notable among Habermas' critics is Nancy Fraser, who argues that Habermas' ideal public sphere is more theoretical than realistic. In theory, from her perspective, the notion of a universally accessible public sphere is nice, but it doesn't square with social facts. Taking a more "realistic" or functionalistic approach to her understanding of the public sphere, she maintains that certain groups have always been denied access. Fraser views the reality of the public sphere as stratified. She means that some people have more and/or greater access than others. Class, race, gender, and whatever else are matters always salient during interaction. She writes:

> In stratified societies, arrangements that accommodate contestation among a plurality of competing publics better promote the ideal of participatory parity than does a single, comprehensive, overarching public. [19]

As such, she, in effect, reimagines the ideal speaking situation. All are not assimilated into one regime of discourse. Instead, "subaltern counterpublics," as she terms them, "invent and circulate counterdiscourses to formulate oppositional interpretations of their identities, interests, and needs." [20] In other words, counterpublics are groups with shared identities that struggle in the public sphere for recognition of their interests.

Fraser addresses a matter that is very important to our argument. Just how alternative are these counterpublics? More to the point, are they so foreign as to be misunderstood? Do they speak in foreign tongues? Do they employ their own logic? Indirectly addressing these questions, she writes, "In my view, the concept of a counterpublic militates in the long run against separatism because it assumes a *publicist* orientation." [21] They seek to communicate with and influence "widening arenas." Albeit indirectly, this assertion matters to our overarching argument because it implies the necessity of *understanding* between publics. Conceding that understanding between publics is necessary doesn't grant Habermas's implied universal manner of reasoning. It does give ground, though. Do various publics get to operate according to their own logic? Can propagating nonsense be construed as an acceptable disruptive counterpublic campaign? Whether the necessity of understanding means either assimilating others linguistically and logically, or embracing multicultural literacy, is irrelevant to our point. In other words, our position on coarseness is consistent with *either* point of view. If understanding each other can be considered a basic necessity of a public sphere that aspires to function at all, then there are grounds for criticism.

The "rub" lies in being able to judge or criticize public acceptability of discourse. Who gets to determine if one statement is acceptable and another statement is coarse? Is there a normative standard that we can draw on? We accept that there isn't such a universal standard. However, we do assert that surrendering the will or desire to evaluate the acceptability of public discourse runs the risk of opening the public to cacophony; without it, how can one even produce a judgment in a controversy? In any given context, provided it isn't used either to rhetorical advantage or to silence voices, public participants should consider the effects their messages have on the communication environment. The quality of public discussion should be a phenomenon worthy of careful evaluation and discussion if only to ensure that strong counterpublic arguments encounter capable, reasonable, empathic, and open-minded audiences willing to and capable of listening.

To sum, it is important from our perspective to maintain that messages in public controversies make sense and aspire to truthfulness because the alternative can be harmful and counterproductive. Alternatively, all that mainstream authority need do is co-opt this manner of counterpublic discourse in order to foster confusion and contribute to communication glut. Under these circumstances, no arguments gain traction. Very little breaks through.

ACCEPTABLE DISCOURSE?

To get to the heart of the matter, is telling someone publicly to "fuck off" acceptable? In answering with an emphatic "Yes!" we look again to Nancy Fraser; counterpublics are not just alternative publics—alternative realities. As she explains, they don't so much enclave themselves as find themselves enclaved. Their differences cause them to be denied access. Thus, they perform *contestation* as a way to demand access to the public sphere. They agitate. For example, illegal Mexican labor is a group that is formally denied access to our public sphere. In 2006, the AP estimated that five hundred thousand people marched in Los Angeles to protest a crackdown against illegal immigrants.[22] Many of the protesters were illegal immigrants, but their numbers made it impractical to round them up. They publicly flaunted their presence as a way to tell the system that it was broken. And this agitation is absolutely necessary for ushering issues perceived as "private" or group specific into the public.

Another excellent example emerges from the historical debates about women's reproductive issues. Those who initially championed women's reproductive rights were shocking; they were often met with disgust. Women advocates were viewed as compromising their femininity and as destructive to society. Were they coarse? Were they behaving coarsely? To the extent that they were addressing these matters at all would cause some to characterize what they were doing as coarse. That the matter dealt with female genitalia probably didn't help. That it often dealt with abortion, prophylaxis, and sex—explicitly or implicitly—made matters even worse. This is an instance that clearly lies on the borderland between coarse expression and contestation, and thus is appears to some worthy of criticism. Yet, it is necessary to note that contestation *necessitates* disruption of the public sphere in order to work. Early advocates for women's rights had to be shocking in order to be listened to; for some it was shocking that women would ask to be listened to. Today, matters of women's reproduction are universally accepted as public issues. Even opponents of feminism don't shy away from these matters in public forums. In fact, these once-shocking issues are today almost always raised in public by feminism's *opponents*—those seeking to repeal abortion rights, rights to prophylaxis, rape protections, and so on. A Republican in the House of Representatives recently proposed requiring poor women to be beaten during their rapes in order to qualify for publicly funded pregnancy intervention[23] —hardly the effort of a conservative seeking to keep sensitive matters relegated to the private sphere. To sum, disruptive public performance is a *necessary* part of democracy. It will always exist and will always be evidence of the constructive nature of democracy, so it would be absurd for us to argue that it should be otherwise.

In their analysis of the anti-fur campaign in the mid-1980s, Olson and Goodnight illustrate in detail the necessary role of contestation or "oppositional argument" in social controversy.[24] They examine how, in a place and time during which people are inclined to accept without question the presumptions of capitalism and fashion that have people wanting and wearing fur clothing, those opposing it can stand a chance to undermine those assumptions by using oppositional argument. It is through protest and disruptive displays, among other methods, that the marginalized get listened to. They can't rely on traditional means of argument because the deck is stacked against them. To be more precise, oppositional marginalized groups perceive "rules of reasoning and division of grounds . . . to be but rationalizations of oppressive power conditions."[25] Olson and Goodnight explain that the value of oppositional argument is that it has the capacity to "provoke reexamination of the norms of personal conduct and challenge[s] the range of publicly acceptable means of communication."[26] Thus, oppositional argument expands the public sphere, causes us to question exclusionary communication norms, and can cause us to reconsider the assumptions underlying the matter being discussed. Kendall Phillips goes further, explaining that oppositional arguments and/or "disruptive tactics" "create a space where alternative discursive and material systems may be proposed," and creates a moment in which an identity can be formed and can assert itself by resisting assimilation or homogenization.[27]

To further consider the boundary between coarse communication and contestation we ask, "What if the nature of the issue contested *involves* coarse behavior?" We aren't asking about a message coarsely crafted in order to demand attention. But what if the topic itself is considered private or risqué? Diogenes of Sinope, it is recorded, would enter the marketplace to masturbate in order to criticize society's values and conventions. Masturbation is one of the most private things people do. It's not only sexual, but is, unlike sex itself for most, considered largely taboo. Diogenes's point was to criticize the arbitrariness of sexual norms. Anyone with a young child knows that their child had to *learn* not to manipulate him/herself around others— take off the diaper and away they go! Anyway, the public/private distinction is a cultural convention, and is not intrinsic to our genetic coding—at least as far as we know. This is an example in which public sexuality or prudish authority and convention are at the center of the controversy. Even in an instance like this, we don't believe contestation should be criticized as coarse. It contributes to the debate inasmuch as it is the subject of the debate. Nevertheless, we don't believe that today's advocates of public masturbation are going to get very far.

We see a related and very real example in the controversy surrounding gay pride parades. It's too simplistic to maintain that there is any one argument being articulated by gays, lesbians, transgendered people, or straight people in gay pride parades, but underlying many of the controversies regarding these counterpublics is sexual liberalism. On the conservative side, some LGBTs desire to mainstream and acquire the right to marry. Others seek to entirely upset conservative sexual conventions, believing that the gay–straight dichotomy and the tradition of monogamy are not supported by observation of human behavior. A conservative person would find many of the displays at a gay pride parade to be sexually provocative, and would likely consider them shocking or coarse. This is, however, a form of contestation; it shocks. But because its content is consistent with its point, we maintain that this example falls within the boundaries of acceptable public discourse. Their arguments necessitate their displays.

Central to our claim that coarse public expression warrants criticism is recognizing expression that *isn't* necessary for public engagement of issues that defines the communication environment down, expression that functions

to crowd public deliberation, and mainstream expression that mimics oppositional appearance and technique. We believe there is an important difference
between public expressions that betray the indifference of a hypertrophic ego
and expressions that communicate ideas and function to expand the public
sphere. Consistent with our position, Chantal Mouffe writes that we *can*
"distinguish within a given regime of truth between those who respect the
strategy of argumentation and its rules, and those who simply want to impose
their power."[28] Power, in our opinion, includes both political and economic/
commercial power.

We propose that public expression becomes harmful to the public, ultimately to democratic processes, however broadly or narrowly defined, when
expressions are made with little mind to their impact on their recipients and/
or the communication environment. When the benefits of public expressions
can be traced back solely to the individual who expressed them (e.g., profit,
fame, hits, votes, viewers, comments, downloads), when they fail to expand
the public sphere, and when they show no consideration given to what the
expressions contribute to the repertoire of public expression, we deem them
coarse. These expressions don't simply disappear into the ether. They contribute to the communication environment, they expand our repertoire of
expression, and they shape our attitudes. As such, people should be held
responsible for what they say.

REFEUDALIZATION AND OUR COMMUNICATION
ENVIRONMENT

Coarseness is a symptom of the larger problem—the hypertrophic ego and
the societal attitudes and mechanisms that foster and encourage it. Though
we don't recommend censoring coarse messages, we quite clearly condemn
them as a significant social problem. Generally, we believe that coarseness
functions in the service of a form of refeudalization of which Habermas
warned. We propose that cynical players (i.e., corporatist plutocrats) employ
coarse discourse. The communication of nonsense has been embraced as an
essential component of the modern communication techniques of leadership.
We outline three notable effects of coarseness. First, coarseness begets
coarseness—thus normalizing it. Second, once coarseness becomes normalized, it contributes to a noisy public sphere. Third, coarse rhetoric is expropriated by elites, generating a public sphere marked by constant contestation.
Coarseness both derails mainstream communication and crowds out and con-
fuses the messages of counterpublics.

Chapter 2

COARSENESS BEGETS COARSENESS

Television, radio, print, and the Internet all vie for the attention of increasingly fragmented audiences. Combine this media scramble with the American notions of the free market and the marketplace of ideas, and you realize an environment in which the pressures to loosen standards for public expression are constant and overwhelming. Audience demand for puerile content certainly can't be greater than investor demand for profit. Television programs sixty years ago were considerably tamer, and yet they had enormous audiences. It is reported, for instance, that 72 percent of homes with televisions tuned in to the birth of "little Ricky" on *I Love Lucy* in 1953; that's forty-four million viewers.[29] By contrast, *American Idol*'s best-viewed episode, its 2006 finale, drew thirty-six million viewers. That's with more than double the population's size and considerable growth in the number of both homes with televisions and televisions in homes. Though its viewership continues to drop, *American Idol* remains television's most-watched program. It is unlikely that *I Love Lucy*, regardless of the quality of its writing, could compete successfully *today* against the "unscripted" drama of *American Idol*. Could Lucy's zany schemes draw a larger crowd than the early-season mocking of desperate and psychologically challenged people who butcher songs while a panel of millionaires laugh at and mock them? Besides, the talent it took to write *Lucy* is considerably more expensive than the cost of desperate, young, aspirant pop stars.

And younger consumers, the most lucrative and present-oriented viewers, are changing their habits from television in favor of the Internet and videogames—significantly richer media. The Internet functions as a television with limitless channels. Today's video games are rich multiplayer environments that enable friends to virtually run around and kill one another, or coordinate in the killing of strangers, all while talking through headphones. The five best-selling PlayStation 2 games were *Vice City* games that allowed the player to complete mafia challenges that involved killing people, exploding things, and drug dealing. One version allowed a person to "charge-up" energy by having sex with prostitutes in a car. If the player unlocked a secret code, s/he could open a bonus sex mini-game in which the player films a "homemade" porn film. Such games are rated, and the restriction of the sale of these games to minors is voluntary on the part of the retailer.

LOSS OF CONVERSATIONAL CONTINUITY

Next, we believe that the fragmented communication environment in which we now live has compromised our society's ability to sustain prolonged conversations. Regardless of a reader's position on Habermas or his/her own notions of the imperialism of Western rationality, it is doubtless to us that anyone could be indifferent to a cacophonous public communication environment. In *any* context, it becomes nearly impossible to shift the consensus away from the status quo by way of the expression of good ideas *if* a steady conversation about the merits or harms of change can't be sustained. Edward Hall notes that some societies, China for example, plan hundreds of years ahead. American business, by contrast, plans quarterly, or every three months. In such a relatively present-oriented setting, we are also immersed in a milieu that encourages impulse buying as the norm. Combine that with fragmented and contentious bickering, and the odds on a sustained public discussion about anything plummet. The latter is consistent with what Maggie Jackson suggests in *Distracted*—that we are surrounded by distracting, buzzing, and attention-competing noise. Our minds, she maintains, get reprogrammed to seek more and increasingly novel stimuli. [30]

The media, in a capitalistic setting, can't be blamed for doing what it needs to attract attention. After all, it must sell advertising. Still, the *rationale* for this manner of public communication doesn't inoculate us from the consequences of the communication it serves up as a model and helps normalize. Since coming into its own during the first U.S. invasion of Iraq in 1990, one would think that channels devoted to twenty-four hours of daily news (e.g., CNN) would have facilitated in-depth, evidence-based public discussion of substantive issues in a manner greater than was seen in previous decades. This attitude, however, presupposes that people have ever wanted to sit for lengthy recitations and exchanges on public matters. Much of what CNN, MSNBC, Fox, and other news channels have done is increase competition and divide marketshare. Thus, broadcast news outlets that once devoted relatively more time to substantive news coverage no longer have the luxury of such an indulgence, particularly following the Reagan-era repeal of Federal Communication Commission (FCC) requirements for public service broadcasting. News outlets must fight for marketshare *and* profit, and not just with other news outlets. If one imagines a wifi'd laptop as an interactive television/real-time mall/portable arcade with limitless content, competition for audience can be more aptly described as a mad scramble. Is it any surprise that televised news has become laden with breezy celebrity host chatter, combative guest exchanges, computerized visual displays, and gritty and graphic crime reports? It makes for interesting television. Who doesn't want to find out where a local sheriff found an arm following the nightly lottery numbers?

We correct Neil Postman only slightly, "I raise no objection to television's junk. The best things on television *are* its junk."[31] Though great at producing junk, we still take issue with the product and its effects. Our issue with the junk is that it doesn't even *poorly* dwell on issues of public policy long enough to generate audience salience and attitude formation. Noted political scientist Richard Zaller has demonstrated that attitude formation is more resilient when a person believes s/he has enough information to support an attitude.[32] Cycling through current events in a manic pursuit of novel matter does little to inform viewers in such a way.

And what if fostering a coarse public communication environment *is* intentional. What if it isn't solely the product of market forces? David Brock argues in *The Republican Noise Machine* that such an effort *is* intentional. He maintains that the GOP has strategically built the policy and apparatus that enables it to control discussion and to mute facts in our present communication environment.

> The Right's premeditated undermining of the media as a public trust in favor of crass commercial values, its coordinated attacks on non-commercial media, and the Republican-led drive for greater consolidation of media ownership have all but wiped-out liberal and left-wing views and voices in entire sectors of the American media. . . . unchecked right-wing media power means that in the United States today, no issue can be honestly debated and no election can be fairly decided.[33]

But if we step back further and examine the entire communication environment, it appears as though the reach of "crass commercial values" goes well beyond the news. If we combine the news with the rest of the flashy noise and stupidity occupying the public sphere, there's little surprise that we find ourselves, as Maggie Jackson says, with an eroded "capacity for deep, sustained, perceptive attention."[34] Politically, such a degraded communication environment is *not* in the interests of the classes that find themselves most in need of public influence and government attention.

CO-OPTED RHETORIC OF CONTESTATION

Above, we introduced the idea that one of the complications with Habermas's ideal public-speaking situation is that it, as Nancy Fraser and Kendall Phillips put it, has never existed. Fraser made various other arguments, but one of her central positions is that counterpublics necessitate contestation as a form of public discourse. This form of communication is intrinsically inconsistent with the ideal public-speaking situation precisely because it is intended to disrupt it. Denied equal access to the public sphere as well as audiences willing to listen, counterpublics must fight and disrupt public tranquility in order to be heard at all.

From our perspective, this form of disruptive communication is necessary for genuine democracy to exist at all in a modern setting. However, central to our argument is the idea that we *must* be willing to critique communication that is harmful to public discussion (whatever form that may take). So, whose communication should be critiqued? We maintain that the rhetoric of contestation isn't defined by its form, but by the context. When privileged elites adopt this rhetoric (e.g., Tea Party rhetoric), legitimate contestation by underprivileged communities can become indistinguishable from that of mainstream voices. Equip these elites with their own media outlets (e.g., Fox News, talk radio, and the Internet) and the entire technique of disruption becomes worthless. The rhetoric of contestation is weakened by making its tenor ubiquitous. It's bad enough, for purposes of message, that a protest is held almost every day in Washington, DC. Combine the protests of politically impoverished counterpublics with the growing number of mainstream, privileged advocacy groups busy working to sound just like them and Americans end up immersed in perpetual disruption.

In this book, we maintain that the rhetorical strategies of underprivileged communities have been expropriated by mainstream advocacy, and have thus slowed, and in some instances begun to reverse, the progress various groups have gained through their historical struggles in the United States. The problem isn't just the noisy and contentious environment; it is that upon closer inspection, the rhetoric is more than mere noise. This facet of public coarseness is antidemocratic.

NOTES

1. Chantal Mouffe, *The Return of the Political: Radical Thinkers* (New York: Verso, 2006).
2. Nancy Fraser, "Rethinking the Public Sphere: A Contribution to the Critique of Actual Existing Democracy," in *Habermas and the Public Sphere*, ed. C. Calhoun (Cambridge: MIT Press, 1999).
3. Hans-Georg Gadamer, *Philosophical Hermeneutics* (Berkeley: University of California Press, 1977), 9.
4. Gadamer, *Philosophical Hermeneutics*, 13.
5. Kendall Phillips, "A Rhetoric of Controversy," *Western Journal of Communication* 63 (1999): 490.
6. James Bohmann, *Public Deliberation: Pluralism, Complexity, and Democracy* (Cambridge: MIT Press, 2000), 205.
7. Benjamin Barber, *Strong Democracy: Participatory Politics for a New Age* (Berkeley: University of California Press, 1984), 175.

8. Susan Herbst, *Rude Democracy* (Philadelphia: Temple University Press, 2010), 126.

9. Lester Olson and Thomas Goodnight, "Entanglements of Consumption, Cruelty, Privacy, and Fashion: The Social Controversy over Fur," *Quarterly Journal of Speech* 80 (1994): 249–76.

10. Jake Tapper, "Coming out Shooting," Salon, May 2, 1999, www.salon.com/1999/05/02/nra/.

11. Montgomery, Alicia, "PETA on the Spot," *Salon*, August 30, 2000, www.salon.com/2000/08/30/giuliani_peta/.

12. Lola Ogunnaike, "Sex, Lawsuits and Celebrities Caught on Tape," *New York Times*, March   19,   2006,   query.nytimes.com/gst/fullpage.html?res=9C07E6DB1E31F93AA25750C0A9609C8B63&pagewanted=all. See Lorenzo Benet, "Kim Kardashian Sues over Sex Tape," *People*, February 21, 2007, www.people.com/people/article/0,,20012494,00.html. See Devon Thomas, "Kendra Wilkinson Sex Tape Video: "People Are Going to Judge Me and Stuff," CBS News, June 1, 2010, www.cbsnews.com/8301-31749_162-20006408-10391698.html&
usg=AFQjCNEgNUSWiwSls03yCFkjvkF6tLK0CA.

13. Alan Wolfe, "Hobbled from the Start," Salon, December 15, 2000, www.salon.com/2000/12/15/trust_4/.

14. David Weigel, "Rand Paul Telling the Truth," *Washington Post*, May 20, 2010, voices.washingtonpost.com/right-now/2010/05/rand_paul_telling_the_truth.html.

15. Elisabeth Noelle-Neumann, *The Spiral of Silence* (Chicago: University of Chicago Press, 1993).

16. Tunku Varadarajan, "In Defense of Tea Parties," *The Daily Beast*, January 10, 2010, www.thedailybeast.com/articles/2010/01/11/in-defense-of-tea-parties.html.

17. David Brooks, "The Tea Party Teens," *New York Times*, January 5, 2010.

18. Jurgen Habermas, *The Structural Transformation of the Public Sphere*, trans. Thomas Burger and Frederick Lawrence (Cambridge: MIT Press, 1991), 27.

19. Fraser, "Rethinking the Public Sphere," 122.

20. Fraser, "Rethinking the Public Sphere," 123.

21. Fraser, "Rethinking the Public Sphere," 124.

22. "Immigration Issue Draws Thousands into Streets," MSNBC, March 25, 2006,www.msnbc.msn.com/id/11442705/ns/politics/t/immigration-issue-draws-thousands-streets/.

23. Nick Baumann, "The House GOP's Plan to Redefine Rape," *Mother Jones*, January 28, 2011, motherjones.com/politics/2011/01/republican-plan-redefine-rape-abortion.

24. Olson and Goodnight, "Entanglements of Consumption, Cruelty, Privacy, and Fashion," 249–76.

25. Olson and Goodnight, "Entanglements of Consumption, Cruelty, Privacy, and Fashion," 249–76.

26. Olson and Goodnight, "Entanglements of Consumption, Cruelty, Privacy, and Fashion," 249–76.

27. Phillips, "A Rhetoric of Controversy," 494. (We don't believe our arguments are consistent with Kendall Phillips, but our arguments are informed by his positions about the nonexistence of a stable public sphere and a standard mode of reasoning.)

28. Mouffe, *The Return of the Political*, 15.

29. Christopher Anderson, "I Love Lucy," Museum of Broadcast Communications, www.museum.tv/archives/etv/I/htmlI/ilovelucy/ilovelucy.htm.

30. Maggie Johnson, *Distracted* (Amherst, NY: Prometheus Books, 2009).

31. Neil Postman, *Amusing Ourselves to Death* (New York: Penguin, 1986), 16.

32. John Zaller, *The Nature and Origins of Mass Opinion* (Cambridge: Cambridge University Press, 1992).

33. David Brock, *The Republican Noise Machine* (New York: Crown, 2004), 12.

34. Johnson, *Distracted*, 13.

Chapter Three

Coarseness in U.S. Politics

Boehner says there will be major political consequences for pro-life Democrats who break from the Stupak bloc. "Take [Rep.] Steve Driehaus, for example," he says. "He may be a dead man."

—Robert Costa, March 18, 2010, *National Review*[1]

Analyzing *where* coarseness manifests directs our attention immediately to
the political scene. Many treatments of coarseness and incivility look first at
entertainment, and while entertainment is certainly affected by these trends,
we encourage the reader to consider the political effects of incivility and
absurdity before examining others because we believe it has the greatest
material implications. Exempting the rhetoric of contestation from our criticism, plenty of political discourse is coarse enough to warrant concern.
Rudeness, for instance, has become a political mainstay of late. For instance,
at the 2011 CPAC conference former Vice President Dick Cheney told the
audience, "All right, sit down and shut up."[2] Andrew Breitbart called liberals
"hate-filled, racist sheep," and "monsters."[3] Ann Coulter likened Democrats
to cancer.[4] All of this came *after* the Gabrielle Giffords shooting and *after*
the show of seating-civility seen during the 2011 State of the Union Address.
In addition to *bogus* contestation, contemporary politics is replete with instrumental or outcomes-oriented communication—a modern-day sophistry
that functions to produce support and/or acquiescence however possible.
Fear appeals, stupid appeals, flak, yelling, force, politics as titillating entertainment, and a refusal to listen dominate contemporary politics. The latter is
no better demonstrated than by recent comments Texas House Representative Ron Paul made to CNN's Anderson Cooper:

> Well, the people's business isn't getting done . . . I don't think it's because
> people don't compromise enough, I think it's because they compromise too
> much. And we don't have enough people standing on principle. [5]

Standing on principle resonates positively with many people. After all, if you don't stand for something you'll fall for anything, right? The problem with it is that standing on principle means starting dialogue or debate without assuming your opponent has anything worthy to say. This statement presupposes that different and opposing principles aren't represented in government by other reasonable people. This and other varieties of rhetoric position the other as an object. This is well illustrated by Wisconsin Governor Scott Walker's rhetoric during his state's 2011 budget standoff: "The bottom line is we are trying to balance our budget and there really is no room to negotiate on that because we're broke." [6] Voices representing standpoints other than those of one's principles aren't treated as equal, reasonable, or human, rhetorically rendering the opponent's arguments easier to resist and ignore.

Concerning ourselves with the state of the communication environment, we warn against dehumanization and absurdity begetting more dehumanization and absurdity. If this type of discourse becomes the norm, we lose the spaces and atrophy the skills necessary for the reasonable consideration of issues. This sentiment is shared by Frances Fox Piven, who has been demonized regularly by Fox's Glenn Beck for supposedly crafting a left-wing masterplan for a worldwide socialist takeover. In a response to these attacks she writes:

> The sheer complexity of our economic and political system makes democratic
> choice and deliberation difficult if not impossible. Democratic possibilities
> depend crucially on the ability of the public to understand what is happening to
> our society and why, and especially on the ability of the public to decipher the
> role of government policies. [7]

And, we fear, not only is mainstream discourse undermined, but counterpublics both lose a public sphere to disrupt and get drowned out by ever-present contestation—a cacophony of public opposition and phony controversy perpetrated by the hegemon to crowd out and confuse the demands of the marginalized. At best, the status quo remains frozen.

At its base, we believe the phenomenon of political coarseness is facilitated by the player mentality, the notion that the world is simply made up of lifeless units to be manipulated by those with the power to do so. Explaining why Congressional retreats, created for the purpose of restoring and fostering civility in Congress, failed miserably, Don Wolfensberger stated the following:

> I would submit that incivility, at least in Washington, is not the central prob-
> lem some think it is, but rather a sporadic symptom of a deeper, core problem,
> which is the great divide between the political elites of the two major political
> parties. Those divisions are partly driven by ideology, but mostly driven by the
> quest for permanent majority control of the government. Yes, it's all about
> power, as much of politics is. [8]

Elites are the players, the power players who have greatly influenced U.S. and world politics. They are creatures who view themselves as transcending national borders, viewing such borders as remnants of a bygone era and obstacles to commerce, preferring political stability, according to Nicholas Shaxson in *Treasure Island*, to political freedom.[9] Players don't participate in politics to uphold virtues or perpetuate standards of discourse. They make investments and they demand returns. Players demand what they pay for. Billionaire David Koch, for instance, represents the quintessential player. Even in the realm of formal research, he demands that results fit his world-view.

> David Koch has acknowledged that the family exerts tight ideological control.
> "If we're going to give a lot of money, we'll make darn sure they spend it in a
> way that goes along with our intent," he told [Brian] Doherty [an editor of
> *Reason*]. "And if they make a wrong turn and start doing things we don't agree
> with, we withdraw funding."[10]

David Koch, part-owner of Koch Industries, a major extraction and energy company, is in this quotation referring to money given to think tanks, such as George Mason's Institute for Humane Studies, the Cato Institute, and Think Progress. Independent researchers are quite clearly compelled to produce research that is consistent with the ideology of the funder.

David Koch and his brother Charles are huge players in industry and in politics. Jane Mayer's piece in the *New Yorker* titled "Covert Operations" outlines how they've created an enormous network of institutions that trumpet libertarianism—the central philosophy of which is an articulation of the player mentality. In short, these brothers promote the idea that no shared or collective interests outweigh the right of the individual to do what s/he wants and they promote this ideology with an enormous fortune that was bequeathed to them by their father. If a mechanism exists to rein in the excesses of our system many libertarians insist, it is Adam Smith's invisible hand—a mythical metaphysic that makes all things right. Just as in the product marketplace, the libertarian assumption holds that in the marketplace of ideas the *best* idea is the idea that wins the day—regardless of how much assistance the idea may have had along the way.

If it can be said that those contributing to elections demand results, it sensibly follows then that any and all techniques will be employed to the extent that their use doesn't limit the chances of winning. We believe this player mentality or ethic has permeated the political process at various levels; specifically, we consider how the player mentality has resulted in coarseness in politician, media, and citizen communication and behavior. Generally, what we find is an attitude implicit in messages made across all three of these entities that reflects an indifference or ignorance about the consequences of messages on anything other than short-term outcome. It is purely instrumental. Coarse political communication is rapidly degrading both our communication environment as well as the perception and the reality that political causes, for anything other than that which is advocated by plutocrats, can successfully be addressed by our political system.

In the sections that follow we address a number of political communicative phenomena. One that has been addressed elsewhere involves political affect or viscerality; many argue, and we partially concur, that politics has become an increasingly emotional affair—across the board. There are arguments on both sides of this issue, and we don't wade in too deep. Instead, our point is more that the perception and/or pursuit of a calm and rational norm in politics has been dispensed with by nearly all parties—except academics (who are consequently framed for their relatively reserved comportment as elites, and often dismissed for it). In his warning about the emotional and illogical shift in U.S. politics Neil Postman advised that it will render "the application of empirical tests, logical analysis or any of the other instruments of reason . . . impotent."[11]

This irrationality often manifests as anger—the sound of our politics is at a constant heated pitch. Once more, people may embrace political anger, believing that when anger is warranted the system *should* be made to pay attention and address it: for instance, teachers' anger over state threats to end tenure or small business owners' anger over a sales tax increase. However, we think anger works in a different way; it is employed enthymematically. The anger implies that a well-evidenced reason must have warranted it. For instance, let's say that a radio talk show host is angry at Obama over the citizen uprising in Egypt. The host is beside herself with anger. In this scenario time need not be wasted explaining the reasons for anger. This anger isn't issuing forth from counterpublics; it is top down. Recently, following the near-fatal shooting of Arizona Congresswoman Gabrielle Giffords, Fox News talk-show hosts were advised to "tone it down" by its president and former Nixon, Reagan, and Bush media consultant Roger Ailes.[12] The anger is coming from working-class free-market advocates, who've been socialized by a vast network of institutions funded by self-interested capitalist billionaires and millionaires. This emotive form of discourse is an enormous distraction from any prolonged engagement of a public issue. It works through the dehiscence of thoughts and feelings—absurdity, conspiracy, suspicion, accusations, and anger. And, as stated, it crowds out marginalized voices.

POLITICIANS AND COARSENESS

Politicians, the media, and voters make up the three components of the political system that we believe have been most important in the spread of public coarseness. We transition first to politicians because they are central to allowing these changes to take place. If politicians perceived the problem of coarseness as significant and had the will, they could change how politics is performed in the United States. Only, we fear that politicians inclined this way get selected out by the funding mechanisms of our system—they lose to politicians who *are* willing to adapt to the newer communication environment. As Mike McCurry stated of the 2004 presidential campaign for John Kerry, "We ran the last best campaign of the twentieth century. Republicans began what it takes to run campaigns in the twenty-first century."[13] Certainly, that included technological innovation, but there was nothing technologically innovative about Swift Boat Veterans for Truth or their third-party advertisements—lying is timeless. It was simply, at that point in history, a new depth in tactlessness. Swift Boat advertisements illustrate the downward "innovation" of U.S. political rhetoric.

We don't, however, direct our criticism at campaign funding because we believe that the notion that this is broken is common knowledge. Worse, we believe, are the effects that contemporary campaign funding has on the foundational attitudes of the campaigning industry and politicians. The voices of those contributing to candidates are the voices of the rich. The American Political Science Association's Task Force on Inequality and American Democracy explained that nearly all political contributors in 2000 earned over $100,000.

> Campaign contributors are the least representative group of citizens. Only 12 percent of American households had incomes over $100,000 in 2000, but a whopping 95 percent of the donors who made substantial contributions were in these wealthiest households.[14]

The task force added that the wealthy are disproportionately more likely to belong to a politically oriented organization, to communicate with political officials, to participate in community problem-solving efforts, and (consistent with our argument about hegemonic contestation) to protest—often thought of as the publicity mechanism of the marginalized. Based on these and other findings the task force concluded that the concerns and thoughts of the elite are much more often addressed by politicians than are those of the lower classes. Larry Bartels summarized additional research in *Unequal Democracy*, writing:

> Elected officials are utterly unresponsive to the policy preferences of millions of low-income citizens, leaving their political interests to be served or ignored as the ideological whims of incumbent elites may dictate. [15]

All of this exposure and influence, we maintain, normalizes the attitudes of the elite for the political class.

The attitudes of politicians that we address here are those of the player: irresponsibility and insular thinking. Specifically, irresponsibility means having to respond to no one. Community, it is presumed within the player mentality, is more of a mass aggregate—individuals buzzing around pursuing their own interests. Lee Fang of Think Progress, in an ambush interview following the swearing in of John Boehner as Speaker of the House, asked David Koch what he thought of the Supreme Court's Citizens United decision. Koch, who has funded the conservative nonprofit group and hosted strategy dinners for Citizens United that included Justice Antonin Scalia and Justice Clarence Thomas, refused to answer:

Fang: What do you think of Citizens United? Has it helped your influence?

Koch: Citizens United?

Fang: The Supreme Court Decision.

Koch: Oh . . . Hm . . .

Fang: I know you had a meeting last summer with Glenn Beck and several other conservatives. Could you tell the public what you discussed at that meeting?

Though he was more receptive to several previous questions in the exchange, Koch refused to respond. [16] While we have problems with ambush journalism (discussed later in the chapter), the Jane Mayer piece "Covert Operations" gives reason to believe that avoiding transparency is par for the course with Koch, players, and politicians alike.

The second component of this player mentality is related to the first. The player, and politicians increasingly, we fear, operate with a model of an impermeable self; they don't listen. Standing on principle, refusing to listen to others, and ridiculing opponents are part of this. Another element involves emphasizing the communion of identities between candidate and voter at the expense of issue-oriented communication. That is, communicating with voters *strictly* in terms of identity. Perhaps no one did this more bluntly than failed Delaware Senate candidate Christine O'Donnell in her political spot that was likely designed to blunt criticism for her past use of witchcraft. Titled "I'm You," O'Donnell, instead of demonstrating that she was similar to voters, just flat out said it—"I'm not a witch. I'm you." We recognize that failing to identify with voters is done at the peril of the politician. Ideally, people want to vote for someone they know and trust. Because a large and modern society can't accommodate that amount of intimacy, politicians must brand themselves as likeable, typical, and familiar. It takes a modern system of experts and technology to facilitate the perception of familiarity between rich politicians and modest-living voters. It also takes some cynical machinations to create the impression of an empathetic leader who *also* pitches him/herself as inflexible and strident.

Considering irresponsibility first, we look at the demands that rich campaign contributors place on politicians. Players, or big-money contributors to political campaigns, are going to insist on using every effective technique at the candidate's disposal to improve the preferred candidate's chances of winning. Large contributors, political interest groups (e.g., NARAL, Club for Growth), and political practitioners (e.g., campaign staff) are not politicians, but they play an inordinate role in choosing, financing, and influencing politicians. Thomas Ferguson and Joel Rogers argue in their book *Right Turn* that it is best to understand the outcomes of elections as the result of investment by large contributors. Contributors "invest" in politicians that they believe will provide the largest return.[17] George Soros and his MoveOn.com group is one example of a hard-left contributor who both funds candidates directly, but has also created a left-leaning a-partisan network of volunteers that can be channeled to assist in campaigns (doing essentially what parties used to do). Contributors are extremely important in terms of direct funding of candidates as well as mobilizing voters. Likewise, David Koch does the same thing for the right. Of the largely Koch-funded Tea Party, Obama advisor David Axelrod says, "What they don't say, is that, in part, this is a grassroots citizens' movement brought to you by a bunch of oil billionaires."[18] In both instances, working outside the party structure allowed these men to operate free of democratic influence. It is as though they run privatized political parties.

Irresponsibility compounds political extremism. Contributors, as well as the groups they help fund, play a very important role in driving politics to ideological extremes. The Tea Party has played a central role in politics since the election of Barack Obama. It has mobilized thousands of conservatives to both protest President Obama's policies and to support austerity-minded libertarian political candidates. Koch-funded Americans for Prosperity, for instance, trains Tea Party protest participants to engage the political system, among other things.[19] It helped organize Tea Party support for Wisconsin Governor Scott Walker and was responsible for helping nominate U.S. Senate candidates *not* backed by the GOP establishment, including now-Senator Rand Paul of Kentucky and less successful Sharron Angle of Nevada. And even when the Tea Party favorites are not successful (e.g., Angle, O'Donnell), they reap successes in less apparent ways. Though these candidates may have trouble getting elected in their general elections, Allen Abromowitz of Emory University says of the Tea Party,

> I think generally what we've seen across the country is that even when the Tea Party candidates have not been successful, in many cases, they have forced the other major Republican candidates to move to the right.[20]

The Club For Growth has had a similar impact on Republican politicians. The Club For Growth is an organization that seeks to limit government in its hope of fostering economic growth. It is widely known for bankrolling conservative challengers against targeted centrist Republicans in their primaries, in an effort to either replace the incumbent or to drive the incumbent further to the right. It conducts a "RINO Watch," targeting Republicans In Name Only.

The National Association for the Repeal of Abortion Laws (NARAL) is known on the political left for driving candidates to the left. This group has often had the unintended effect of making Democrats unelectable in relatively more conservative areas. Encouraged strongly by NARAL's vetting process to support antiabortion positions, Democratic candidates either bow out altogether or lose because of their hard-left stance on the issue. Both NARAL's funding and/or blessing are often necessary to win the primary, thus causing a leftward swing. Both political donors and the groups they fund have generated a primary environment in which candidates emphasize how ideologically pure they are.

Many successful campaigns import campaign practitioners who are experts in winning elections but who know little of the constituencies for whom they are hired to craft appeals. These people are mercenaries. They are responsible to no one but the candidate and/or the party. Their job is to win, and nobody gets points for being polite. Whereas some people may have the impression that campaign staff-building is a local, organic, or grassroots process, it is nothing of the sort—particularly at the national level. Campaign professionals are rarely local. They are hired out of national publications like *Campaigns and Elections*. Many others are provided directly by the national parties. Sometimes party financial support is contingent upon the candidate accepting national party staff or preferred contractors, in order to ensure consistency with party agenda.[21] The result is that candidate intuition and or familiarity with the constituency is ignored in favor of technological knowledge of how campaigns are won and lost. While intuition may do little for a candidate (though the successes of once-Senators Russ Feingold and Paul Wellstone, who refused much national assistance, suggest otherwise), candidate successes end up coupled with a campaign-homogenizing effect; the campaign agenda of Massachusetts becomes the campaign agenda for Kentucky. Local organization and participation become almost meaningless when outsourced outsiders come to town with their models, data, and cookie-cutter strategies rendering local organizations anachronistic and quaint. Does anyone under sixty years of age know what a party councilman is?

The assumption in the above writing assumes candidates also emerge locally, ostensibly starting as lower-level public servants and working their way up. The degree to which this has changed has contributed to the irresponsibility of politicians from their constituents. Changes in the funding processes for candidates have allowed rich candidates to bypass the mechanisms that once gave candidates experience and built trust with communities. We don't pretend that the rich haven't always been inordinately represented in national politics.[22] What has changed since the 1960s has been the weakening of the party (local and national) apparatus (as well as a more critical press) that kept politicians answerable to local constituents.[23] It is now easier for a multimillionaire to fund his/her *own* campaign than for him/her to rely on party funding. And, their own seed money deems them "viable," thus attracting more dollars from contributors. This siphons money away from other candidates. Even the voluntary spending limits imposed when accepting national matching dollars have become too restrictive; candidates like George W. Bush and Barack Obama ignored voluntary spending limits in order to use money in excess of the federal matching fund limits. Enormous amounts of money combined with the power of modern media have allowed politicians to become free agents.

The free-agentry of politicians brings us to our second observation about coarseness among politicians. Politicians share with players, we argue, an insularity or impermeability to the public. Our point is not so much an extension of the irresponsibility observation; instead we claim that politicians abstain from listening to constituents in the first place. Political free agents no longer *need* to make career-long overtures about being humble, reluctantly drafted, selfless agents of public service. Not only do they no longer need political experience, their lack of experience is cast as an asset—it reinforces their independent, outsider branding; this has been on the rise since Watergate and Jimmy Carter's successful presidential bid in 1976.[24] Politicians no longer need to be intimately familiar with how politics classically gets done.

The coarseness in political free-agency is not in the use of quaint metaphorical colloquialisms (e.g., Ross Perot's "Raise the hood and go to work"). Instead, because the lower and middle classes end up with so little access to the political system, their rich representatives resort to distraction, the use of identity appeals, and anger to short-circuit concerns regarding everyday material issues. Ever since monarchs surrendered power to democracies, the aristocracy has had to appeal to immaterial and metaphysical issues to get voters to vote against their own material wellbeing. God and nationalism are two tired but effective commonplaces to which politicians often return when they intend to offer little else. When one defines him/herself according to God and nation, their vote ends up being an endorsement of their identity. Of identity, cognitive linguist George Lakoff writes:

> People do not necessarily vote in their self-interest. They vote their identity. They vote their values. They vote for who they identify with. They may identify with their self-interest. That can happen. It is not that people never care about their self-interest. But they vote their identity.[25]

Thus elections become a choice of self versus other. As such, combative political discourse becomes necessary to create an other against whom the voters' identity can be contrasted. Politicians and their surrogates are increasingly reminding voters of who they are through a process of identifying who the villains are. Voters shouldn't be feminine (e.g., Sharron Angle told Senate Majority Leader Harry Reid to "Man up,"[26] while New York gubernatorial candidate Carl Paladino told New York's then-Attorney General and fellow competitor Andrew Cuomo, "Andrew, for the first time in your life be a man."[27]). Voters shouldn't be fascists (e.g., Keith Olbermann stated of President George W. Bush, "If you believe in the seamless mutuality of government and big business, come out and say it! There is a dictionary definition, one word that describes that toxic blend. You're a fascist!"[28]). They shouldn't be communists (e.g., Michael Savage said of Obama that he "is a neo-Marxist fascist dictator in the making"[29]). Nor should they "pal around" with terrorists, according to former vice presidential candidate Sarah Palin.

Villainizing the other to both reinforce voter identity and instill the motivating force of fear in voters has become de rigueur for today's mainstream candidate. This is a visceral manner of communicating that isn't excused by exceptions made for counterpublic forms of arational public contestation. Candidate statements flattering voter identity is a phenomenon that is felt, not thought, by the receiver. "I like her!" one might say. Numerous people said of Bush, "He's someone that I could have a beer with." Who we'd like to have beer with is rarely a matter for careful formal consideration—it's something immediately felt. This is consistent with the observation made above that candidates have become increasingly informal and personal in their messages. And why not? It's journalists like Joe Klein who write,

> I want a president who has intimate, personal knowledge of human frailty, who has been humbled by what Woodrow Wilson once called his own "imperious passions." Who has the wisdom that comes from failing, falling down, and getting up.[30]

Unfortunately, this kind of confidence in our candidates doesn't come from their having public political experience. It comes from *personal* trials. People don't want to know about what kind of sausage a candidate ushered through Congress. People, like Klein, want to know if they had DUIs or mistresses.

Make no doubt about it, these demands shape candidate rhetoric. The desire to know a person's "real self" seems to have elevated personal revelatory expression about public reason. Research showed that many in the public supported George W. Bush in 2004 because he was consistent.[31] They didn't necessarily agree with him, but they *felt* they liked that he had conviction. Consistency, like steadfastness in principle, is a quality that many people like to see in themselves, and many recognized more of what they wanted to be in Bush than in the often-depicted "flip-flopping" John Kerry. Being authentic, disclosing one feelings, being real and consistent—these are the tropes of the contemporary political scene. Stephen Colbert riffed on this in his roast of President George W. Bush at the 2006 White House Correspondents' Dinner:

> Guys like us, we're not some brainiacs on the nerd patrol. We're not members of the factinista. We go straight from the gut. Right, sir?[32]

And it's this gut-based rhetoric, we suspect, that likely gave Sarah Palin, the rogue candidate of once-maverick Senator John McCain, her widespread appeal among the political right. Her talk rarely appeared to be carefully crafted. It was blunt and ham-fisted. This is the language of contemporary politics.

While one might think that poorly filtered rhetoric of the "authentic" politician would give rise to more instances of apology, it seems that just the opposite is the case. Apologies appear to compromise the toughness and independence of the politician. Rarely are one's absurdities, when pointed out, treated as legitimate grounds for criticism. These instances often function as an opportunity for those criticized to redirect attention to their opponents' hypocrisies, resulting in a "she did it, so can I" confusion of the original matter. Besides, apologizing cedes the news cycle to the opposition. Thus, regardless of how rude, disrespectful, or insensitive a politician's comments are found to be, politicians quite often dismiss and redirect. Sometimes the press is blamed for distracting viewers with content the accused deems "irrelevant." Rush Limbaugh termed this the "drive-by media" phenomenon after journalists put his show's "satire" song *Barack the Magic Negro* under the microscope. The messenger (the critic) is characterized as complicit in the use of a red herring. This attitude toward apology is reflected in Sarah Palin's publicly Tweeted advice to radio self-help guru Dr. Laura Schlessinger following her use of the N-word during one of her shows. "Don't retreat . . . Reload!!!" she advised Schlessinger.

Finally, politicians and political groups are rendered safe from sustained scrutiny for their absurd statements because of widespread voter complicity. Doublespeak comes from the mouths of politicians and their surrogates, but it is ignored or even encouraged by many of the people "on the ground." The outcome is Orwellian communication that no one seems to care about. The receiver doesn't question a politician's words because s/he "knows" that the politician means something else. For example, the aforementioned Koch brothers have funded the Americans for Prosperity Foundation. The name is one of those think-tank names meant to sound like an august, nonpartisan, and academic research foundation. This particular group hosted a Tea Party event in Texas billed as a "populist uprising against vested corporate power."[33] It seems like the perfect event to mobilize the unemployed and those disgruntled with the state of American business. The speakers, however, advanced the cause of the *corporate* donors who underwrote the event. They railed against Obama and "special interests." While criticism of special interests is usually directed at high-earning market segments dominated by just a few corporations (e.g., Big Oil, or Big Pharma), in this case it referred to those groups that rely on government for assistance (e.g., senior citizens and the poor). Sarah Palin does something similar, playing with double meaning, in her response to the BP oil spill in the Gulf of Mexico. To it, she responds on Facebook, "Unless government appropriately regulates oil developments and holds oil executives accountable, the public will not trust them to drill, baby, drill. And we must!" It's a surprising point from her, until you remember that she actually supports *less* regulation of energy exploration. Her point here is to turn the blame for the BP mishap onto government; in other words, government's lack of oversight caused the oil spill, she's implying. The point of the statement, while explicitly calling for more effective regulation, is to foster mistrust of government and to divert blame toward it.

This double-speak is very common. George W. Bush proposed solving the problems faced by Social Security by privatizing it. He proposed breaking the nation from its oil "addiction" by promoting further exploration of ethanol (among other things), the production of which is highly dependent upon fossil fuels. The Healthy Forests Restoration Act of 2003 allowed lumber companies access to national forests to remove large-diameter trees while ignoring the brush and small growth that contributes the most fuel to forest fires. Bush's Clear Skies Initiative was based on the idea that "economic growth is key to environmental progress, because it is growth that provides the resources for investment in clean technologies." Though the title of the bill *implied* that its purpose was to tighten environment pollution regulation, it was *intended* to foster economic growth, as the bill itself stated, by loosening caps on various environmental pollutants.

There is always a lot at stake in elections. It is difficult to envision politicians being successful by bucking a system that largely goes unquestioned. Attitudes of irresponsibility and imperviousness largely fly below the radar of critics. The result is that coarseness, incivility, and absurdity in politics is often lumped into expressions of dismay as people consider just the symptoms of coarseness (e.g., vulgarity, mean-spiritedness, stupidity). A political system that continuously rewards irresponsibility and insularity in its politicians will, we fear, eventually celebrate the emergence of politicians who are extremely unempathetic and unsympathetic—a harsh version of federalism blended with a cold plutocracy.

MEDIA AND COARSENESS

The second I realized I liked being hated more than I liked being liked—that's when the game began.

—Andrew Breitbart, March 25, 2010, *Time*[34]

The "media" draws a lot of academic criticism of late. A problem with this criticism, particularly informal sorts of criticism, is that it assumes that there is such a monolithic thing *as* the media. For decades one was safe assuming this meant newspapers, radio, and television. Relatively uniform assumptions could be made about those three media, such as that they were well-funded and were governed by long-lasting journalistic traditions. The news arms of radio and television broadcasters both functioned under FCC guidelines, requiring them to do public service in exchange for their broadcast bandwidth. Today, when talking about "the media" these assumptions of uniformity aren't valid. Not only did the Reagan administration repeal various FCC rules that resulted in broadcasters orienting their news divisions toward profit pursuits, but the advent and competition of the Internet gave ownership the excuse to insist upon defining journalism downward.

Our political system probably wouldn't be able to sustain contemporary coarse politics if it weren't for the demise of traditional media; mass media's desperation for audiences and profit make it vulnerable. Would Sarah Palin survive politically in an era of Walter Cronkite? Would she have even been chosen as a candidate for vice president or as Alaska's governor? While we can only speculate about journalism's past tolerance for today's absurdity, Dan Rather's demise hints at the fate of the old rules in the new milieu.[35] Various changes in the mass media industry have enabled change in contemporary politics. Some would say that journalism has been significantly compromised. Others claim that media's "democratization" is an improvement. Either way, few doubt that significant changes have occurred. Many of these changes have occurred because of innovations in media delivery. Fewer and fewer people are reading newspapers.[36] People on trains and subways download newspapers and magazines to their eReaders. People can read the news through websites instantly on their iPhones and other electronic delivery devices. IPads may eventually render print on paper obsolete.

Because of these changes, confusion between traditional journalism, for-profit journalism, advocacy journalism, and other forms of journalistic activity have blurred its meaning. The quality of one's journalism is irrelevant if no one is willing to pay for it. Blogs are almost entirely free reading. In some instance they offer outstanding investigative journalism; still, they are better known for titillating and opinionated screeds on matters of little relevance to the operation of the commonweal. As we write this, HuffingtonPost.com, a nonsubscription left-leaning site that shares journalism, opinion, and a blog-blend of the two, lists the following story topics on its front page: sports, "The View" for men, a body stolen from a mausoleum, donut burgers, Heidi Montag's breast implants, and a "fire tornado" caught on video. These are hardly the topics that need covering in order to equip the populace to make informed decisions about public matters. It certainly calls to mind Thoreau's quip about the prospects of mass communication in 1854:

> We are in great haste to construct a magnetic telegraph from Maine to Texas, but Maine and Texas, it may be, have nothing important to communicate . . . We are eager to tunnel under the Atlantic . . . ; but perchance the first news that will leak through the broad, flapping American ear will be that the Princess Adelaide has the whooping cough.[37]

Remnants of genuine news ethic compete for eyes, ears, and click-through traffic against porn, TMZ, and bombastic partisan news that is made-to-order.

So, imagine how difficult it must be to refrain from covering titillating news about politicians. The electability of politicians often depends upon their life narrative. Revealing and/or constructing a glowing narrative is essential to a politician; concurrently, a politician's past is a rich source of provocative infotainment. The life and times of a politician can be a soap opera of sorts. Revealing the skeletons hidden by a politician can help a news source to compete for the eyes being won by alternative media. Thus, news sources lower the bar to provide images like CGI reenacts of Al Gore's alleged sexual harassment of a masseuse, TV news reenacts of gay bathroom sex solicitations by a U.S. senator, intimate details about John Edwards' sex life, disclosures from South Carolina Governor Mark Sanford's love letters to his mistress, or Representative Mark Foley's texted questions to his congressional page about his penis. And these stories aren't just brought to us via obscure blogs; this includes long-respected outlets like *Time* magazine and ABC News. Today, breaking candid news brings click-through traffic, Digg counts, "shared" Facebook posts, and Tweets. Getting the juicy stuff is absolutely necessary to maintaining a news outlet's relevance.

And if politicians aren't leaving evidence of their bizarre behaviors around where journalists can find it, journalists *generate* news by ambushing politicians with unexpected questions while they walk about in public. The tactic is used to good journalistic effect if a politician is trying to avoid being confronted on a matter of significance, but is stonewalling. Katie Couric was often criticized by the political right for her 1992 surprise interview of George H. W. Bush during a White House tour with the first lady. In her defense, she asked the president questions about public policy, and he knew, after all, that he was stepping in front of a camera with a journalist. Today, political activists like Jason Mattera are promoted by advocacy news outlets like Breitbart.com for ambushing politicians with prepared questions mixed with hyperbole, absurd assertions, interruptions, and limited time for response in order to enhance the appearance of the politician as flummoxed. Mattera performed one such stunt with Minnesota Senator Al Franken (who he called Senator Smalley later in the video, a snide reference to his Saturday Night Live sketch character named Stuart Smalley):

Mattera: Which portions of the health care bill lower costs? Is it the provision giving $7 billion to fund jungle gyms or the provision mandating that employers provide time off for breastfeeding?

Franken: Uh, give me—

Mattera: You should know.

Franken: Give me the jungle gyms.

Mattera: Right here, the jungle gyms—

Franken: Yeah

Mattera: —is on 1184.

Franken: Yeah, show it to me right now.

Mattera: Okay, 1184, to provide physical activity opportunities to promote healthy lifestyles. So why is that the job of the federal government?

Franken: Okay, now. Let me—

Mattera: Why is that the job of the federal government?

Franken: If you won't let me answer—

Mattera: —to create an army of monkey bars? Go ahead, answer it. [38]

In this video, posted at Mattera's website and ostensibly edited either by Mattera or with his approval, Mattera baits the senator by opening with "appreciate your remarks in there. You were awesome." Mattera did something similar to Representative Charlie Rangel, introducing himself as from Brooklyn outside a Capitol elevator before saying:

> I was wondering . . . why the hell do you drive a taxpayer subsidized Cadillac, use four rent-controlled apartments below market rate, and failed to pay taxes on rental properties? [39]

These are legitimate questions, but Rangel was being investigated formally for these accusations. Mattera didn't ask *if* Rangel did these things. He asked *why*, presupposing that he'd done them. This isn't journalism. It is a bogus expression of antiauthoritarian rage—the disruptive bogus-marginalized rhetoric that constitutes much of coarseness. Still, the video gets spun out on Fox News. Sean Hannity praised the video; "Jason Mattera, that is priceless. That is priceless!" [40]

Ambush interviewing goes on quite often. Local television news affiliates often use this method to get obstinate politicians and businesspeople to answer questions when they refuse to be interviewed. The video was dramatic, and it left the impression that the politicians were hiding something. In the Mattera cases, these people were not contacted beforehand and had demonstrated no resistance to being interviewed on the topic. Alex Lawson ambushed former Senator Alan Simpson, cochair of President Obama's White House Deficit Commission, to ask him about Social Security reform proposals. The modus operandi is very similar, and the interviewer manages to elicit some vulgar language from the senator. The exchange ends up with the tone of an ambush, but Simpson, much to his credit, reins it in and ends up having a somewhat-valuable exchange on the topic. Bill O'Reilly's ambush reporter, Jesse Watters, regularly provides ambush features for the Bill O'Reilly Show. In one instance, a journalist and critic of O'Reilly named Amanda Terkel, who hadn't been contacted previously for an interview was stalked, she claims, outside her home, trailed to another state, and ambushed as she emerged from her car to begin her vacation. It was another case, like Senator Simpson's, of the ambush getting turned on the reporter because Terkel seemed poised and cool-headed.

Watters: Did you actually ever hear the Radio Factor segment in question?

Terkel: Yes.

Watters: So what was the Mel Gibson component to Bill's analysis?

Terkel: I don't believe I highlighted the Mel Gibson component.

Watters: Do you know what the Mel Gibson component was?

Terkel: No.

Watters: Why not?

Terkel: Because I didn't highlight it.

Watters: Because you didn't hear it, did you, because you're just dishonest.[41]

O'Reilly used the tape in his broadcast, but it generated sympathy for Terkel, who used it as an opportunity to call O'Reilly out for blaming rape victims for being raped.

Clearly, the point of this tactic is to reveal the otherwise-collected politician as unprepared, avoidant, and rattled. This is made most evident by another Watters interview with Florida judge J. Rogers Padgett. Ambushed in a convenience store, Watters stopped Padget from closing his car door by placing his arm and body in the way while continuously asking the judge questions. While blocking the door Watters says, "Give me a break, Judge. We looked at the record. You owe us an explanation here. Your salary is paid for by the taxpayers. Judge, even the defense attorney thought this was outrageous. Judge, with all due respect you have an obligation to talk to us here. You're a public official."[42] Padgett was ambushed by O'Reilly because the judge had refused an interview on the show. Ignored in this is that sitting judges are barred by law to discuss pending cases. Moreover, according to a Florida defense lawyer, Padgett was required by law to release the person in question, a child molester, because no evidence of flight risk had been provided. All of this would have come to light if *The O'Reilly Factor* was a journalistic program. It isn't journalism, but it is an influential part of today's media and it shapes public discussion.

The media's capacity to shape public discussion is important to note. Other than as profit generators, these alternative media outlets aren't well defined and yet they are legitimized by the relatively short news segments that bookend them. Are they news? They certainly *make* news. They often catapult stories ignored by the mainstream media into the public scene. Drud-gereport.com broke the Monica Lewinsky story. DailyKos.com broke the *"macaca"* story involving Virginia Senate candidate George Allen. Glenn Beck broke the Van Jones "Communist in the White House" story, calling Van Jones a "self-avowed radical revolutionary communist."[43] Glenn Beck also brought us the bogus edited ACORN video. Net-based Breitbart.com, a right-wing news purveyor, provided the "artfully" edited video that implicat-ed the USDA's Shirley Sherrod as a racist. Fox aired the story. *Fox & Friends* reported the story, ran the doctored pimp video, and allowed Laura Ingraham to denounce Sherrod, and ask, "where was the media on this?" Interestingly, these new news-like entities, like news talk radio, news talk television, politically slanted news outlets, news aggregating websites, and blogs operate according to a different standard than do journalists. Glenn Beck knows this well, stating to *Forbes* magazine, "I could give a flying crap about the political process . . . We're an entertainment company."[44] Even Fox News defines its news hours as following their "editorial" content, in-cluding Beck, Hannity, and O'Reilly.

Regarding the mass media, in general, the boundaries of what can or should be covered have been defined downward. Whether it is constant rota-tion of Vice President Joe Biden telling the president that the healthcare legislation is a "big fucking deal," allegations of an affair involving Arizona Senator and former GOP presidential nominee John McCain; rumors about a McCain affair with a black woman; discussions of Obama's worshipping habits; allegations of drug use by Obama, Bush, and Clinton; Bush's DWI; Bush's drinking; Bill Clinton's sex habits; or speculation of Hillary Clinton's sexual preferences. Little is off limits. And while traditional journalistic out-lets may not pick these stories up at all, spinning them in less traditional media causes them to bleed over to the public discussion. When Rush Lim-baugh, in a clever blend of nonjournalistic meme-spreading with paralipsis, states, "How can we be Islamophobic? We elected Obama, didn't we?" the comment continues to spread the meme that Obama is a Muslim. Granted, he didn't actually say "Obama is a Muslim," but that's his "alibi." Limbaugh gets to defend himself by saying he never stated it. And in some outlets, this irresponsible commentary is aired more during the day than the news; quite literally on Fox, their news-dedicated hours take up nine hours out of twenty-four. Even *if* the journalists resist airing bogus news, it becomes virtually impossible to hold back the tide of absurdity.

So, once personal slights, misinformation, lies, and innuendo enter the media stream, it isn't denounced. Public relations experts will advise a com-pany faced with a rumor to not dignify the rumor with a response. Doing so graduates the rumor from the realm of rumor to a genuine news story. The official attention legitimizes the story, gives it a real source, and allows journalists to cover it. What should someone like Obama do when faced with a story that he wasn't born in the United States? What should President Bush do when, once again, accused of going AWOL? If you respond, it becomes a real story. If you ignore it, it goes undenied. Failure to deny a story actually feeds into conspiracy logic. Why won't he deny it? Regardless of Obama's denials and outright claims that he's Christian, a Pew Research Center survey indicates that 18 percent of respondents believe he's a Muslim.[45] Today, a *majority* of conservatives claim to believe he's a Muslim.[46]

This new media environment enables people to find the news they *want* to find. If they don't get it from their network news, they go to cable. If they don't get it from CNN, they get it from Fox or MSNBC. If they don't get it from the *New York Times*, they get it from the *Wall Street Journal*. If they don't get it from the news, they get it from news talk radio. If they don't get it from radio, they get it from blogs. And if the news doesn't fit your world-view, you create one that will—like BreitBart.com, Glenn Beck's online news source named TheBlaze.com, or Tucker Carlson and Neil Patel's The-DailyCaller.com. If the media they have doesn't deliver the content and tenor desired, there are other outlets. The result is that we are increasingly separating ourselves out into news consumption communities.

In *Echo Chamber* Kathleen Hall Jamieson and Joseph Cappella explain that people increasingly find themselves in media "echo chambers,"[47] a phenomenon predicted by Cass Sunstein in *Republic.com* (he termed it "balkanizations").[48] Writing specifically about what they term "right-wing media" (e.g., *The Rush Limbaugh Show*, the *Wall Street Journal*, and Fox News), Jamieson and Cappella write that these sources "developed the capacity to wrap their audience in an insulated media enclave of information and opinion."[49] Jamieson and Cappella did not examine any "liberal" enclaves, but we suspect they exist as well. Though conservatives might contend that mainstream news supplies liberal-angled information, we suspect that while mainstream journalism has a traditionally progressive-populist bent,[50] liberals turn to specific liberal sources (e.g., NPR, the *New York Times*, *The Rachel Maddow Show*). As such, both sides operate in news enclaves, and so both the political left and right should heed their warnings; among various important observations, Jamieson and Cappella warn that these insular communities can foster outrage by engaging emotion and the replacement of argument with ridicule and *ad hominem*.

Assumptions about news production have changed significantly over time. Our politics are today shaped in part by the fragmentation and provocativeness of our mass media. Moreover, journalism no longer perceives itself as following a fly-on-the-wall model. The very process of selecting a story reveals bias in the process of attending to the world. News stories can also be retold in countless different ways. Not only are journalists aware of the fact that prejudice is always operative in their reportage, so are their audiences. Of the many consequences of this awareness, journalism is subject both to audience criticism and audience performance in the news. The following section outlines several ways with which active audiences actively shape the news.

CITIZENS AND COARSENESS

> Our goal is to make the gathering look as greedy and goonish as we know that it is, ding their credibility with the media and exploit the lazy reporters who just want dramatic shots and outrageous quotes for headlines.

—Mark Williams, February 20, 2011, *Mother Jones* [51]

During the healthcare debate and the Tea Party protests that accompanied it the media did what one would expect it to do: it aired its most heated moments. The images were unsettling and gripping. The images crafted by the participants also exploited the needs of the media to provide attractive content; it was done so in order to help advance an agenda. The media performed its role and citizens performed theirs. Citizens came prepared to produce a show for the cameras. The performance wasn't, in many ways, visible, unlike protests people have seen from the 1960s. Town hall forums and city meetings were disrupted by disgruntled voters. The events, the delivery, had a truth-spoken-to-power semiotic quality to them. But if one looks closely at the rhetoric of these events, there were striking differences with events from the sixties. Most notably, there were few if any linear and rational objections to the legislation expressed in these venues, but no observer could walk away without a strong sense of opposition to it—the enthymeme of political anger.

On August 7, 2009, Democratic members of Congress began their recess and braced themselves for disrupted town hall meetings held to discuss, among other issues, changes being proposed to healthcare policy. A woman named Katy Abram attended a town hall meeting hosted by Senator Arlen Spector on August 11, 2009. We look at her rhetoric because, among others, she received relatively more attention and her words don't represent the most heated and disruptive of those heard during these protests. Her performance was also not much unlike that of many other protesters. After being featured on Sean Hannity's show on Fox News, Ms. Abram began to channel her unlikely fame to promote small-government candidates she supports (she now has a website at www.katyabram.com and a blog). At that event, she said the following:

> I am a Republican, but I am, first and foremost, I am a conservative. I don't believe this is just about healthcare. It's not about TARP, it's not about left and right. This is about the systematic dismantling of this country. I'm only thirty-five years old. I've never been interested in politics. You have awakened the

sleeping giant. We are tired of this. This is why everyone in this room is so ticked off. I don't want this country turning into Russia, turning into a socialized country. My question for you is, what are you going to do to restore this country back to what our founders created according to the constitution?[52]

Her performance was better than average, and the degree to which it wasn't polished added to its authenticity. The problem is that if someone views the town hall as a legitimate forum for the exchange of information, her comments didn't fit. If, as she requested, the country had been "restored" to what the founders created, Ms. Abram wouldn't be allowed to speak publicly. She could be thrown in jail. From an argumentation standpoint, her point simply begged the question. What did she want restored? Inasmuch as the healthcare proposal under consideration at that time utilized private insurance companies, a version of a proposal crafted by Republicans in 1993,[53] in what sense was healthcare being socialized?

The point is that Ms. Abram wasn't looking to have questions answered. She was *performing* protest. The goal was to create a scene to attract free media and to send the message to people at home of a disgruntled critical mass. In this sense, Katy Abram did a fine job. If one reads the instructions for town hall protests then listed at operationembarrassyourcongressman.com, a "guerilla website" of unknown origin, protestors were advised:

Again, let me emphasize that Operation EMBARRASS YOUR CONGRESS-MAN is a peaceful operation. We don't condone violence in any way. Don't harass, intimidate, or otherwise do anything threatening towards anyone! (No sense in acting like a community organizer or a member of ACORN). Simply use your freedom of speech in public forums to accomplish our mission.

The success was that these encounters made the news. Healthcare-reform opponents won free media by generating a story about rage. The matters for concern were always moving targets, making it impossible for a public debate on specific issues to begin. Nevertheless, Sean Hannity ran his show with the banner at bottom reading, "Tempers Continue to Flare at Townhall Meetings over Healthcare." The theme of Hannity's own remarks focused on leaders failing to listen. What they were ignoring, other than rage, was left less clear.

To be fair, people on the left do this sort of thing all of the time. Karl Rove was dogged during a recent book signing tour by antiwar protesters who interrupted him to call him a war criminal. Jodie Evans, cofounder of Code-Pink, attempted to make a citizen's arrest for war crimes. During the confrontation at one signing a woman yelled, "The only comfort I take is that . . . you are going to rot in hell." Jay Bookman of the *Atlanta Journal Constitution* criticize this and similar events as "street theater."[54] These performances are likely to have the unfortunate effect of making politicians less interpersonally or publicly accessible. Note that George W. Bush made many of his 2004 campaigns stops at tightly controlled, ticketed venues at which attendees had been vetted. Many of his presidential speeches were delivered from military bases at which it was *illegal* of the audience to voice opposition. It is also worth noting that there is little value in public accessibility if politicians aren't made to hear the thoughts of their constituents.

Street theater isn't new, and it's probably always been messy. It is a necessary part of the democratic process: speaking truth to power. Its purpose as a component of social movement is consciousness-raising, to awaken people to their plight, protest a moral offense, and/or to generate abuses of power as authorities seek to shut down the "rabble-rousers" (i.e., to provoke confrontation for the cameras or the papers). The town hall protests did more than employ the techniques of protest, but they mimicked them. These events were made to *look* like protests. They tap the familiar frames of 1960s protest, and in doing so cast Democratic office holders as entrenched power while offering the money-backed interests of protesters the guileless countenance of spontaneity and magnanimity. In other words, these protests differed because they were bogus, simulating a relationship between protester and power that didn't reflect reality. The coverage and the volume cultivate an overrepresentation of the position. In these instances, the protesters weren't being quieted; there was no reason to yell if, in fact, they simply wanted their questions answered. Their behavior suggests that this wasn't the intent, and they certainly didn't achieve the effect. In one case, however, Representative Kathy Castor wasn't allowed to speak by protesters among her Tampa Bay constituents. Protesters chanting "Tyranny!" kept Castor from beginning, and she was ultimately escorted out of the building.

In these contexts, citizens also appear to understand their importance in the process of meme spreading. Imagine a meme as a beach ball at an outdoor concert. If each person doesn't play his or her part, the ball falls and the fun stops. In politics, the spread of information and the diffusion of ideas occurs in a similar manner. People need to say it for others to hear it. What's not said falls out of favor. As Elisabeth Noelle-Neumann explained in her explanation of her Spiral of Silence Theory, when ideas aren't encountered, audiences believe they are out of favor, and so they themselves don't voice them. Silence compounds itself. Mass media play an important role in this process, but it isn't only the responsibility of opinion leaders via mass media to perpetuate beliefs, ideas, and talking points. Citizens need to play their role. Listen to call-in shows, C-Span, Rush Limbaugh, Rachel Maddow, and talk in public. At one town hall hosted by Representative Tim Bishop a woman inside protested, "I don't want to be shoved into a government-run socialistic program."[55] That the program requires people to purchase *private* insurance never gets a hearing. That was the case with numerous people attending town hall meetings and organized protests throughout the country.

Complaints about communism, fascism, insurance for illegals, government-funded abortions, all of which were false, were continuously spread despite the content of the bill. While one could argue that these efforts forced legislators to address these concerns, these memes *continue* to be spread despite the fact that they are patently false. Expressions of surprise at the absurdity and tenor of the town hall protests were almost uniformly met with the retort that "We're just trying to get our questions answered." In one instance, Representative Barney Frank was asked why he supported a Nazi policy (the woman equated a cut in Medicare to the Nazi T4 euthanasia program). Frank asked her, "On what planet do you spend most of your time?" After insisting that Frank answer her question, he said, "It is a tribute to the first amendment that this type of vile, contemptible nonsense is so freely propagated."[56] And despite the passage of the bill and the complete absence of any provision that can be equated with euthanasia, the meme still spins in the public. On August of 2010 Glenn Beck described an FDA decision to ban Avastin, shown to have no life-extending benefits for cancer patients, as a death panel decision—continuing the death panel meme begun by Sarah Palin during the 2008 presidential race.

Finally, with respect to the role of the citizenry in coarseness, efforts by pundits and other opinion leaders to spread nonsensical points would likely shorten their careers if not for a complicit audience. There appears to be an ethic that has audiences demonstrating unflinching unity in the face of candidate hypocrisy and/or absurdity. We do not mean to imply that voters are stupid or at all duped by the candidates. Instead, as savvy citizens, we believe they are participating in the campaign by saying what they believe is the right thing—as though they'd been briefed by the same operatives used by the campaign. This was probably best demonstrated during Sarah Palin's run for vice president. On a number of levels, she'd been shown to be an inadequate candidate. She possessed little political and historical knowledge and she was prone to saying nonsensical things. John McCain put Republicans in the unenviable position of pretending the queen had clothing. Citizens performed a pageant, pretending to ignore all of her inadequacies while trying to recode her ignorance as an asset. The extent to which audiences are willing to participate in these charades is rather shocking. Take, for instance, Laura Ingraham, who was quoted on Fox News on December 21, 2009 saying of the of the Park51 Cordoba House mosque development in downtown Manhattan, "I can't find many people who have a problem with it," and "I like what you are trying to do." After it was made an issue of by right-wing groups, Ingraham revisited the issue on Fox News, complaining that Imam Feisal Abdul Rauf's comments about America were insensitive and that no proof had been given that all of the money supporting the project was free of Iranian and terrorist contributions. The irony of ironies is that the project had been supported, in part, by co-owner of Fox News' parent company News

Corporation Saudi Prince Al-Waleed bin Talal. Nevertheless, there's been no word of a drop in credibility either for Ingraham or Fox. We suspect that supporters of Fox will know their role in this, and they'll remain faithful.

NOTES

1. Robert Costa, "Exclusive: House Minority Leader John Boehner on the Health-Care Vote," *National Review*, March 18, 2010, www.nationalreview.com/corner/196465/exclusive-house-minority-leader-john-boehner-health-care-vote/robert-costa.

2. Gabriella Schwarz, "Cheney, Rumsfeld Face Jeers and Cheers," CNN, February 10, 2011, politicalticker.blogs.cnn.com/2011/02/10/cheney-rumsfeld-face-jeers-and-cheers/.

3. "Brief Time Out from Heated Discourse Has Ended," *Toledo Free Press*, February 14, 2011, www.toledofreepress.com/2011/02/14/brief-time-out-from-heated-discourse-has-ended/.

4. Liz Sidoti, "CPAC Speeches and Fiery Attacks Suggest 2012 Campaign Has Begun," *Huffington Post*, www.huffingtonpost.com/2011/02/13/cpac-speeches-fiery-attac_n_822677.html.

5. *Anderson Cooper 360 Degrees*, February 16, 2010, archives.cnn.com/TRANSCRIPTS/1002/16/acd.01.html.

6. Kate McCarthy, "Wisconsin Governor Scott Walker: We're Broke and Can't Negotiate," ABC News, last modified February 21, 2011, abcnews.go.com/blogs/politics/2011/02/wisconsin-governor-scott-walker-were-broke-and-cant-negotiate.

7. Frances Fox Piven, "Crazy Talk and American Politics: Or, My Glenn Beck Story," *Chronicle of Higher Education*, February 10, 2011, chronicle.com/article/Crazy-Talk-American/126334/?sid=cr&utm_medium=en.

8. Don Wolfensberger, speech on incivility, Seminar on Civility, Society, and Politics, Drake University, Des Moines, IA, September 19, 2007.

9. Nicholas Shaxson, *Treasure Island* (London: Bodley Head, 2011).

10. Jane Mayer, "Covert Operations: The Billionaire Brothers Who Are Waging a War against Obama," *New Yorker*, August 30, 2010, www.newyorker.com/reporting/2010/08/30/100830fa_fact_mayer.

11. Neil Postman, *Amusing Ourselves to Death* (New York: Penguin, 1986), 127.

12. Stephanie Condon, "FOX News' Roger Ailes: "Tone It Down," CBS News, January 10, 2011www.cbsnews.com/8301-503544_162-20028077-503544.html.

13. Dennis W. Johnson, *Campaigning in the Twenty-First Century: A Whole New Ballgame?* (New York: Routledge, 2010), 6.

14. "American Democracy in an Age of Rising Inequality," report by the American Political Science Association, 2004, p. 7.

15. Larry Bartels, *Unequal Democracy* (Princeton, NJ: Princeton University Press, 2010), 2.

16. See Lee Fang, "Pollutocrat David Koch Refuses to Answer Questions about Citizens United Secret Right-Wing Meetings," Think Progress, last modified January 12, 2011, climateprogress.org/2011/01/12/pollutocrat-david-koch-refuses-to-answer-questions-about-citizens-united-secret-right-wing-meetings/.

17. Thomas Furguson and Joel Rogers, *Right Turn* (New York: Hill and Wang, 1987).

18. Mayer, "Covert Operations."

19. Felicia Sonmez, "Who Is 'Americans for Prosperity?'" *Washington Post*, August 26, 2010, hvoices.washingtonpost.com/thefix/senate/who-is-americans-for-prosperit.html.

20. Aliyah Shahid, "Tea Party Candidates, Joe Miller, Clint Didier, Jane Norton Try to Knock off Republicans across U.S," *NY Daily News*, July 3, 2010, www.nydailynews.com/news/national/2010/07/03/2010-07-03_tea_party_candidates_joe_miller_clint_didier_jane_norton_try_to_knock_off_republ.html.

21. Jerome Armstrong and Marcos Moulitsas, *Crashing the Gate: Netroots, Grassroots, and the Rise of People-Powered Politics* (White River Junction, VT: Chelsea Green Publishers, 2006).

22. Brian Montopoli, "237 Millionaires in Congress," CBS News, November 6, 2009, www.cbsnews.com/8301-503544_162-5553408-503544.html.

23. Thomas Patterson, *Out of Order* (New York: Vintage, 1994).

24. Judith Trent, "Presidential Surfacing: The Ritualistic and Crucial First Act," *Communication Monographs* 45 (1978): 290–91.

25. George Lakoff, *Don't Think of an Elephant: Know Your Values and Frame the Debate—The Essential Guide for Progressives* (White River Junction, VT: Chelsea Green Publishers, 2004), 19.

26. Huma Khan, "'Man Up Harry Reid': Sharron Angle Attacks, Questions How Reid Made Money," ABC News, October 15, 2010, abcnews.go.com/Politics/vote-2010-elections-sharron-angle-attacks-harry-reid/story?id=11886670.

27. Michael Grynbaum and Michael Barbaro, "Paladino Is Taunting in a Letter to Cuomo," *New York Times*, September 19, 2010, www.nytimes.com/2010/09/20/nyregion/20paladino.html.

28. Keith Olbermann, "A Veto of the FISA Bill 'Endangers Americans,'" MSNBC, updated February 14, 2008, accessed April 22, 2011, www.msnbc.msn.com/id/23173388/ns/msnbc_tv-countdown_with_keith_olbermann/.

29. "Savage: Obama 'Is a Neo-Marxist Fascist Dictator in the Making," Media Matters for America, March 6, 2009, mediamatters.org/mmtv/200903060012.

30. Joe Klein, *Politics Lost: From RFK to W: How Politicians Have Become Less Courageous and More Interested in Keeping Power than in Doing What's Right for America* (New York: Broadway Books, 2007), 12.

31. Dalia Sussman, "Poll: Bush Has Likeability Edge on Kerry," ABC News, accessed June 28, 2012, abcnews.go.com/politics/story?id=120664&page=1.

32. Stephen Colbert as quoted in "Stephen Colbert's Blistering Performance Mocking Bush and the Press Goes Ignored by the Media," Democracy Now, May 3, 2006, www.democracynow.org/2006/5/3/stephen_colberts_blistering_performance_mocking_bush.

33. Mayer, "Covert Operations."

34. Steve Oney, "Citizen Breitbart: The Web's New Right-Wing Impresario," *Time*, March 25, 2010, www.time.com/time/nation/article/0,8599,1974949,00.html.

35. Corey Pein, "Blog-Gate," *Columbia Journalism Review* 1 (January/February 2005): 30–35.

36. "Daily Newspaper Readership Trends-Age (1998–2007)," Newspaper Association of America, accessed February 21, 2011, www.naa.org/docs/Research/Age_Daily_National_Top50_98-07.pdf.

37. Henry David Thoreau, *Walden: A Fully Annotated Edition*, compiled by Jeffrey S. Cramer (New Haven, CT: Yale University Press, 2004), 50.

38. Jason Mattera, "Does Al Franken Even Know What Was in the Health-care Bill He Voted For? Um . . . Nope," YouTube, accessed February 21, 2011, www.youtube.com/watch?v=VFXr3i5_y1A&feature=player_embedded#at=37.

39. Jason Mattera, "Rep. Charlie Rangel Swears at Jason Mattera over Scandal Questions," YouTube, accessed February 21, 2011, www.youtube.com/watch?v=rdtFWCrCh0s&feature=related.

40. Sean Hannity, "Waking Up the 'Obama Zombies,'" Fox News, March 25, 2010, www.foxnews.com/story/0,2933,590004,00.html.

41. Keith Olbermann, "Countdown with Keith Olbermann," YouTube, first broadcast March 24, 2009, accessed February 21, 2011, www.youtube.com/watch?v=rdtFWCrCh0s&feature=related.

42. Bill O'Reilly, "The O'Reilly Factor," YouTube, first broadcast December 22, 2009, accessed February 21, 2011, www.youtube.com/watch?v=rdtFWCrCh0s&feature=related.

43. "Van Jones Is an Avowed, Self-Avowed Radical Revolutionary Communist," *Tampa Bay Times* (PolitiFact), last modified September 8, 2009, accessed February 21, 2011, www.politifact.com/truth-o-meter/statements/2009/sep/08/glenn-beck/glenn-beck-says-van-jones-avowed-communist/.

44. Lacey Rose, "Glenn Beck Inc,"

Forbes, last modified April 26, 2010, accessed August, 8, 2010, www.forbes.com/forbes/2010/0426/entertainment-fox-news-simon-schuster-glenn-beck-inc_print.html.

45. "Growing Number of Americans Say Obama Is a Muslim: Religion, Politics, and the President," Pew Research Center, August 19, 2010, pewresearch.org/pubs/1701/poll-obama-muslim-christian-church-out-of-politics-political-leaders-religious.

46. Robert Schlesinger, "Poll: Birthers Now Make Up a Majority of Republican Primary Voters," *U.S. News & World Report*, February 16, 2011, www.usnews.com/opinion/blogs/robert-schlesinger/2011/02/16/poll-birthers-now-make-up-a-majority-of-gop-primary-voters.

47. Kathleen Hall Jamieson and Joseph Capella, *Echo Chamber* (New York: Oxford University Press, 2008).

48. Cass Sunstein, *Republic.com* (Princeton, NJ: Princeton University Press, 2009).

49. Jamieson and Capella, *Echo Chamber*, 4.

50. Michael Schudson, "The Concept of Politics in Contemporary U.S. Journalism," *Political Communication* 24 (2007): 131–42. See also Herbert Gans, *Deciding What's News: A Study of CBS Evening News, NBC Nightly News, Newsweek, and Time* (New York: Pantheon, 1979).

51. See quotation in Adam Weinstein, "Tea Party Leader Plan to Infiltrate Union Goons," *Mother Jones*, February 20, 201, www.stumbleupon.com/su/5XoJRB/motherjones.com/mojo/2011/02/tea-party-leader-plan-infiltrate-wisconsin-seiu-wiunion.

52. "Angry Patriots Confront Turncoat Senator Arlen Specter at Town Hall Meeting," You-Tube, accessed February 21, 2011, www.youtube.com/watch?v=jV1jmvMHsS0.

53. Maggie Martens, "Chart: Comparing Health Reform Bills: Democrats and Republicans 2009, Republicans 1993," *Kaiser Health News*, February 24, 2010, www.kaiserhealthnews.org/Graphics/2010/022310-Bill-comparison.aspx.

54. Jay Bookman, "Even Karl Rove, Wrong as He Is, Has a Right to Be Heard," ajc, last modified March 30, 2010, accessed February 21, 2011, blogs.ajc.com/jay-bookman-blog/2010/03/30/even-karl-rove-wrong-as-he-is-has-a-right-to-be-heard/?cxntfid=blogs_jay_bookman_blog.

55. "Tim Bishop Protest, Setauket, NY," YouTube, accessed February 21, 2011, www.youtube.com/watch?v=UOLs7Cybnqw.

56. "Barnie Frank Floored by Nazi Insult at Town Hall," YouTube, accessed February 21, 2011, www.youtube.com/watch?v=OjF4YjvJLe4.

Chapter Four

Coarseness and Reason

In a republican nation whose citizens are to be led by reason and persuasion and not by force, the art of reasoning becomes of first importance.

—Thomas Jefferson, 1824, *Letter to David Hardin*[1]

The central issue in all the arguments about the public sphere is the capacity of participants to reason. Can the public hope to reason well? Can reason prevail? Reason is a form of thinking that is separate from content knowledge. The existential problem of not sharing the same knowledge or of not having valid or enough knowledge is one issue. But another is whether people sharing the same valid facts can reason well and accept the logical conclusions that rational discourse demands. Too often emotional interests become obstacles to reasoning. While experts in logic agree on the rules of argumentation such as the excluded middle, the law of noncontradiction, and others that guide discourse in courts of law, for instance, where one may object to a statement because it is misleading, harassing, illogical, or untrue, and have it stricken from the debate, many people who participate in self-governance are ignorant of how to think logically. They fall victim to various fallacies such as confusing correlations with causation at a rate that makes public debate inadequate for deriving intelligent decisions. Consequently, public policy and people suffer.

Relativists like to question if a uniformly understood notion of "reason" even exists. Is reason privileging for those groups better versed in it (whatever *it* is at the moment)? Are decisions the product of reason or irrational tricks of persuasion? What is less often considered is the degree to which the public sphere even fosters and encourages reasoned thought at all. In this section, we don't consider the public contributions of the marginalized. We discuss *mainstream* talk. How can we expect people to communicate reasonably in a milieu filled with nonsense? What is compromised by opening mainstream dialogue and debate to marginalized voices, those ostensibly less rational, if the majority of mainstream public discourse writ large is itself absurd, inconsistent, and contradictory?

And what if those best trained in logic are ostracized as being "out-of-touch" intellectual "eggheads?" Name calling, the irrelevant *ad hominem* attack, is a typical gambit used to disqualify a person's source credibility, rendering them mute. The merit of their claims and reasoning is not even considered because of who they are: an "egghead," a "liberal," a "wing-nut," and so forth. Many intellectuals feel muted by belligerent lines of argumentation that are uninformed and irrational yet loud and popular. While current conservatives attack public broadcasting, for years it was the major forum for the most reasoned exchanges in U.S. mass media between political opponents; *Firing Line* hosted by William F. Buckley, Jr. from 1966 to 1999 (and later Michael Kinsley) a legendary conservative thinker who founded the conservative journal *National Review*, and who, toward the end of his illustrious career as an intellectual lion from the conservative perspective decried the decline in the quality of public discourse, be it among chanting left-leaning "hippies" or sophistic ill-informed conservative politicians. Keep in mind that his erudite prose and oratory was in English, his *third* language, which he did not learn until he was seven, while we observe today orators who can barely muster a line of reasoning in their only primary language.

Today, few outlets for such high-quality oratory remain. One might cite Charlie Rose, host of the interview show of the same name, Bill Moyers, host of *Bill Moyers' Journal*, Terry Gross, host of *Fresh Air*, and Diane Rehm, host of the *Diane Rehm Show*. They all offer forums for experts to inform us and for high-quality examination and cross-examination of issues. But they are all distributed by one organization. Just like Buckley's *Firing Line*, they are all distributed by the not-for-profit Corporation for Public Broadcasting. Where profit is the motive, oratory and forensic prowess is abysmal. And in the for-profit media the attack on rigorous deliberation has been orchestrated as explained by Naomi Oreskes and Eric Conway in *The Merchants of Doubt*[2] and *Doubt is Their Product* by David Michaels.[3]

By comparison with *Firing Line*, today's talk TV and talk radio amount to little more than bullying on primary-school playgrounds. The point here is not whether conservatives or liberals are more rational in their thinking and discourse, but whether their debates are. The crisis in rationality impacts the form of discourse itself and the quality of public policy decision making generally. However, the decline tends to be more pronounced, as one might guess, on the side of those who attack intellectual achievement and rigor, which tends to be the political right more than the political left.

A good example was in a "debate" between Princeton economist Paul Krugman and Bill O'Reilly mediated, barely, by Tim Russert on NBC's *Meet the Press* in 2004. During this meeting at a neutral forum, O'Reilly bragged about his own bestselling books and attacked Krugman's books and columns in the *New York Times* as being nothing by fear-mongering false-hoods about the George W. Bush administration's economic policies. Krug-man was warning in 2004 that the U.S. economy was heading for disaster and he turned out to be completely correct. But his attempt to reiterate his analyses of the empirical facts was not only mocked but totally disrupted by O'Reilly's constant interruptions and refusal to yield the floor. He verbally assaulted Krugman and the *New York Times* with repeated *ad hominem* at-tacks and sweeping claims of liberal bias without even one empirical exam-ple. When Krugman tried to talk facts, statistical measures of the economy and analytical examination of them, he was cut off as O'Reilly, who called him the "top Bush hater," described all of his work as "absolutely dead, one hundred percent wrong," and instructed Krugman to do his own research. Four years after O'Reilly accused Krugman of being "completely wrong" and of not doing his own research, Krugman was awarded the Nobel Prize in Economics. Within the span of thirty seconds during this same "debate" O'Reilly called the media watchdog group Media Matters "Fidel" and the "Klu Klux Klan."

As the show continued, O'Reilly became increasingly belligerent, point-ing his finger in Krugman's face and leaning toward him. Krugman is a lot smaller person than O'Reilly's hefty 6'4" frame. This is important because the "debate" quickly degraded into a confrontation dominated by physical intimidation, aggressive nonverbal movements, and increasingly louder and personal incriminating insults from O'Reilly. Krugman, in his frustration, literally stopped trying to talk and threw his head back and stared at the ceiling. Finally, the host of the program, Russert, who had said almost noth-ing while O'Reilly attacked the academic, finally said "Come on guys," and ended the debacle which had almost no elements of traditional rational dis-cussion. Those who watched learned nothing about the state of the economy from the exchange.

Given a normal distribution, the most rational thinkers and the best in-formed always constitute outliers, a minority. Leadership is always a minor-ity position. The real question is that if the majority of people are less in-formed and less rational in their reasoning skills, then when it comes to picking leaders will they go with the person that makes them feel most comfortable, the person they feel they know better and are familiar with, or will they support the oddball outlier? One of the most predictive questions of electoral success asked of voters is, "Who would you rather have a beer or hotdog with, candidate X or candidate Y?" Repeatedly voters pick the person most like themselves; with him they feel a common bond and familiarity even if that feeling is based on false information. Consequently, in any population the numerical majority of people will pick leaders who reflect their own capacities and avoid those who make them feel inadequate, stupid, or uncomfortable. Most fear, or at least are suspicious of, difference. The key to the intellectual leader is to be able to code switch, to be able to communicate his/her personality as common while possessing extraordinary skills. Hence, since the modern era all over the world, including in dictatorships, from Marcos in the Philippines, to Mao, to Lincoln, to Reagan, and Clinton, leaders stress their "common roots," their "average guy" origins.

It's cool to be common, "down to earth," to share common experiences, values, and beliefs. Therefore, such a "normal" person is presumed to be able to better understand the plight of the "common" person. This why George W. Bush downplayed his privileged private-school New England upbringing while stressing his aw-shucks Texas connections and why, during the 2008 presidential election, a professor of constitutional law from an elite university would come out looking not-so-good in the eyes of millions when confronted by Joe Wurzlebacher, an emotional, unemployed, and lesser-educated plumber who improbably believes, like so many in America, that he too may one day join the statistically insignificant, miniscule ranks of billionaires. The problem of democracy recognized by logicians from Plato to Bertrand Russell is that if people vote based on emotional identification with celebrity candidates rather than analytical assessment of their past actions and ideology, social policy will not be rational. Today, an entire industry of experts in sophistic persuasion techniques that emphasize pathos over logos and even ethos have come to dominate the democratic process itself. Their skills are available to those who can afford them. Media costs money and in today's world campaigns are media driven. Messages do not, therefore, compete on an equal playing field adjudicated by logical consistency and empirical validity alone. The "marketplace of ideas" is a damned expensive place to do business.

O'Reilly may be capable of cool-blooded reasoning but in a world where public discourse and political activity has been converted to mass entertainment, packaged, branded, and sold for advertising dollars, his sort of pyrotechnics sells. This form of talk may be bad for decision making and bad for an electorate charged with selecting its own leaders, but it is good for cable broadcasters.

Much of today's public talk of policy is irrational and anti-intellectual. In fact, we maintain that those who fancy themselves the champions of cold, paternal rationality—conservatives—are the worst perpetrators of manipulative stupidity on the scene today. We contend that capitalists, those with the most political and pecuniary privilege and power, and conservatives, their representatives, marshal non-sense as a means to their ends. And these folks *are* the mainstream; these are the people who benefit from the perpetuation of the regime of rationality being imposed on others who seek power. We argue, however, that conservatives on the other hand merely adorn themselves with the accoutrements of privilege so as to afford their arguments the presumption of reasoned, coolheaded objectivity. Whereas Cheris Kramarae's Muted Group Theory maintains that the less privileged, no matter how well-reasoned, are perceived as less credible than the mainstream,[4] the privileged, no matter how absurd, are received by audiences as relatively more credible.

And while any given instance of irrationality may appear to be an isolated instance of stupidity or the cynical use of any means to an end, taken together these instances amount to a logic all their own. Ronald Reagan argued for a stronger America while bargaining with terrorists and circumventing the constitution. George W. Bush insisted on invading Iraq before he had cause. Glenn Beck explained the overthrow of Hosni Mubarak as a part of a worldwide Socialist scheme that even Bill O'Reilly had to criticize as without evidence. While each can be critiqued as irrational, we argue in this chapter that there *is* an underlying logic. Considered together, each instance shared a central element—a market logic, akin to Jules Henry's "pecuniary logic."

> A false statement made as if it were true, but not intended to be believed. No proof is offered for a pecuniary pseudo-truth and no one looks for it. Its proof is that it sells merchandise; if it does not, it is false.[5]

Henry was critiquing market reasoning, suggesting that its reach has extended well beyond the marketplace of goods and services. For our purposes, *market logic* refers to the efficacy of a statement in gaining public compliance or acquiescence. Market logic doesn't sell products so much as it propagates ideas. It is an amoral version of Mill's "marketplace of ideas:"[6] if a communicative technique works, it must have been good.

Today, market logic produces purely instrumental communication in contexts far beyond that of the economic marketplace, and the only test of veracity is that a message "work." If your task is to get viewers, then why not use nudity, sex, and violence? After all, it works! If your goal is to save souls, why not cleanse dogma of community, sacrifice, and responsibility? Get rid of dogma altogether while you're at it! After all, it works! If you seek to garner support for policy or avoid blame for its failures, why not lie, manufacture evidence, make character attacks, or use straw arguments? And when the standards for public discourse decline enough, voices of technical knowledge (i.e., scientists, lawyers) and the accounts of witnesses and experts are treated with cynicism. An expert is "just another person," with "just another opinion." Relativism rules.

The Supreme Court's Citizens United ruling springs forth from this market logic. The *Citizens United v. Federal Election Commission* decision of 2010 overturned the McCain-Feingold Act's "electioneering" limitations on corporations and unions (and consequently ended the efficacy of contributor disclosure rules that make campaign spending transparent). The legal basis for these speech limitations was based upon the *Austin v. Michigan Chamber of Commerce* decision. In it, the court introduced the idea that corporations that had amassed tremendous amounts of wealth could distort the "political marketplace."

> Regardless of whether this danger of "financial *quid pro quo*" corruption . . . may be sufficient to justify a restriction on independent expenditures, Michigan's regulation . . . aims at a different type of corruption in the political arena: the corrosive and distorting effects of immense aggregations of wealth that are accumulated with the help of the corporate form and that have little or no correlation to the public's support for the corporation's political ideas.[7]

This concern is with the economic marketplace affecting the marketplace of ideas, or "political marketplace." To this, the Citizens United court asserted in the opinion's syllabus:

> This Court now concludes that independent expenditures, including those made by corporations, do not give rise to corruption or the appearance of corruption. That speakers may have influence over or access to elected officials does not mean that those officials are corrupt. And the appearance of influence or access will not cause the electorate to lose faith in this democracy.[8]

Unfortunately, the Citizens United opinion begs the question about the distorting effects of corporate electioneering. Instead of addressing this matter, it asserts once more that corporations are individuals, the strict scrutiny standard for limiting speech rights, and the chilling effect of election speech regulations (e.g., Political Action Committees or PACs). The court made a number of other arguments critiquing the logic of the Austin decision, but failed to address concerns about distortion. In fact, it merely asserts that the public is to be the only judge of the worthiness of speech; "Factions should be checked by permitting them all to speak . . . and by entrusting the people to judge what is true and what is false."[9] Thus, ideas that "win" are true. Inequities of wealth and/or access are irrelevant to the outcomes of public sphere discussion. Within this framework, then, it could be reasoned that *stupid* arguments, provided they are the most widely adopted, are not only the *best* ideas, but are true.

On its face, this manner of understanding "truth" is absurd. After all, we shouldn't jump in lakes because all our friends are doing it. Determining what is right, good, best, or true in any instance is always an intrinsically tricky matter. Despite the inherent difficulty, our task, particularly in a democratic governmental system, is always to *try* to get it right. Perhaps, that is assumed by the Supreme Court in the Citizens United decision. Clearly, the court values a system unencumbered by government more than it does short-term remedies to the system's flaws. Still, this can't be construed as an endorsement of a winner-takes-all communication environment; it's just the best that can be done by government without allowing the government undue influence in the outcomes of public discussion. Just because government should limit its influence to providing information to facilitate knowledge-able debate, it is still incumbent upon think-tanks, journalists, bloggers, educators, or work-a-day taxpayers to employ, improve, and perpetuate what they understand to be the best practices of sense-making. What is true or best can never be confused with what is most widely accepted, lest we surrender our democracy to communication technicians with the skills to manufacture consent and those with the resources to hire them.

In this chapter we make an argument for reason by historically contextualizing the present moment as a human achievement of reason over complacency, mythology, fear, blind trust in authority, and viscerality. Yet, we argue that today's prevalent attitude that embraces market logic places many of those achievements at risk. Much of mainstream political discourse is just plain nonsense, and the detractors of nonsense, when they gain traction, are dismissed as elitist prigs. This, then, is followed by a discussion of market logic and its implications—namely the role market logic is playing in installing a regime of pharaonic rule.

THE HISTORY AND VALUE OF REASON

The opposite of coarseness is consistent refinement. The opposite of coherence is incoherence. When things are incoherent and inconsistent we cannot make logical decisions. This truth was clearly argued around 1150 by Ibn Rushd (Averroes) in his most important work, *The Incoherence of Incoherence* (*Tahafut al-tahafut*), a defense of Aristotelian thought written in dialogue form, which is important because it presents the formation of knowledge itself as a product of dialectical, free argument and cross-examination. It is also important because this book helped to reignite the flames of reason in a very dark Europe. Averroes was defending Aristotle against al-Ghazali's claims in *The Incoherence of Philosophers* (*Tahafut al-falasifa*). Averroes quotes passages by al-Ghazali and then rebuts them. In his book al-Ghazali argued that Aristotelian thought, especially as presented in the writings of Avicenna, was self-contradictory and an affront to the teachings of Islam. Averroes' counterpunch was two-pronged: first he argued that al-Ghazali's claims were simply inaccurate representations Avicenna, even self-serving, and second that regardless, Avicenna's rendering itself was a distortion of Aristotle's thinking so that al-Ghazali was attacking a straw man.

This is not merely a footnote to history for this would be one of the seeds that would help Europe pull itself out of the coarseness of the Dark Ages. It is important for two reasons: it recalls how, thanks to Alexander the Great, Greek philosophy, especially logic was spread far and wide throughout Asia and the Middle East where it was preserved while Europe retrograded and forgot or lost much of what the Greco-Romans had achieved, and second, that what was at stake was the ability to think clearly, analytically, logically, coherently. This ability is at the core of all human achievement. It is vital to a democracy where everyone is expected to make voting decisions. European utopian thought was different from all other cultures that linked utopia to supernatural, mystical perfection. Enlightenment ideas of radical European intellectuals were largely perceived as a threat to imperial power. From the Habsburgs, the royals of England and Spain, to the Czar, serfdom was normal.

But in the United States leaders were studying the utopian ideas, including the radical notion to promote education and rational thinking among the masses. This was the model in Prussia, but largely lacking in the rest of Europe. This radical agenda presumed universal education. Analytical skills had to be taught. And as the history of Europe proved, such skills can be lost and when they are, society and individuals suffer—most especially democratic societies.

In the middle of the nineteenth century, a member of the Massachusetts State Legislature and a former tutor of Latin and Greek and a librarian at Brown University, Horace Mann, proposed legislation mandating compulsory and universal education for all Massachusetts children. At his own expense he had traveled to Prussia to study their curriculum and upon return to the United States he wrote a report that was widely read in Massachusetts and also reprinted across the United States.[10] The King of Prussia, taking an idea from Martin Luther, who advocated compulsory education, instituted a tax-based compulsory education system that including teacher training, national testing of students, and a national curriculum. Affluent children could continue on to advanced private education, which was essentially out of reach for the general public. Mann borrowed from the Prussian model and pushed it further. His idea was to form normal universities to support common education for children of all classes. He wanted everyone to have a common educational experience that would support a democratic ethos.[11]

It was to be tax supported in order to enable all children, no matter how poor, to have access to education. Mann and his fellow legislators realized that democracy requires citizens who can read, write, and reason, otherwise you risk having illiterates and ignoramuses making policy that affects everyone. This move, which was copied across the United States, set the stage for not only a great democracy but also for a great leap forward in industrialization. Because there was no tax-based compulsory education in most of Europe at the time, within a generation, the truly radical result was that educated American workers became the backbone of an industrial giant that rose to compete with and generate more wealth than the old European empires. Industrialists in the United States soon were making trips to Europe to buy their castles and ship them block-by-block to be rebuilt in the United States (e.g., England's Agecroft Hall and Spain's Cistercian Monasteries) over to places like Rhode Island to be reconstructed along with much of their interior art and furniture. In two generations, thanks in part to a literate workforce, the United States caught up with and surpassed Europe in industrial wealth and power. But even more importantly, the wealth in the United States spread throughout the population and as the average person could read, books opened their minds to all sorts of possibilities and new expectations. Election after election supported the building of hundreds of universities and thousands of primary and secondary schools, as well as museums of science, industry, and art. The arts along with industry flourished. Carnegie donated a large proportion of his wealth to the building of libraries in every town in America. Books were free for loan.

American industry was beyond competitive for it was built on the monopoly that invention affords the inventor, not just the endless cuts in labor costs until one ends up with slavery. Edison, Goodyear, Eastman, Ford, Rockefeller, Vanderbilt, and other names of innovators and inventers were plastered across the landscape, something utterly missing in Europe until decades later. The United States became refined, while Europe, with its few old universities that were bastions of elitism rather than gateways to social advancement as in the United States, declined. The stage was set for endless wars on the continent. Meanwhile the United States had its own struggle to overcome darkness as the South lagged behind the North in reforms.

Now there is a huge inconsistency. Old conservative capitalists were nationally, even regionally patriotic. They, like Teddy Roosevelt, cared about the plight of poorer Americans and aspired to military service. Roosevelt promptly quit a nice job as Secretary of the Navy the instant he had a chance to serve at the relatively low rank of Lieutenant Colonel in Cuba. Many of his Ivy League friends eagerly joined him. A generation later, his niece Eleanor would be a staunch progressive and marry her distant cousin Franklin Roosevelt who served in World War I while their son subsequently served in World War II (while Franklin was president). Meanwhile many others such as the

Kennedys and Bushes served in the military and other civil services. Today, capital, as Karl Marx predicted, has gone global and so too have allegiances (hence his call for an international labor movement).

The superrich today are global citizens, and as such, they have more in common with each other than with their poor "countrymen."[12] The old class concept of the bourgeois is obsolete. Today the world has seen the emergence of the global player who is not conservative in the old law and order sense but the opposite. These are people who flee from all laws and regulations in order to pursue maximum profits and so we see them operating all over the world, shipping production and jobs literally overnight to places that have no environmental or labor protections. As Donald Trump put it in an interview on CNN, if the United States does not lower its taxes we will, he warns, have rich people leaving the United States in "droves."[13] They already have, at least on paper. Off-shore tax shelters for both wealthy individuals and companies like Halliburton, not only in some instances violate U.S. law, but ignore any notion of patriotic allegiance to all Americans.

At home in the United States, where wealthy conservatives may still enjoy a relatively safer domestic environment, they have been promoting a relentless assault on public education. In of all places, the United States, "conservatives" have been attacking the very foundation of what made the country great. Why? In part because nationalistic patriotism has been swept aside by globalism.[14] Entrepreneurs today do not have to live or fight with their workers. Instead the race to the bottom for the cheapest labor and least regulation is global and so local and national allegiance has given way to global capitalism. Marx's old reasoning maintains; it is not in the entrepreneur's interest to support tax-based programs to help all Americans because he or she no longer needs them. This is logical, from a very egocentric point of view. What we have is a basic conflict of interest between the exploiter and the exploited in a class system.

So the industrial base is eroding while entire towns, ones that were once the envy of the world, such as Detroit, the home of the automobile; Buffalo, the home of mass electrical generation; Rochester, the home of mass photography; Akron, the home of the tire industry, Kansas City; the home of aviation, and so forth are becoming ghost towns of mass dereliction. Salaries have stagnated[15] even for traditional professions such as teaching, so that people are not building new domiciles but struggling to make do with older and older hand-me-down homes, schools, roads, bridges . . . infrastructure that was once the envy of the world.[16] Grand department stores have been replaced by abandoned shopping malls. Main Street America is boarded up. Once grand railway stations, the commoner's mass transit, have either been torn down or stand long abandoned. True entrepreneurialism at the local level has been decimated. Strip malls and warehouse "big box" retailers now dot the landscape. The further we get away from the liberal notion of com-

munity and embrace the winner-takes-all, "bigger is better" social Darwinism of anonymous society, the more coarse our very landscape becomes.
Schools now have armed police for hall monitors and metal detectors at the
doors. Drug-sniffing dogs check lockers. Music and arts education are fast
disappearing. Such shifts correspond to changes in our civic environment and
polity.

COLLAPSING REASON IN MAINSTREAM DISCOURSE

Part of this chapter is about logic but illogical behavior in moral terms means
ignoring the absurd—cynicism. Logic is precise, structured, unyielding. Two
plus two equals only four. We say in logic, "if and only if . . ." Morality used
to be seen this way too. But increasingly the logic of behavior is anything
goes so long as it continues to sell. For the folks in Houston, the tens of
thousands who lost their stock-based retirements at Enron, are they angry
that their company was a shame of deceit and lies, that their daily commute
and routine was a farce, or that it stopped working as a massive Ponzi
scheme? Bernie Madoff reported from prison that the banks "had to know"
about his scheme.[17] So long as the money flowed, the market logic was
sustained. But, what of culture? What of truth? What of real logic in the real
world?

At the same time we have one Heisman Trophy winner being stripped of
his trophy for taking illicit money from pro agents[18] while another wins the
same award despite the fact that his father was shopping him around college
teams for $180,000.[19] It is claimed by his reverend father that the player who
was found guilty of cheating in three classes at the University of Florida and
of stealing a laptop before spending a year in football purgatory at a no-name
junior college, knew nothing of such sordid dealings. One has to wonder that
if Michael Vick were not making millions and being cheered by fanatical
supporters, would he still be on the straight and narrow? What if he were just
a "regular guy?" How much reward for being a good citizen does it take
these days to get someone to act like a decent human being? Or are we
increasingly rewarding people for being stupid and mean? Reality television
would support the latter thesis with primetime coverage of drunken midgets
urinating and a bisexual reality star road testing male and female "contest-
ants" for the job of celebrity partner.[20]

Today we can listen to hours and hours of tapes of President Richard
Nixon, a Quaker, cuss up a storm in the Oval office while plotting cover-ups,
hit lists, and other fundamental threats to our democratic process. No wonder
Dwight Eisenhower lost his temper when the RNC selected Nixon, the friend
of faux communist hunter Joseph McCarthy, whom Eisenhower personally

worked to bring down, and Charles "Bebe" (Baby) Rebozo along with other mafia confidants in Florida and Cuba, to be his running mate in the 1952 presidential election. Nixon had been introduced to Rebozo by Florida Democratic Senator and famous signatory to the "Southern Manifesto" protesting desegregation of public schools. George Smathers worked in the Senate to dilute equal rights laws promoted in congress by the Eisenhower administration. Coarseness and people contradicting their own interests and the agendas of their own leaders is not new.

In 1995 the federal government was literally shut down due to a hardline stance taken by the Speaker of the House, Newt Gingrich. He refused to let the federal budget be voted on and passed in part because he claimed to have been personally offended by President Clinton during a flight to and from Yitzhak Rabin's funeral in Israel.[21] Gingrich was born to a seventeen-year-old who divorced almost immediately after Newt's birth.[22] Not unlike his hero Ronald Reagan, who as a child lived on federal welfare (the Works Progress Administration),[23] Gingrich, himself, married his twenty-six-year-old high-school geometry teacher at the age of nineteen and[24] later told her of his plans to divorce her while she was in the hospital being treated for cancer.

Gingrich often stooped to sex politics, a favorite of conservatives. He led the charge to impeach Clinton over an affair with a Whitehouse aide, while he himself was having an affair with an aide of his own, and by circulating a memo insinuating that House Speaker Tom Foley was gay, coupling his name with gay Congressman Barney Frank's.[25] Meanwhile his half-sister, twenty-three years younger than him, Candace Gingrich, is a gay-rights activist just as is one of Dick Cheney's daughters, the same Cheney who for years sided with antigay elements in the Republican Party. Such contradictions between public policy positions and personal interest abound. Cheney also ridiculed gun-control activists' concerns about domestic safety until he himself shot a friend in the face while hunting in 2006 (report of the incident to the local law enforcement was delayed and speculation linked the delay to possible alcohol consumption being a factor in the accident—drinking while hunting).[26] Reagan too had been an arch defender of gun rights until he and his press secretary James Brady were shot. Then their tunes changed and their wives pushed doggedly to get the Brady Handgun Violence Prevention Act passed.[27] It was finally signed into law by Clinton (November 3, 1993) as the first act instituting federal background checks on firearm purchasers in U.S. history.

While Minority Leader of the House under Gingrich and a coauthor with Gingrich of the campaign document *Contract with America*, Dick Armey famously called Barney Frank "Barney Fag."[28] Gingrich famously campaigned against others for their lack of "personal responsibility" and integrity. Believing that welfare was the major cause of unwanted immigration to the United States and discouraged people from seeking work, while also arguing that illegal immigrants were taking American jobs, Gingrich relentlessly pushed a major bill he authored called Personal Responsibility and Work Opportunity Reconciliation Act. After two previous vetoes by Clinton it finally passed in 1996. The trimmed-down bill replaced the Aid to Families with Dependent Children (AFDC) program, which had been in effect since 1935, and led to the restructuring of the U.S. welfare-assistance program.[29] Gingrich now hosts and partially funds pro–right-wing documentaries and wrote a book in 2009, arguing that the United States is a uniquely and exclusively Christian country; *Rediscovering God in America*. Friends with Jerry Falwell, Gingrich was twice invited to be the commencement speaker at Falwell's Liberty University (others include former Republican candidates for President Steve Forbes, John McCain, Ron Paul, and Mike Huckabee), which was saved from bankruptcy in 1994 by an infusion of cash from self-proclaimed deity, founder of the Unification Church, and convicted con man Sun Myung Moon.[30] Playing up to the conspiracy theory that President Barack Obama is not born American, in 2010, Gingrich stated that Obama could only be understood by people who "understand Kenyan, anti-colonial behavior."[31]

Thanks to political activists cynically claiming self-righteous justifications, we can read the Independent Counsel Ken Starr's report on the Bill Clinton/Monica Lewinsky affair after "conservatives" attempting to impeach Clinton called it the worst thing to ever happen in the White House and demanded that the full "closed" testimony, every vile and private detail of it, be published on the Internet for all to read. Why? For the sake of justice and transparency or for pure political assault via personality assassination?

The ultimate in irrationality is absurdity, which means a self-contradicting position. Deputy White House Counsel to Clinton Vince Foster had complained of how depressing the political environment was.[32] His suicide became a partisan football adding to the toxic environment, kicked around by Starr who also led an investigation into Foster's death while "conservative" pundits and politicians suggested that Clinton himself had had his childhood friend killed.[33] What more was left to Foster but to roll in his grave over such utter cynicism? Clinton had brought heat to the tobacco industry, forcing its executives to stand in public before Congress and one by one incredulously claim that nicotine is not addictive. Starr, a former tobacco lobbyist and lawyer led the counterattack.[34] It was not limited to the Monica Lewinsky affair. Starr had tried to prosecute the Clintons for a failed real estate deal in Arkansas and in the process, because she would not testify the way he wanted her to, Susan McDougal of the Whitewater Development Company served the maximum of a year and a half in prison for contempt of court, eight of those months in solitary confinement. She refused to capitulate to Starr's demand that she change her testimony and "lie" just to get out of jail.[35] She, like Clinton in his impeachment trial, was eventually acquitted but only after tremendous abuses of the legal system. This is getting government off our backs? What we have here is absurdity: the ultimate in illogic.

Why does our culture now not only tolerate such behavior but reward it? Those who pushed for publication of the Starr Report online were reelected, even cheered by conservatives across the land. Those who supported Starr's misuse of power against McDougal claimed to hate abuse of government authority. And Starr, the tobacco lawyer who grew up in north-central Texas, the son of a preacher in the Church of Christ, was rewarded with the dean's position at Pepperdine University's School of Law. Pepperdine is affiliated with the Church of Christ. At this writing he is president of the Baptist-affiliated Baylor University in Waco, Texas.

Toleration of immoral behavior (and is not abuse of power immoral, especially by an unelected political appointee?) is enabled because our late-modern culture with its profound dissociation has separated what is legal from what is moral. Two years after the collapse of the financial industry with its massive fraud on Wall Street no one has been convicted. In the early 1990s the worst economic scandal since World War II in U.S. history, second now only to the current disaster, the Silverado Savings and Loan debacle, lead to over seven hundred savings and loans failing in the southwest.[36] Ronald Reagan's 1986 Tax Reform Act profoundly affected the real estate markets and his push to deregulate the industry allowed savings and loans to do what banks alone had been qualified to do in granting real estate loans. The deregulation allowed savings and loans to do banking but without the banking regulations.[37] The massive collapse required over $160 billion in taxpayer bailouts authorized by President George H. W. Bush. Two of the president's sons were directly involved, including the future governor of Florida and current presidential aspirant Jeb,[38] and Neil Bush. L. William Seidman, former chairman of both the Federal Deposit Insurance Corporation (FDIC) and the Resolution Trust Corporation, stated, "The banking problems of the '80s and '90s came primarily, but not exclusively, from unsound real estate lending."[39] In 1996 the FDIC published a report entitled "Lessons from the Eighties."[40] Did we learn anything?

Under President George W. Bush, who had been governor of Texas and directly involved in the savings and loans crisis, promoted the same deregulatory mentality and it predictably led to a similar real estate bubble, only this time on a national scale affecting world markets. So far the bailout bill for the U.S. taxpayer for this second disaster is over $2 trillion dollars and counting. During this time of "conservative" leadership, we also saw the greatest Ponzi scheme in history with Bernie Madoff and his children stealing over a billion dollars from investors despite the fact that regulators had been repeatedly informed that something with Madoff's operation was wrong.[41] During the same time we saw Enron collapse and outrageous pictures taken for fun at Abu Ghraib published, making people all over the United States and the world wonder what is going on with this culture.

Those who claim to be conservative, to be "law and order" types, have perpetrated some of the largest frauds in U.S. history. Examples are countless but for our purposes we will simply note the illogic of having the regulator and the regulated be essentially the same person or partners in corporate interest. As a tiny example consider the auditing firms of Ernst & Young, Price Waterhouse Coopers, Deloitte & Touche, and Arthur Andersen, and their well-documented conflicts of interest with those they were to audit such as Lehman Brothers, AIG, Nortel, WorldCom, Tyco International, and so forth. In each case billions of dollars were lost due to a lack of private-sector oversight as well as decades-long attacks by "conservatives" on evil government oversight (law and regulations) especially involving the Environmental Protection Agency and the Securities and Exchange Commission. Their budgets gutted, they lacked staff to do the job and were repeatedly led by political appointees of conservative administrations who hated the missions of the very agencies they were tasked to lead and who put pressure on career law enforcers to relax their efforts. This is absurd.

MARKET LOGIC

The more the logic of pure capitalism prevails, the poorer most individuals become, and so the poorer the environment becomes. Labor populations are pitted against each other in strident efforts to sell themselves and entire dying communities become easy pickings for exploitation. What has emerged is a logical quagmire. The more the logic of capital accumulation prevails the more globalism expands in search of ever-cheaper labor. But labor is people. Labor is community. Market logic increasingly comes into direct contradiction with the logic of community, which includes reciprocity, sharing, and nurturing. The irony seems to be, that in the search for ever more business-friendly environments, the more poverty spreads due to concentrations of wealth. Even Marx did not see this coming quite as it has unfolded. He thought capitalism, with its ability to harness greed to the task of production, would raise all boats, would supply all needs to all people, leading to socialism. But he underestimated the power of greed as hoarding. He thought that once people had all they needed then surplus would ease fears and tensions, leading naturally to open sharing. He failed to understand ego-identity with having more than the other guy . . . far more than one could ever possibly need.

Old conservative ideologies, which Marx was assuming, used to temper such greed with doctrines of shame and notions of noble sacrifice, notions reinforced largely by Christianity. Being a pillar of the community, a powerful person with paternalistic duties, was once the great ambition of the entrepreneurial class. See, for instance, the residents of Gramercy Park, including Cyrus Field, who convinced his wealthy neighbors to help him build the first trans-Atlantic telegraph cable not just for the earnings potential but for the good it would bring to humanity and also for the sheer romance of the new marvel. This class of people really did believe that the flower of capitalism should be greater prosperity for all. They believed in a general progress and community building. They believed in a Calvanist doctrine that hard work and making money was to serve a higher set of goals essential to healthy individuals, families, communities, and countries. Gramercy Park was the epicenter not only of wealth in New York City but also of philanthropy and institutions such as The Federation of Protestant Welfare Agencies. Gramercy Park became a model for upper-class subculture copied in city after city across America up to the 1960s. It was the children from such families that formed the "hippies" and Peaceniks that insisted on equal opportunities and made the workingman's denim into a cultural icon of universal ware. The new player class is utterly different. Its religion is the hedonic calculus of egocentric pragmatism. To this new group, altruism is not only illogical but nonexistent. The rise of the player class presents a sea change in culture (beliefs, attitudes, values, motives).

The player class, which has transcended the old bourgeoisie, has no such spiritual dimension: no checks on total domination or moral self-discipline. What is rational is what sells. Market is logic. This is what President Nixon's White House Counsel John Dean is hinting at, but in some ways fails to fully expound, when he speaks of conservatives without conscience.[42] What he fails to see is that there can be no such thing as a conservative without a conscience. Players are *not* conservatives. They are radical egoists who see all rules, laws, obligations, duties, and regulations as nothing but quaint old-fashioned obstacles to total self-expression and desire attainment.

The irony here is that the most ruthless exploiters are not those who rose up, "bootstrap" style, through their own innovation or luck. These old-style "captains of industry," who built the country, were dedicated to their communities. For instance, Ernest W. Marland once controlled one-tenth of the world's oil. He founded Marland Oil (what is now Conoco) in Ponca City Oklahoma when he hit his first gusher in 1911. He pioneered employer-paid insurance for his employees, including eye and dental care, and he built four hundred homes for them. He lavished money on his small town, believing that it was his duty to elevate his employees and community. Little Ponca City for a time had more paved streets per capita than any other town in America. He built schools and lavish parks. But then he was invited to a meeting with J. P. Morgan in New York City. Marland believed Morgan wanted to invest in his oil company. Instead, upon entering Morgan's office Marland was confronted by an army of lawyers and Morgan explained the details of a forced acquisition of his company. The oilman was legally out-maneuvered and lost his company in a hostile buyout. He had to vacate his estate and move with this wife into the artist's studio on the estate. He ran for governor of the state as a Democrat and won.[43] After his death his widow Lydie moved away and during the 1960s participated in anti–Vietnam war protests.

The conservatives who originally built American industry were not ac-countants, scientific managers, or marketing majors. They knew and had passions for their particular industries. They were not corporate capitalists (financiers). They literally built and developed the economy and they saw their prosperity bringing with it an obligation to stewardship. By contrast, the modern master of business administration (MBA) is not an inventor or inno-vator. S/he is less inspired by an idea or innovation than by pure profit, no matter the means. Modern MBAs switch jobs at will. But the inventor/build-er of industries cannot simply stop being the maker of cars or airplanes. This is who they are, what they know, and what they care about. The modern player is a generic, empty vessel, quick to shift allegiances as a formalist. All that matters is the quantification of capital value. The new expert MBA claims to be able to manage tomato growing just as well as violin making, arms sales, or pest extermination. Everything is reduced to a single quantity: the bottom line, a business opportunity, a source that is exploitable. Market logic is pure empty form. This is also how labor, as a market, is treated. Workers, here or there, make no difference. The modern manager does not see herself as an integral part of any community. Cohesion is maintained largely out of a threat of poverty. This anonymity and disconnectedness, as the primatologist and student of human behavior Desmond Morris,[44] and also Jean Gebser,[45] note, enables a person to not care, to be a dissociated disinter-ested actor, to abandon what Morris has called the "delicate balance" be-tween cooperation and competition. Morris says:

> With the loss of the person-to-person tribal pattern [which sustained the spe-cies for countless generations up until the rise of complex societies], the com-petitive/co-operative pendulum began to swing dangerously back and forth, and it has been oscillating damagingly ever since. Because the subordinate members of the super-tribes became impersonal crowds, the most violent swings of the pendulum have been towards the domineering, competitive side. The over-grown urban groups rapidly and repeatedly fell prey to exaggerated forms of tyranny, despotism and dictatorship. The super-tribes gave rise to super-leaders, exercising powers that make the old monkey tyrants look posi-

tively benign. They also gave rise to super-subordinates in the form of slaves, who suffered subservience of a kind more extreme than anything even the most lowly of monkeys would have known. [46]

As the scale of economic activity expanded, decisions began to be made that affected larger and larger populations, decisions that directly affect people on other continents: people the decision makers will never know, see, or care about. The logic of bottom-line accounting has no existential content. Thus market logic contradictions existential rationality. The result is sledgehammer generalizations that seem well informed but that operate blindly.

When it comes to cognition we refine our thinking with logic. For our emotional lives refinement takes on the qualities of sympathy and empathy. Logic makes ever-finer distinctions in reasoning. Fine thinking or reasoning is precise thinking or reasoning. Precision comes from making distinctions, for precision is the result of fragmenting things like space, time, and problems into ever-smaller parts.

The smaller a unit of measure the more precise the measurement. If one says, "I will see you on Sunday," that is good, but if you can tell another what hour you will arrive that would be even better. And if you could tell what minute, the precision would be appreciated. Likewise, if you tell a friend you will meet her in Idaho, that's nice but what city, what street, and what address makes the whole process of meeting much more precise. Justice has also been refined by degrees such as the profoundly important distinctions between murder in the first, second, or third degrees and manslaughter in the first, second, and third degrees. [47]

The opposite of precise thinking is imprecise thinking, which involves not attending to detail, gross generalizations, and a disregard for accuracy in facts. Willful blindness to the actual in favor of an oversimplified virtual, a kind of statistical hubris by averages, is an example that has become commonplace. A perfect instance of this attitude is hedge fund speculation, specifically the methods used by Long-Term Capital Management Corporation in 1998, which nearly lead to a collapse of world markets because they would not take into account actual contingencies (facts in the real world), such as Yeltsin devaluing the ruble. The Nobel Prize winners running the company arrogantly relied on their computer formulations to work no matter what. But the longer they let the computer trading go, the deeper in trouble they got with massive debt piling up exponentially until the U.S. government, at the behest of other major brokerage firms and banks, had to step in and stop them, and just in the nick of time as it turns out. They were literally just a couple of trading cycles away from implicating world markets in a meltdown. [48]

Even worse is incoherent and absurd, meaning self-contradictory, thinking. The logical laws of the excluded middle and of noncontradiction allows us to avoid being absurd and in ethical terms it allows us to identify illogical arguments and either absurd or cynical people who can do great damage when we are trying to make policy decisions involving the expenditure of scarce and precious resources such as spending public funds, our honor and respect, and the blood of our youth sent off to war.

Someone who claims to be an objective analyst of events and who, at the same time, celebrates economic hardship and promotes the purchasing of gold from a company he himself represents and which experts in the field of investment in precious metals repeatedly note overcharges its customers with nearly 40 percent commissions, someone like Glenn Beck, is a danger to society.[49] It is widely understood that his general spiel is as a fear monger. Those who follow his advice and then try to get their money back, however, realize that over a third of their investment was taken in commissions by the company who pays Beck to advertise for them. He also regularly distorts or misstates facts in order to convince Americans to vote illogically, against their own interests. People and society overall are harmed by his persuasive oratory and the source credibility he has gained from his appearances on the Fox News Channel.

There is an irrational conferral of status to anyone who appears on television and makes lots of money. Such irrational status is summed up by the advertising phrase, "as seen on TV" implying, irrationally, that appearing on television by itself makes a person or product more trustworthy and valuable. In Beck's case he selectively presents only some of the information about the value of precious metals in an economic environment that sees stocks and bonds falter. Some of the rest of the story would include the fact that one can purchase gold far more cheaply at any number of other brokerages than the one he represents. Glenn Beck is a "conservative without conscience."[50]

Beck's bosses have repeatedly shown themselves to be utterly cynical. They have created and sustained this danger. Rupert Murdoch, the number-one shareholder and founder of Fox News, and the second-largest holder of stock in the cable operation, Saudi Royal Prince Alwaleed bin Talal, both use their media empire to preach free-market ideology. Fox News doesn't have an evening news segment like most news networks, choosing instead to air opinion-based programs. The same is true of the *New York Post*, one of America's oldest newspapers that was founded by Alexander Hamilton and which Murdock purchased in 1976 and promptly changed into a tabloid with "conservative" editorial and labor policies, but with anything-goes sensational content.[51] *Columbia Journalism Review* stated that under Murdoch's ownership, "the *New York Post* is no longer merely a journalistic problem. It is a social problem—a force for evil."[52] The *Post*, it explained:

is written and presented so as to appeal to the basest passions and appetites of the hour. The front pages regularly play to two emotions: fear and rage. And all too often what follows is meant to turn white against black, the comfortable against the poor, the first world against the third. [53]

In 1988, Murdoch, who claims to be a law-and-order conservative, was forced to sell the *Post* due to cross-media ownership regulations when he purchased WNYW-TV to launch the Fox Broadcasting Company. In 1993, during George H. W. Bush's tenure as president, the FCC made an exception to its own regulations and allowed the president's supporter and personal friend, Murdoch, to violate the cross-media ownership rules and repurchase the newspaper. [54] In 2007 Murdoch bought the largest circulation newspaper in the United States, the *Wall Street Journal*. During negotiations he promised to not interfere with the daily running and editorial policy of the paper, but within a year the managing editor Marcus Brauchli resigned under pressure. [55] Much of the original staff has since left. This is Murdoch's pattern; lie, purchase, replace experienced journalists with young people with little or no journalism experience or training, cut news content, boost ad content, and use the property as a platform for political campaigning in the guise of objective news reporting. Murdoch did the same thing in 1981 when he purchased the *Sunday Times* and *The Times* of London (which began publishing in 1785) and immediately fired the editor William Rees-Mogg. [56]

The overall point here is that powerful people extend their power through control of messages mediated on a mass scale and that a profound contradiction has been realized. That in some cases, usually extremely conservative news outlets, "the more you read the less you know," as Bruce Selcraig described the Gaylord Family newspaper, the *Daily Oklahoman*. [57] When powerful people purchase mass media outlets not because they are interested in journalism but instead to propagate their own personal political biases, this is called "news narcissism." Narcissism is an irrational preoccupation with the self. As the former dean of Berkeley's school of journalism Ben H. Bagdikian noted, the owner of a business may feel justified in calling the shots however he or she likes but news as a commodity is unique. News affects how informed a populace is and that is critical in a democracy. [58] If one owns a shoe factory or is a car manufacturer or retail jeweler and one insists on making only pink shoes and lousy cars and wildly overpriced jewelry, such irrational entrepreneurial behavior has no effect on the decision making citizens must perform when they vote. News is not shoes. Also, as the United States has continued its slide into marginal literacy, there is less and less competition among serious news outlets. Americans used to have access to at least two, often three or more daily newspapers, and they read them. Today, reading is declining and standardized tests repeatedly show that Americans are less and less able to comprehend what they read, especially if it has complex arguments or scholarly content.[59]

The modern world is complex and becoming more complex by the day. Good decisions often require intricate logic and the critical capacity to discern poor quality information from high-quality information. Decisions require precise thinking and evidence gathering. The ancient Greeks realized this and invented philosophy to combat what they called sophistry. To the Greeks, sophistry was a way of talking that made a person or an audience dependent on the speaker. This is the type of talk gurus practice. Instead of telling or teaching people how to read and critically reason, the guru maintains his position by keeping people ignorant and telling them "all they need to know." In this process the sophist actively seeks to keep people ignorant and dependent on him. Instead of teaching people how to fish, the guru gives the people fish and thereby controls them. This is the stuff of cult formation and behavior.

Plato knew this and thus made the distinction between false and true rhetoric in the fifth century BCE. False rhetoric seeks to enslave and by implication give the master narrator, the speaker, power. True rhetoric seeks to impart the truth even if it may harm the relationship between the speaker and hearer. True rhetoric meant to free the hearer of delusions. Thus, a parent may tell a child not to marry someone because the parent truly believes such an act is not in the best interest of the child, even if that means risking conflict with the child. Gurus do not risk conflict by stating unpopular or inconvenient truths. Instead their speech is meant to aggrandize the audience to them, often through forms of flattery such as saying to Americans, "America is the greatest country in the history of the world," even though in 2010 it ranked last and next to last in five dimensions of health-system performance,[60] and had continually declined since its peak in the mid-1970s as a leader in education. Today it ranks eighteenth among thirty-six nations in secondary education.[61] During the same three decades by 2009 the United States had fallen from the top five to being ranked thirtieth out of thirty-one countries in infant mortality, beating only Slovakia, while Singapore led the thirty-one countries studied.[62] Despite medical advances, infant mortality in the United States had risen 36 percent since 1984.

While it is impossible to say that one culture is "better" than another, it is objectively possible to say is one society is efficient or deficient in terms of being able to endure and self-replicate. No society has remained successful while attacking its own intelligence. It is irrational to attack intellectuals, but conservatives, especially fundamentalist Christians, do just that—from Ronald Reagan's denigration of college professors in the California university system to televangelists Pat Robertson. Intellectuals in Reagan's administration struggled. He had as his first budget advisor David Stockman, who was universally praised for his brilliance. But Stockman, who later decried the "triumph of politics [read sophistry]" over facts, himself reported publically that Reagan did not read nor understand the budgets he was presented with.[63] Reagan regularly confused lines and claims he had read in fictional movie scripts and speeches written for him by General Electric public relations people while he was a paid spokesperson for the corporation.[64] While president of the Screen Actors' Guild, Reagan handed over lists of members to the House Un-American Activities Committee,[65] effectively ruining several peoples' careers and lives while pretending to be representing their interests. All were innocent of the charges he leveled at them of being Soviet-controlled puppets who had infiltrated Hollywood in order to poison America. Such horribly ignoble behavior—which prompted his first wife, Actress Jane Wyman to leave him for "mental cruelty"—betraying his friends and office, is seen as either noble by his "conservative" fans or just conveniently forgotten.[66] When running for president, Reagan would feign ignorance of the ignoble "dirty tricks" and lies the man who helped him get elected, Lee Atwater, perpetrated. Atwater would later confess that he had done horrible things to Reagan's and later G. W. Bush's political competitors and, while facing his own mortality, pleaded for forgiveness.[67] Ed Rollins[68] writes of Atwater's profound influence on how party politics took a sharp turn toward negative rhetoric and took politics to a new level of disregard for others or the facts. Atwater collapsed during a fundraiser for Phil Gramm in 1990, which led to his diagnosis of cancer. Gramm, a Texas senator and protégé of Alan Greenspan, who in turn used to literally sit at the feet of Ayn Rand in her apartment in New York City,[69] was the architect under George W. Bush of massive deregulation of the financial industry, which set the stage for our present global financial crisis. Gramm along with other conservatives finally succeeded in repealing the 1933 Glass-Steagall Act, which was part of the effort to restore confidence in and discipline to the financial sector back during the Great Depression.[70] In a stark look at how to "rig an election" by the Republican "operative," Allen Raymond marks the rise of the "great communicator" Reagan as the turning point in political campaigning as a win-at-all-costs philosophy.[71] Atwater called it the "scorched Earth" approach, a claim also made by David Brock in his 2003 book *Blinded by the Right* in which he recounts how he abandoned all fairness and empirical fact to attack Anita Hill for testifying against President George W. Bush's Supreme Court nominee Clarence Thomas. Brock, long-time acquaintance of others in the Republican "noise machine" such as Ann Coulter and Lora Ingraham, also said of the latter that she was "the only person I knew who didn't appear to own a book or regularly read a newspaper."[72] Nevertheless, she pontificates away on Fox and other mass platforms as an opinion leader.

This anti-intellectualism may be one of the biggest problems with the coarsening of discourse. The utter disregard for facts, the truth in general, and science in particular is often cast by conservative talkers as somehow a form of effeminate weakness or mushy-headed liberalism. For example, Reagan's Surgeon General C. Everett Koop would recount frustrations regarding Reagan and others in his administration refusing to take universal health care, AIDS, secondhand smoke, and other issues seriously.[73] "America's family doctor" would later publish a book about Christian doctrine and medical science.[74] Not incidentally, Stockman has recently come out publically to chastise Tea Party and other "extremists" on the right for their dangerous combination of ignorance and arrogance, especially in their uninformed attacks against Obama's banking reforms and their demands to extend Bush tax cuts.[75] Stockman argues that the country is in danger by following ignorant and incompetent advice from people like Limbaugh, Sarah Palin, and "Joe the Plumber."

Reagan's son[76] and his official biographer[77] suspect that while "Dutch" was still president he was already showing signs of mental deterioration due to Alzheimer's disease. Reagan famously and erroneously believed that once launched, intercontinental ballistic missiles could be recalled. Such ignorance is dangerous. One of the most troubling trends in news narcissism has been the use of massive media power to rewrite history. A good example of a flagrant disregard for facts and the truth has been the systematic distortion of Reagan's legacy,[78] as well as the claim that America is a "Christian nation."[79]

Similarly, numerous and various sources reported on a general and disturbing lack of intellectual curiosity on the part of President George W. Bush before and while in office. This trend is growing among conservatives. See, for instance, the constant personal attacks by conservatives in Congress on scientists reporting their findings supporting the thesis of global warming. They include House Representative and Chair of the House Energy and Commerce Committee from Texas Joe Barton and Republican Senator from Oklahoma James Inhofe. Both used their power to initiate government-sponsored investigations of the employees, research projects, and funding sources of Boulder, Colorado's National Center for Atmospheric Research (NCAR) and its parent organization, the University Center for Atmospheric Research.[80]

Increasingly, the opinion leaders for millions of Americans are neither news gatherers nor intellectuals nor even rigorous students of political science, law, or natural sciences. They are people like Rush Limbaugh, Sean Hannity, and Glenn Beck. Coming out of very conservative rural Washington, libertarian conspiracy promoter Beck is a drug and alcohol addict. He claims to have gotten high every day for fifteen years beginning when he was sixteen. He has also been suicidal. His great achievement before hitting it big

on Fox was being "self-educated."[81] He took one college class and dropped
out before it finished. Hannity's achievements before being picked up by Fox
were dropping out of college twice and being a bartender, and ironically,
having his first broadcast gig as a volunteer at the University of California's
KCSB saved for him by the local ACLU who came to the defense of his free-
speech rights despite their objectionable nature, which prompted his managers to fire and then reinstate him. Thanks to the ACLU, we have Hannity
misinforming millions of people on a daily basis on radio and television. [82]

Limbaugh's great record, other than avoiding the draft due to a cyst on his
butt, consists of dropping out of Southeast Missouri State after two semesters
of failing grades and going east to become a rock 'n 'roll DJ under the
pseudonyms "Jeff Christie" and "Rusty Sharpe." He was repeatedly fired[83]
until deregulation of broadcast laws during the "law and order" Reagan administration eliminated the "fairness doctrine." Limbaugh never has guests.
His shtick is to make straw arguments and then tear them apart without the
person or group he identifies with them being present to defend themselves.
This is of course is antidialectical, antidemocratic comportment and simply
dishonest and also cowardly. With the deregulation of the number of radio
stations any one person or group can own from seven to an unlimited number. Limbaugh's network, Clear Channel Communications, now syndicates
him over all nine hundred of its stations from coast to coast, exposing his
views to the largest radio audience in the United States. Limbaugh's sophistry satisfied Cincinnatian Terry Jacobs, who ran a small media group of
religious stations. Jacobs, owner of Jacor Communications, pumped Limbaugh and when Jacor was sold to Clear Channel Communications, the owner of Clear Channel, the Texas archconservative and advertising magnate
Mark Mays loved his rhetoric. In October 2007, forty-one Democratic U.S.
senators sent a letter to Mays, asking him to renounce Rush Limbaugh for
calling all soldiers who disagreed with the Iraq War "phony soldiers." Mays
gave the letter to Limbaugh who used it as a foil on his show, ultimately
putting it up for auction on eBay,[84] an event heralded on Fox News in a news
report describing Limbaugh as having the "Midas touch."[85] Keep in mind
that this ridicule of soldiers came from a man who took 4-F status to stay out
of the army. In 1999 Limbaugh's bid to buy an NFL team was met with so
much opposition from players and owners that the sale was blocked and
Limbaugh withdrew his offer. The NFL Players executive director DeMau-
rice Smith and the commissioner of the NFL Roger Goodell issued a joint
statement that the league seeks to unify American spectators by rejecting
discrimination and hate mongering.[86] In June 2006, Limbaugh was detained
and questioned for travelling with unprescribed drugs into the United States
from the Dominican Republic[87] and for doctor shopping for a narcotics addiction.[88] His listeners seem not to care about the hypocrisy, which is the
nature of the problem with an uncritical flock.

Not all of the problem can be blamed on the gurus. What we are dealing with is a larger cultural issue that has been spreading for the past thirty to forty years. Two GOP presidents who were and are still hailed by conservative followers as stalwarts in defense of law and order and of the United States conspired to break the law and sell missiles to the very terrorist state that had held our embassy staff hostage for over a year in Tehran, Iran.[89] Several members of the Reagan administration were charged by the Special Counsel and long-time Republican Judge Lawrence Walsh, with multiple felony counts of conspiracy, lying to Congress, obstruction of justice, and altering and destroying documents pertinent to the investigation. There was evidence that even before he was elected Reagan and members of his campaign had negotiated with the Iranian hostage takers, telling them not to release the embassy staff until after the election, assuring the President Jimmy Carter's efforts would not help his reelection efforts. Soon after Reagan was inaugurated he countered Executive Order 12170, issued by Carter, to freeze about $8 billion of Iranian assets in the United States, with Executive Order 12294, which suspended all litigation against Iran.[90] Not only did Reagan reward the Iranians but we now know he also agreed to sell arms to them as part of the overall deal. Years later, in his autobiography *This American Life*, Reagan himself admitted to authorizing the shipments to Iran.[91]

Many were convicted, but when Reagan's vice president was elected president, George H. W. Bush pardoned them, including several high-ranking individuals convicted of lying under oath about the arms sales to Iran and diversion of funds to the Contras in Nicaragua, such as Oliver North, John Poindexter, Elliot Abrams, Caspar Weinberger, and so on. In fact, Bush's son named several of the men his father pardoned (e.g., Elliot Abram, found guilty of withholding information from Congress about the Iran-Contra scandal, was ironically appointed senior director of the National Security Council's Office for Democracy, Human Rights, and International Operations by George W. Bush) to high-level jobs in his own administration.[92] Such incoherent behavior is not held up to scrutiny by the masses. Walsh had amassed evidence linking George H. W. Bush himself directly to the illegal activities but his mandate expired under President Bill Clinton, who declined to extend the investigation, claiming that it only served to aggravate partisan conflict. Little did Clinton know that his own lies under oath, not about breaking the law and selling arms to our enemies but about sexual relations, would not meet with such gentility and discretion. Walsh was very frustrated with the decision, which prematurely terminated his investigation.[93]

Robert Jay Lifton, the preeminent authority on cults and cult behavior in the twentieth century, agrees with Plato's basic distinction between true and false rhetoric. Philosophers did not seek to impart empirical truths to the next generation because facts change. That is why of all books, science books go out of date the fastest. Rather, philosophers teach their beloved students method that will allow them to root out error and to protect themselves against the enchantment of charismatic speakers. The weapon of choice is logic and a critical mindset that is suspicious of claims until and unless they can be verified.

PHARAONIC RULE

This deification of Reagan is extremely interesting and a very—it's scandalous, but it tells a lot about the country.

—Noam Chomsky, February 17, 2011, *Democracy Now*[94]

Ancient Greek communities, like all peoples from that time, tended to be ruled by living gods. This form of authority is called pharaonic rule and it means that the ultimate authority is not temporal but eternal and whatever the pharaoh, emperor, or supernatural chief says is an infallible edict as gods cannot be wrong (even when they contradict themselves).[95] The power structure of most such societies was and is today in places like North Korea made up of a priestly class of people who derive their power directly, often by touch itself, from the god-king. The magic power of association is manifested in mass circulated photos of such supporters literally standing with the dictator. If they fall out of favor, they are expunged from photos, or as in ancient times their names and faces are obliterated from statues, mosaics, sarcophagi, hieroglyphs, and so forth. While such purges were easy to detect before because photo alteration was clumsy, today with digital manipulation, a person can be added or removed from a photo in such a way that it is increasingly difficult to catch the fraud.

If there is no truth, there can be no liars.[96] In a world of digital manipulation one of two disastrous consequences are given: (1) people are duped by the faked photos or video and may make horrible decisions to follow the liars to war or some other calamity, or (2) people realize that images can be faked and so they stop believing anything. Neither scenario is positive for society, and yet we are now in this "postmodern" terrain. The priestly class constitutes the enforcers of the system. As we continue in this chapter, we will refer to such people as "mindguards," a type of person who is a fervent (though sometimes subtle), and an often irrational defender of the faith, whatever that might be. The term "mindguard" comes from Irving Janis's theory of groupthink.[97] Herein, we integrate and synthesize Janis's theory with Elisabeth Noelle-Neumann's theory of the Spiral of Silence. The result is the spiral of groupthink. The thesis argues that with the megaphone effect whereby an extremely small group of people, such as Rush Limbaugh, Sean

Hannity, Bill O'Reilly, and others can form a united front of dis- and misinformation on a scale never before seen. They form a consistent, although possibly incoherent (when compared to objective facts), picture of the world. In the process the psychological effect is one of groupthink on a mass scale by daily and hourly repetitions of the same, often even identical, talking points about a particular interpretation of the world. They are the mindguard priests of electronically mediated and amplified groupthink. To borrow from George Gerbner, by using initially fax machines and now e-mail list serves and Twitter accounts, they orchestrate daily, sometimes hourly campaigns to "cultivate" a particular picture of the world.[98] Even particular rhetorical phrases are repeated by multiple people on the same day to create the impression of a false common reality or mass movement as described in the Spiral of Silence theory.

The priests in theocratic dictatorships are alone granted the right to interpret the god-king's edicts and impose the will of the god-king on everyone else. Curiosity and questioning of such edicts is considered blasphemy and also as a seditious activity. We saw something of this in Republican primaries across the nation in 2010 as incumbents with voting records in Congress that deviated from the Club for Growth's orthodoxy were targeted and "cannibalized" by their own party, as Arlen Specter put it in his farewell speech to the Senate to which he was elected five times.[99] Former George W. Bush speechwriter David Frum described the manner with which conservative think tanks treat people who break from orthodoxy, "We don't pay you to think, we pay you to repeat."[100]

The illogicality of purification purges is that they can never be concluded. There is always something imperfect about anyone. Just as Nazis may have liked to purify the Aryan race, if they had succeeded and everyone was six feet tall with blonde hair and blue eyes, then to be Aryan would have lost all meaning for meaning and identity comes from difference. But such physical as well as ideological pogroms that are orchestrated campaigns to exterminate diversity (difference), eventually leave no one standing and eliminate any possibility of innovation. This is the sort of coarseness and stupid ambition we are increasingly seeing.

The ultimate show of illogic is a system that is not only no longer self-sustaining but suicidal, for self-destruction is the ultimate expression of absurdity. An example of such suicidal decisions coming out of a fervor of ecumenical proportions for ideological purity was noted by Specter who, in the same speech chastised Supreme Court Chief Justice John Roberts and Justice Samuel Alito for "eroding the constitutional mandate of separation of powers," by reversing federally imposed campaign finance regulations for corporations and unions. Specter argued that in their ruling on the case *Citizens United v. Federal Elections Commission*, the court had wantonly undermined the democratic system itself by, "Ignoring a massive congressional record and reversing recent decisions." Specter argued that Chief Justice Roberts and Justice Alito had contradicted their own conservative stance toward consistency in oath taking and repudiated their confirmation testimony by providing the key votes to permit corporations and unions to secretly pay for political advertising—thus further undermining the basic Democratic principle of the power of one person, one vote. Specter argued that in his confirmation, "Chief Justice Roberts promised to just call balls and strikes and then he moved the bases."[101]

The god-king and his visors and priests were spiritual beings as well as political beings. They are "know-it-alls." They had all the answers to all the questions. They could tell the populace everything and could not be questioned. Their voice was law. Then, in ancient Greece, half a millennium before Christ, along came a small group of people including Thales, Anaximander, Diogenes, and Socrates, who questioned conventional answers and pushed for natural explanations to things. They demanded reliability, meaning consistency. They demanded validity in claims. They were secularists, which means of time, not eternity. They were, in this sense the opposite of people like Chief Justice Roberts and Justice Samuel Alito, who claim to be Constitutionalists, meaning that the constitution is infallible and sacrosanct, even as they make law in their own subjective way. The philosophers held that their statements could be wrong and so truth was contingent upon the best evidence available. They spoke not in terms of divine edict or eternal truths that defy interpretation, but in terms of theory and theses. And they not only allowed questioning and challenges to their claims but encouraged such disputation in the form of dialectical confrontation. No one had the upper hand based on being divine or of being a representative of divine power. Not surprisingly, many philosophers were either killed or expelled by priestly castes of mind guards that populated their city-states. Arlen Specter is in good company.

The philosophers essentially looked at many of the explanations for things in their day, such as the cause of earthquakes, and challenged the priestly supernatural explanations in favor of natural causes. And they began to experiment, to empirically go forth and see for themselves what makes things tick. Their motto was, "show me." If you claim to be able to turn water into wine, fine, but prove it and then show me how to do it. Their approach was inherently democratic, not giving some supernatural privilege to "special people." They doubted the existence of miracles, which are things done that contradict the laws of nature.

These philosophers were, in a sense, know-nothings as they could not begin to search and ask questions until they admitted that they did not already know all the answers. They invented logic so that they could coherently build arguments, cross-examine claims, and test hypotheses. Logic was not only unnecessary for divine edicts, but it was overtly discouraged. Isocrates, a contemporary of Socrates and Plato, invented school so that young people could learn to read, write, and participate in civic life, not based on their divine blood but on their abilities to question toward the best solution for problems. Ultimately meritocracy is based on the methodical, logical process of testing claims. Meritocracy also allows all comers to try: Mill's "free market-place of ideas." School was not necessary for priests except as scribes and the rote learning of sacred texts. This manner of training is exactly what kept China and other Asian nations from advancing until they abandoned their Confucian examination system with its extremely restricted curriculum in the late nineteenth and early twentieth centuries.

And so all over the world, first in ancient Greece, logic begins as a form of enquiry and the struggle between the know-it-alls and the know-nothings has continued down through the ages and across the globe. The struggle between cross-examination of claims and a demand for honesty, reliability, and validity—reason versus blind faith and defense of orthodoxy continues. It is a never-ending struggle because it is eventually a political struggle, a fight for power and a fight for which claims will seize the day. The pendulum between blind faith and the demand for reasons is ever-present and how it swings expresses the battle between competing forms of authority, rational and legitimate or irrational and illegitimate. Legitimate authority is authority that welcomes critical assessment and that stands the test of repeated cross-examination by all comers. It manifests a democratic ethos where all are encouraged to participate. In the modern world, we encourage, even demand, that our children study math and science and learn how to debate. But in other societies authority follows the dictum that stability is prized more than innovation and that for the masses a full stomach and empty head is best. Some have argued that conservative forces in the United States have consistently worked to undermine tax supported universal and compulsory education for this very reason.

The ancient Greek philosophers (know-nothings) called their time ruled by priests and god-kings who claimed to know everything and to terrorize people who questioned the First Sophistic. The First Sophistic was a time when free speech, which is a social requirement for philosophy and science to thrive, did not exist. Instead, fancy, grand, eloquent proclamations and orations were parts of ceremonies conducted by living gods and their entourages. This is homiletics or sermonizing. Rarely, if ever, does a minister, rabbi, or priest stop in the middle of a sermon to take questions or to encourage authentic and sincere debate. Sincere debate means a form of discourse where people come together to examine an issue or problem without prejudgment or belief that the truth is already known. If people engage in discussion believing that they already know the truth, then all questions are merely rhetorical—inauthentic.

During the Catholic Eucharist, the flock is not invited to debate the material properties of the wine and wafers and the meaning of the process. In dictatorships, the priests perform and others listen and watch. Sophists do not invite inquiry. The philosophers, by contrast, liked to walk together and have educated conversations, with everyone chiming in. Sometimes they liked to get a little drunk because that would actually help shyer people to speak up and take on the teacher, the one who led the seminar. Symposium means "drinking party." Challenging authority was encouraged, not punished. And so better and better answers to questions emerged. Progress began and it continued until the fall of Republican Rome when the courts were closed, the Senate silenced and tyrannical dictator god-kings emerged to rule the Empire. This period was termed the Second Sophistic. The age of philosophy was coming to an end. And though Quintillian tried to reinvigorate free speech, debate, cross-examination, marshalling of warrants and facts, and the testing of evidence, he failed and Europe slipped into what Petrarche would, over a thousand years later, call the "Dark Ages." Roger Bacon, Albertus Magnus, Abélard, Petrarch, Alphonso X of Castile and Leon had begun studying the Greco-Roman writers as they were preserved in old libraries and also by Arab scholars in Spain mentioned above, such as Averroes.

NOTES

1. Thomas Jefferson, *The Jefferson Cyclopedia*, ed. John Foley (New York: Funk & Wagnalls, 1900), 664.

2. Naomi Oreskes and Erik Conway, *The Merchants of Doubt: How a Handful of Scientists Obscured the Truth on Issues from Tobacco Smoke to Global Warming* (New York: Bloomsbury Press, 2010).

3. David Michaels, *Doubt Is Their Product: How Industry's Assault on Science Threatens Your Health* (New York: Oxford University Press, 2008).

4. Cheris Kramarae, *Women and Men Speaking: Frameworks for Analysis* (Rowley, MA: Newbury House, 1981).

5. Jules Henry, *Culture Against Man* (New York: Vintage, 1965), 47.

6. John Stuart Mill, *On Liberty* (London: John W. Parker and Son, 1959)

7. Austin v. Michigan Chamber of Commerce, 494 U.S. 652 (1990).

8. Citizens United v. Federal Elections Commission, 558 U.S. 08-205 (2010).

9. *Citizens United v. Federal Elections Commission.*

10. Jonathan Messerli, *Horace Mann: A Biography* (New York: Knopf, 1972).

11. Messerli, *Horace Mann.*

12. Eric Mark Kramer and Tae-Sik Kim, "The Global Network of Players," in *Globalization and the Prospects for Critical Reflection*, ed. J. M. Choi and J. W. Murphy (Delhi, India: Aakar Books, 2009).

13. Donald Trump, interview by Wolf Blitzer, *The Situation Room*, CNN, September 22, 2010.

14. Kramer and Kim, "The Global Network of Players."

15. "Educational Attainment in the United States: 2008," U.S. Census Bureau, accessed March 11, 2011, www.census.gov/population/www/socdemo/aducation/cps2008.html.

16. Robert Frank, *Falling Behind: How Rising Inequality Harms the Middle Class* (Berkeley: University of California Press, 2007).

17. Bernard Madoff, "From Prison, Madoff Says Banks 'Had to Know' of Fraud," *New York Times*, February 15, 2011, www.nytimes.com/2011/02/16/business/madoff-prison-interview.html.

18. "Heisman Trust Calls Report Inaccurate," *ESPN*, last updated September 8, 2010, accessed March 11, 2011, sports.espn.go.com/los-angeles/ncf/news/story?id=5542215.

19. Marcus Vanderberg, "Controversy Haunts Cam Newton's Heisman Quest," The Grio, December 10, 2010, www.thegrio.com/sports/controversy-haunts-cam-newtons-heisman-quest.php.

20. Christopher Rocchio and Steve Rogers, "MTV to Debut New 'Tila Tequila' Bisexual Reality Dating Show October 9," Reality TV World, September 7, 2007, www.realitytvworld.com/news/mtv-debut-new-tila-tequila-bisexual-reality-dating-show-october-9-5753.php.

21. "Gingrich: Snub Caused Impasse—Treatment on Air Force One Blamed," *Seattle Times*, November 16, 1995, community.seattletimes.nwsource.com/archive/?date=19951116&slug=2152925.

22. "The Long March of Newt Gingrich," PBS, accessed March 11, 2011, www.pbs.org/wgbh/pages/frontline/newt/newtchron.html.

23. "American President: An Online Reference Resource: Ronald Reagan," Miller Center of Public Affairs, accessed March 11, 2011, millercenter.org/president/reagan/essays/biography/2.

24. Dale Russakoff, "He Knew What He Wanted; Gingrich Turned Disparate Lessons Into a Single-Minded Goal," *Washington Post*, December 18, 1994.

25. Margaret Carlson, "Getting Nasty," *Time*, June 24, 2011, www.time.com/time/magazine/article/0,9171,1101890619-152038,00.html.

26. Brian Knowlton, "Bush 'Satisfied' with Cheney Tale; Delay in Announcing Hunting Accident Had Raised Questions," *International Herald Tribune*, February 17, 2006.

27. Stephen Holmes, "Gun Control Bill Backed by Reagan in Appeal to Bush," *New York Times*, March 29, 1991.

28. Frank Rich, "Closet Clout," *New York Times*, February 2, 1995.

29. Judi Hasson, "Welfare Enters Whole New World Rules Could Take Years to Settle In," *USA Today*, August 23, 1996.

30. Marc Fisher and Jeff Leen, "A Church in Flux Is Flush with Cash; Moon Linked to Bewildering Array of Entities," *Washington Post,* November 23, 1997.

31. "Gingrich's Daffy 'Insight,'" *Los Angeles Times*, September 17, 2010.

32. David Von Drehle and Howard Schneider, "Foster's Death a Suicide," *Washington Post*, July 1, 1994.

33. Thomas Watts and Righard Whittle, "Rumors about Foster Attacked at Whitewater Hearing; Senate Panel Opens Sessions with Focus on Death of Aide," *Dallas Morning News*, July 30, 1994.

34. James Carville, . . . *And the Horse He Rode In On: The People v. Kenneth Starr* (New York: Simon & Schuster, 1998).

35. Susan McDougal, *The Woman Who Wouldn't Talk* (New York: Simon & Schuster, 2003).

36. Martin Tolchin, "Federal Grand Jury Indicts Ex-Chairman of Silverado," *New York Times*, September 11, 1992, www.nytimes.com/1992/09/11/business/federal-grand-jury-indicts-ex-chairman-of-silverado.html?ref=neilbush, and "Savings and Loan Association," *New York Times*, May 24, 2012, topics.nytimes.com/top/reference/timestopics/subjects/s/savings_and_loan_associations/index.html.

37. Paul Krugman, "Reagan Did It," *New York Times*, May 31, 2009, www.nytimes.com/2009/06/01/opinion/01krugman.html.

38. Jeff Gerth, "A Savings and Loan Bailout, and Bush's Son Jeb," *New York Times,* October 14, 1990, www.nytimes.com/1990/10/14/us/a-savings-and-loan-bailout-and-bush-s-son-jeb.html.

39. Michael Lewis, *Liar's Poker* (New York: Penguin, 1990), 83.

40. "History of the Eighties: Lessons for the Future," Federal Deposit Insurance Corporation, last updated June 5, 2000, accessed March 13, 2011, www.fdic.gov/bank/historical/history/.

41. Binyamin Appelbaum, "SEC Didn't Act on Madoff Tips," *Washington Post*, December 16, 2008, www.washingtonpost.com/wp-dyn/content/article/2008/12/15/AR2008121502971.html.

42. John Dean, *Conservatives Without Conscience* (New York: Penguin, 2006).

43. John Joseph Mathews, *Life and Death of an Oilman* (Norman: University of Oklahoma Press, 1951).

44. Desmond Morris, *The Human Zoo* (New York: Kodansha, 1969/1996).

45. Jean Gebser, *The Ever-Present Origin*, trans. Algis Mickunas (Athens: Ohio University Press, 1985).

46. Morris, *The Human Zoo*, 22.

47. Eric Mark Kramer and Richiko Ikeda, "Defining Crime: Signs of Postmodern Murder and the 'Freeze' Case of Yoshihiro Hattori," *The American Journal of Semiotics* 17 (2001): 7–84.

48. Roger Lowenstein, *When Genius Failed: The Rise and Fall of Long-Term Capital Management* (New York: Random House, 2001).

49. Tanzina Vega, "Be Wary of the Rush to Gold," *New York Times*, May 22, 2010.

50. Dean, *Conservatives Without Conscience*.

51. Anthony Bianco, "The *New York Post*: Profitless Paper in Relentless Pursuit," *Businessweek*, February 21, 2005, www.businessweek.com/magazine/content/05_08/b3921114_mz016.htm.

52. "Doing the Devil's Work," *Columbia Journalism Review* 15 (Jan/Feb 1980): 22.

53. "Doing the Devil's Work," 22.

54. Jayson Blair, "FCC to Waive Rules for Acquisition by Murdoch," *New York Times*, July 21, 2001.

55. Steve Stecklow, "WSJ Editor's Resignation is Criticized by Committee," *Wall Street Journal*, April 30, 2008.

56. "Murdoch's Revolving Door," *Economist*, July 18, 1992, 59.

57. Bruce Selcraig, "The Worst Newspaper in America," *Columbia Journalism Review* 37 (Jan/Feb 1999): 46–51.

58. Ben Bagdikian, *The New Media Monopoly* (Boston: Beacon, 2004).

59. Mark Bauerlein, *The Dumbest Generation* (New York: Penguin, 2008).

60. Karen Davis, Cathy Schoen, and Kristof Stremkis, "Mirror, Mirror on the Wall: How the Performance of the U.S. Health Care System Compares Internationally, 2010 Update," The Commonwealth Fund, accessed March 14, 2011, www.commonwealthfund.org/Content/Publications/Fund-Reports/2010/Jun/Mirror-Mirror-Update.aspx.

61. "US Slipping in Education Rankings," UPI, November 19, 2008, www.upi.com/Top_News/2008/11/19/US-slipping-in-education-rankings/UPI-90221227104776/.

62. Marian MacDorman and T. J. Mathews, "Behind International Rankings of Infant Mortality: How the U.S. Compares with Europe," Centers for Disease Control and Prevention, last updated November 3, 2009, accessed March 14, 2011, www.cdc.gov/nchs/data/databriefs/db23.htm.

63. David Stockman, *The Triumph of Politics—The Crisis in American Government and How It Affects the World* (New York: Bodley Head, 1981). See also William Greider's *The Education of David Stockman* (New York: Signet, 1987), which discusses Stockman's dismay at the lack of curiosity and basic analytical competence he found with Reagan and his entourage.

64. Paul Slansky, *The Clothes Have No Emperor* (Riverside, NJ: Simon & Schuster, 1989).

65. William Hughes, "Ronald Reagan: B Film Actor, Ladies' Man and FBI Snitch," *American Chronicle*, November 12, 2008, www.americanchronicle.com/articles/view/81186.

66. "Timeline: Ronald Reagan's Life," PBS, accessed March 14, 2011, www.pbs.org/wgbh/americanexperience/features/timeline/reagan/.

67. "Gravely Ill, Atwater Offers Apology," *New York Times*, January 13, 1991, www.nytimes.com/1991/01/13/us/gravely-ill-atwater-offers-apology.html.

68. Ed Rollins, *Bare Knuckles and Back Rooms: My Life in American Politics* (New York: Broadway/Doubleday, 1997).

69. Jerome Tuccille, *Alan Shrugged: Alan Greenspan, the World's Most Powerful Banker* (Hoboken, NJ: Wiley, 2002).

70. "Glass-Steagall Act (1933)," *New York Times*, accessed March 14, 2011, topics.nytimes.com/topics/reference/timestopics/subjects/g/glass_steagall_act_1933/index.html#.

71. Allen Raymond, *How to Rig and Election: Confessions of a Republican Operative* (New York: Simon & Schuster, 2008).

72. David Brock, *Blinded by the Right: The Conscience of an Ex-Conservative* (New York: Three Rivers, 2003), 57.

73. C. Everett Koop, *Koop: The Memoirs of America's Family Doctor* (New York: Zondervan, 1992).

74. C. Everett Koop and Timothy Johnson, *Let's Talk: An Honest Conversation on Critical Issues: Abortion, AIDS, Euthanasia, Health Care* (New York: Zondervan, 1992).

75. Jennifer Depaul, "David Stockman: U.S. Is in 'Race to the Fiscal Bottom,'" *Fiscal Times*, October 6, 2010, www.thefiscaltimes.com/Articles/2010/10/06/David-Stockman-US-Is-in-Race-to-the-Fiscal-Bottom.aspx.

76. Ron Reagan, *My Father at 100* (New York: Viking Adult, 2011).

77. Edmund Morris, *Dutch: A Memoir of Ronald Reagan* (New York: Modern Library, 2000).

78. Will Bunch, *Tear Down This Myth: The Right-Wing Distortion of the Reagan Legacy* (New York: Free Press, 2010).

79. Chris Rodda, *Liars for Jesus: The Religious Right's Alternate Version of American History*, vol. 1 (Charleston, SC: BookSurge, 2006).

80. "Hunting Witches," *Washington Post*, July 23, 2005, www.washingtonpost.com/wp-dyn/content/article/2005/07/22/AR2005072201658.html.

81. Alexander Zaitchick, "Common Nonsense: Glenn Beck and the Triumph of Ignorance," Salon, September 21, 2009, www.salon.com/news/feature/2009/09/21/glenn_beck/print.html.

82. Steve Rendall, "An Aggressive Conservative vs. a "Liberal to be Determined," FAIR, November/December 2003, accessed March 14, 2011, www.fair.org/index.php?page=1158.

83. Paul Colford, *The Rush Limbaugh Story: Talent on Loan from God* (New York: St. Martin's Press, 1993).

84. Neely Tucker, "Limbaugh Spin's Reid's Letter into Charity Gold," *Washington Post*, October 20, 2007.

85. "Limbaugh Letter Fetches $2.1 Million on eBay," FOX News, October 21, 2007, www.foxnews.com/story/0,2933,303569,00.html.

86. Chris Mortenson, "Smith Sends E-mail Detailing Opposition," ESPN, October 12, 2009, sports.espn.go.com/nfl/news/story?id=4551010.

87. Bill Hutchinson, "Viagra Holds Up Limbaugh for Three Hours," *Daily News*, June 17, 2006.

88. Tom Zucco, "Rush's Drug Use Has Palm Beach in Tizzy," *St. Petersburg Times*, December 14, 2003.

89. Lawrence Walsh, *Firewall: The Iran-Contra Conspiracy and Cover-Up* (New York: Norton, 1998).

90. "Executive Order 12294—Suspension of Litigation Against Iran," The American Presidency Project, February 23, 1981, accessed March 14, 2011, www.presidency.ucsb.edu/ws/index.php?pid=43455#axzz1GaUpLFkE.

91. Ronald Reagan, *This American Life* (New York: Simon & Schuster, 1990).

92. Mary McGrory, "Conta-Intuitive," *Washington Post*, July 8, 2001.

93. Walsh, *Firewall*.

94. "'Democracy Uprising'" in the U.S.A.?: Noam Chomsky on Wisconsin's Resistance to Assault on Public Sector, the Obama-Sanctioned Crackdown on Activists, and the Distorted Legacy of Ronald Reagan," Democracy Now, February 17, 2011, www.democracynow.org/2011/2/17/democracy_uprising_in_the_usa_noam.

95. Eric Mark Kramer, "Dimensional Accrual and Dissociation: An Introduction," in *Communication, Comparative Cultures, and Civilizations,* vol. 3, ed. Jeremy Grace (Cresskill, NJ: Hampton, In Press), 156–242.

96. Eric Mark Kramer, "A Prolegomena to an Ethic for Digital Deception: Rationale for an Ethic for New Technologies of Ontogenesis: Modernity and Visiocentris," authored by request of the Director of American Forces Information Services, Department of Defense, The Pentagon, accessed April 2, 2011, erickramer.net/download/papers/Kramer-unpublished1.pdf.

97. Irving Janis, *Victims of Groupthink* (Boston, MA: Houghton Mifflin, 1972).

98. George Gerber and Larry Gross, "Living With Television: The Violence Profile," *Journal of Communication* 26 (1976): 172–99.

99. Carl Hulse, "Arlen Specter's Closing Argument," *New York Times*, December 21, 2010, thecaucus.blogs.nytimes.com/2010/12/21/arlen-specters-closing-argument/.

100. David Frum, "When Did the GOP Lose Touch with Reality?" *New York*, November 20, 2011, nymag.com/print/?/news/politics/conservatives-david-frum-2011-11/index3.html.

101. Arlen Specter, "Full Text of Arlen Specter's Farewell Speech," New Mexico Central, accessed March 14, 2011,nm-central.com/blog/?p=1657.

Chapter Five

Art and Cultivated Vulgarity

I do think that the whole phenomenon of Thierry [Guetta] . . . and a lot of
suckers buying into his show, and him selling a lot of expensive art very
quickly is anthropologically, sociologically a fascinating thing to observe and
maybe there's some things to be learned from it.

—Shepard Fairey, 2010, *Exit Through the Gift Shop: A Banksy Film*[1]

How do we get from Diego Rodriguez de Silva y Velazquez's *Portrait of
Pope Innocent X* (figure 5.1) to Francis Bacon's *Study after a Portrait of
Pope Innocent X* (figure 5.2)?

What happened in between the 1650 work by Diego Velázquez and the
1953 portrait by Francis Bacon? In one word, industrialization, which
changed everything from family structure, education, self-identity, transpor-
tation, communication, religion, and the predominant mode of production
from quilts, clothing, and furniture, to eyeglasses, medicines, and pots and
pans. That is how the definition of "genius" and a masterpiece worthy of
gallery space changed from the self-portrait by Peter Paul Ruebens (1623)
(figure 5.3). And this occurred even as we believed we had achieved great
social and cultural progress.

To the poster of professional wrestler Andre "the Giant" by Shepard
Fairey (figure 5.4), whose work has been exhibited in the Los Angeles
County Museum of Art, the Museum of Modern Art in New York, and the
Victoria and Albert Museum in London and sold for great sums. Or Keith
Haring's large acrylic painting *Debbie Dicks* (1984) (figure 5.5).

No event exists in a vacuum including the most revolutionary work of art.
Even as modern artists struggle with what Harold Bloom calls "the anxiety of
influence,"[2] they presume thousands of years of tradition, in Picasso's case,

Figure 5.1.   Diego Rodriguez de Silva y Velazquez (1599–1660), *Portrait of Pope Innocent X* (oil on canvas). Source: Velazquez, Diego Rodriguez de Silva y (1599–1660) / Galleria Doria Pamphilj, Rome, Italy / Alinari / The Bridgeman Art Library.

purposefully reaching all the way back to prehistoric cave paintings for inspiration and stylistic guidance. The "revolutionary" Renaissance thinkers and artists were manifesting not something entirely new but a rebirth of Classical Occidental culture characterized as it is by individualism and ideology. The artists of the time were radical because they began painting pagan themes such as Botticelli's *The Birth of Venus* (c. 1486) rather than Christian themes.

Figure 5.2.   Francis Bacon (1909–1992), *Study after a Portrait of Pope Innocent X* (1574–1655) by Velasquez, 1953 (oil on canvas). Source: Bacon, Francis (1909–1992) / Private Collection / Giraudon / The Bridgeman Art Library.

Botticelli's Venus in the painting was inspired by a copy of a copy. He had the opportunity to study the statue *Venus de' Medici* in the de' Medici collection which was a copy of the earlier sculpture of Aphrodite by the fourth-century BC Attic sculpture Praxiteles. As a result of the sudden embrace of

Figure 5.3.   Peter Paul Rubens (1577–1640), *Self-Portrait*, 1623 (oil on panel).
Peter Paul (1577–1640) / The Royal Collection © 2011 Her Majesty Queen Elizabeth II / The Bridgeman Art Library.

Figure 5.4.   Shepard Fairey, *Andre "the Giant."* **Courtesy of SHEPARD FAIRY/ OBERYGIANT.COM. Used by permission.**

all things pagan from art to philosophy to mathematics (especially by Galileo) the firebrand Dominican friar Savonarola (1452–1498) railed against the sponsors of the new reason and individualism whipping the Florentines into riots of destruction culminating with what came to be called "Bonfires of the Vanities" upon which artists, including Botticelli himself, cast their paintings. Perhaps the most audacious embrace of the rational pagan worldview was represented in Rafael's great fresco *The School of Athens* (depicting all the great Greek philosophers as heroic personages).

Two points are important here. First, as stated, art does not exist in a cultural or historical vacuum. And second, the Renaissance ushered in not only new techniques of art making but two other things: the artist as celebrity, and a renunciation of the collectivism of Medieval Christian Europe expressed in the technique of perspectivism itself. For the illusion of depth space on a two-dimensional plane situates the individual viewer as part of the scene. Perspective articulates the artist's personal view and it also draws the

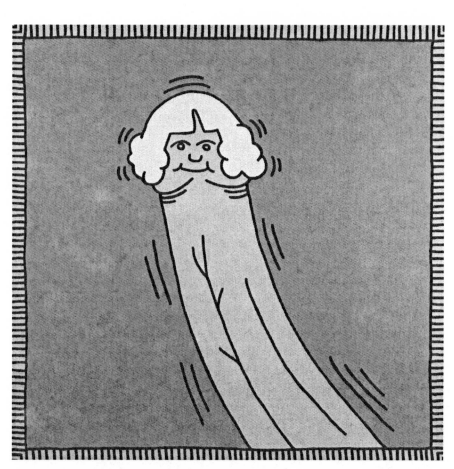

Figure 5.5.   Keith Haring, *Debbie Dick* (1984). Debbie Dick © Keith Haring Foundation. Used by permission.

viewer into that space. Art itself became a mode of personal expression and the greatest artists became heroes. It has been suggested that the word "genius" as we now use it was basically invented to refer to Michelangelo.

During this time people started signing their creations. In fact, when Michelangelo's *David* was first unveiled he overheard someone in the crowd comment that it was executed by another artist. That night Michelangelo returned and by candlelight chiseled his name on the base. During the Medieval period few even had names. Within a short period authorship and artistry became special statuses. Petrarch (1304–1374), a Florentine, discovered a collection of letters that had long been lost from one of the last Classical thinkers, Cicero in 1345, which inspired him to promote humanism. This new movement shifted the emphasis of everything, of life and its purposes, aims, and motives from the eternal soul to the earthly body. Art and other material interests began to flourish. The naked, human form was embraced by artists. Taking pleasure from sensual objects was reignited. And art became the purview of elitism while space fragmented just as the community began to fragment. Around this time the humanist rules were defined by Leon Batistta Alberti (1404–1472) in his book *De Re Aedificatoria*.

Art became urban. Initially it was contracted to represent a group or town, then art was commission for private collections. For instance, Michelangelo's *David* sat outside in the main plaza as a sign of Florentine pride and dominance, and it is there, during one of Savonarola's bonfire riots, that its arm was broken off when a bench was hurled out of a high window of the campanile or bell tower of the Uffizi Palace (a structure designed by Giorgio Vasari who invented the word "Renaissance" and who would, years later, reattach the arm). The banking business of the de' Medici needed administrative space and so they commissioned the Uffizi, which is today a great art gallery. For them the word "*uffizi*" simply meant offices. It was the precursor to the modern corporate headquarters.

As Florentines reinvented money in the form of the gold florin, the Venetians invented double-entry accounting, though it likely originated in the Islamic world. We have extant records of a merchant, Amatino Manucci, using the technique in thirteenth-century Florence but it was systematized and formalized in a book on mathematics[3] by Luca Pacioli (c. 1446–1517) who was a friend of Leonardo da Vinci and who helped him work out the geometry for aerial perspective. Pacioli recognized that accounting involved a ratio between debts and losses and so he argued that accounting was the essence of rationality. This notion of cost-benefit analysis lives on today in the philosophy of utilitarianism, namely Jeremy Bentham's "hedonic calculus"[4] and George Homans Social Exchange Theory.[5] This notion that reason is not virtual, like the eternal soul, but actually embedded in everyday pragmatics changed everything. While the body had been denigrated and flagellated as the despised domain of the Devil during Medieval times, the revolution in thinking rehabilitated not only Aristotle, but the body as the very source of truth and knowledge—sensational empiricism.[6] Werner Sombert states:

> The very concept of capital is derived from this way of looking at things; one can say that capital, as a category, did not exist before double-entry bookkeeping. Capital can be defined as that amount of wealth which is used in making profits and which enters into the accounts.[7]

The imagination that conceived of this artifact and its system of exchange was a revolutionary vision. The de' Medici not only funded art but they became the "bankers of the Renaissance" across Europe with bank branches across the continent. The florin became the engine that drove Europe out of the "Dark Ages"—a term invented by Petrarch. Capital investment displaced barter and this new system financed the development of industry from Britain to Bruges, to Lyon, to Hungary. The de' Medici financed the English kings during the Hundred Years War and the papacy, including the construction of Avignon and the reconstruction of Rome when the papacy returned from the "Babylonian Captivity" in Avignon.

Now, while wealthy patrons such as the Albizzi, Alberti, Borgias, and de' Medici sponsored the new form of artistic culture, there was not yet a market. Patrons kept the pieces they commissioned for their private collections. They collected art and stables of artists. However, it was during this time, with the rise of monetary exchange, the reinvention of money, first in Florence and then elsewhere, that markets arose for art. Once art became a commodity, the source of its value changed dramatically from an inherent sense of beauty to a process of exchange. The value of a work of art was no longer rooted in the mastery of its manifest technique or the beauty of the form. Rather, anything that people were willing to exchange capital for became valued art. So the definition of art changed from inherent quality to commodity exchange. If no one wants a piece then it is of little value and is not considered at the moment to be serious art. A famous example is that of Vincent van Gogh. Of the two thousand artworks he produced including nine hundred paintings, he only sold a couple during his lifetime. Most of them were stored in the back of his younger brother Theo's gallery. Much of his agony was a consequence of abuse by the market. He suffered terrible dissonance because, while he believed in his work, at the same time, being a man of his times, he had internalized the notion that if it does not sell it must not be real art, the dominant ideology at the time, which he learned while working at the Goupil & Cie gallery in The Hague (the third largest city in the Netherlands). Art became vulgarized. Only those who sell are considered "real artists." Borrowing from Jules Henry, art, "true art," became like today's truth in general, that which sells.

Ned Ludd and his followers the Luddites are instructive. They have been maligned by conservative writers, but they were not anarchic mobs. Beginning in 1811, many of the handloom weavers were imprisoned and executed for vandalizing the machines that were being deployed to replace them, not because they dumbly "hated technology," but because they understood what the machine meant: the end of their livelihoods and control over their own skills and labor.[8] They understood the technology because it was designed based on their skills and techniques.

Before industrialization, everything was handcrafted by skilled workers. With industrialization, not only was work life dramatically altered but so too was family life, economic complexity and stress, time, space, motivations, aesthetics, and expectations—culture. At the core of the issue was power manifested in self-determination and social agency, especially in the form of independent work patterns.[9] Growing "conservative" corporate business interests conflicted with the self-control of personal time and motion more than the Church of Rome ever did.

Defenders of the current world will argue that life in the past was awful: brutal and short. Children were chained to machines in factories, asylums and orphanages were hellholes, the great industrial cities saw high levels of mortality due to the smog produced by the coal-fired factories and domestic heating, there were no social "safety nets," and so forth. The irony here is that those who defend the current industrial world, and who in principle defend laissez-faire philosophy (socioeconomic Darwinism), also in principle hate government regulation and social support. But when pushed to the wall the same people will contradict themselves and cite social safety nets for banks and corporations. They also cite social safety nets to make their case that times are better now than ever. This self-contradiction aside, they are wrong. Times are not better now than ever.[10]

As the Harvard economist Leslie Perlow tells us, yes times were horrible after massive industrialization and before the social safety nets and regulations were imposed, but if you go back in time just a little farther, the picture changes dramatically.[11] Before industrialization and the last virtue, as Jacques Ellul calls the "cult of efficiency" in *The Technological Society*,[12] there was no chronic sense of urgency or "time famine,"[13] which has changed the tone and tenor of life profoundly.

Preindustrial Europe saw relative prosperity and equality. Technical prowess is a matter of point of view. Knowing how to heat a home with wood demands more knowledge and technique than turning a thermostat and hoping "something works." Craftsmen back then built their own homes. In many ways they were technically more proficient than people today. Of course medical progress has changed, but that does not address the overall comportment of everyday life, culture and cognitive complexity vis-à-vis capabilities from knowing how to grow your own food and medicines to canning and other productive behaviors.

Preindustrial Europe saw far more leisure time and more satisfaction from work with craft guilds controlling the modes of production and their cities. Everything was handcrafted and much more ornate than today's plastic minimalism. Many mundane objects were worthy of becoming family heirlooms and today fill our antique shops. What we produce today is not likely to do so. We have created a fast, disposable world with Styrofoam cups, plastic toys, framed poster board art reproductions, and standardized cheap kit furniture. Pollution was much less prior to industrialization and the structure that created the ground for industrialization was generally tidy, civil, and prosperous.[14] Young people did not run in urban gangs or spend hours every day on Facebook and videogames but instead began apprenticing to become artisans by age ten or so.

The world before electricity was a relatively quiet, slow, but not simple-minded world. Art, handcrafted objects were everywhere and to become a celebrity of craftsmanship in such a world required years of practice under master tutelage and dedication to the craft, be it stonecutting, cabinet making, violin crafting, carpentry, or portrait painting. Under the system of apprenticeship, which today an internship is a joke, a young person had no tuition to pay but rather learned on the job be it as a muralist, an accountant, or a carriage maker. Everything had to be made by hand and so all hands were busy but skilled. Production, as so many social scientists have argued, was not a drudgery of endless repetition but much more satisfying involving what psychologists call "flow;" a psychological state in which a person loses him/herself in the attentive concentration of crafting things.

Mihály Csíkszentmihályi defines flow as a single-minded immersion in activity based on a completely focused motivation whereby "emotions are not just contained and channeled, but positive, energized, and aligned with the task at hand. The hallmark of flow is a feeling of spontaneous joy, even rapture, while performing a task."[15] To flow means to allow an activity to follow its own course and for as long as it organically needs, not to artificially extend or shorten it because the clock says "time's up." For instance, in a culture that is characterized by organic time rather than instrumental clock time,[16] or in other terms, polychronic rather than monochronic culture,[17] a conversation lasts as long as it needs, not just until the end of the "coffee break" or the end of my appointed and allotted time with my doctor. The same used to be true of production. One worked on a pair of shoes, a hat, a wagon wheel, or a painting until it was finished and correct. According to Csíkszentmihályi, if one is barred from flow, interrupted or hurried, one suffers the ennui of depression or the agitation of anxiety.[18]

Be it harvesting in a field or orchard, spinning wool, or planing wood, much work in the preindustrial world had its own organic pace and involved personal satisfaction and an immersive quality. That is what the Luddites realized was at stake. Once all of their skills were taken from them and manifested in machine assembly, not only they, but other workers were at risk of losing their value, their identities as printmakers, book binders, ceramicists, upholsterers, watchmakers, toymakers, and so on, and ultimately their peace of mind. Today, pharmacists mostly just count pills and put them in bottles. They no longer mix their own medicines and so they are being replaced by less-skilled workers in chain, absentee-owned operations. Violins are made on production lines. Even surgery is moving in this direction.

The motive is largely profit, since because profit is realized with each unit moved, it behooves the owner of the means of production to move as many units as fast as possible. The goal is minimized to "whatever the market will bear" in terms of the lowest quality that will sell at a high margin. In the process, ownership of one's own mode of production, one's own skills, and control over one's own time and motion is lost. Motivation is decimated and with it the joy of creativity and innovation because in a standardized mode of production such variances are not a virtue but a problem to be eliminated. This is not just a problem for individual craftsmen; it becomes a social issue.

Enter the new vandalism-as-art scene. Graffiti artists, street artists such as Shepard Fairey and Banksy, have become the Michelangelos of our time. They can execute dozens of works per night because their art consists of mass-produced posters that they glue onto buildings or stenciled images they spray paint on any surface they can find. They are the masters of reproduction that have an air of romance about them because vandalism is, after all, illegal and so they must work in the dark and run away when police approach. What does that say about our time?

But even they are now lamenting the collapse of what constitutes art *and* the artist. In the documentary film *Exit Through the Gift Shop: A Banksy Film*, which is about Thierry Guetta's fraudulent claim to be an artist, a filmmaker, and then general artist, Banksy documents how, out of naiveté and an effort to be friendly to a roadie (stage hands for bands and art exhibitions), he created a monster.[19] While a rock star may encourage a roadie to take up music, it is difficult and requires hours of practice to play even simple music well. But in the case of Banksy and Guetta, Banksy inadvertently demonstrated that his art could be very easily reproduced because it is not really art at all.

It is instructive that the title of the film itself includes the credit "a Banksy film" because the famous and anonymous London-based street artist Banksy wanted to make it clear that he put this film together, not Guetta. As Banksy says in the film the French immigrant living in Los Angeles, Guetta, turned out to be a "crazy man" with a video camera who taped literally everything in his daily life. It was by sheer accident that upon a return trip to France, Guetta met his cousin who was a graffiti artist. Guetta had no interest in art or street art. But because his cousin existed within the frame of his camera he began to follow him and tape him. Then upon return to the United States, Guetta started taping all the street artists he could, gaining their confidence by claiming to be making a documentary, a work of art about art. But when Banksy's work started to move from the street, the source of its curiosity, into the galleries and command respect and high prices from private collectors, he wanted more exposure. Banksy wanted the "true story" about street art told, in part he claims, because it disappears so quickly.[20]

Sensing a promotional opportunity, Banksy *invited* Guetta to come to London to tape everything about him despite the concerns of Banksy's staff. They were uncomfortable with Guetta because they had worked hard to protect Banksy's identity for years. Banksy was famous for his street art and also for infamous anonymity. Nevertheless, Banksy insisted that Guetta tape him, his processes, his secret studio—everything. Then he asked Guetta where the documentary was, the one Guetta had claimed to be working on for years.

There was none. So Banksy told Guetta to go home with all his tapes and make the true record of his art. After months, Guetta's film *Life Remote Control*, presumably documenting street art in general and Banksy's art specifically, was done. He sent it to Banksy for a viewing. Banksy sat down to watch it. To his consternation it was more Guetta's personal artistic expression than documentation of his own work. Banksy's reaction:

> Auh . . . Ya know it was at that point that I realized that maybe Thierry wasn't actually a filmmaker. And he was just maybe someone with mental problems who happened to have a camera. It just seemed to go on and on. It was an hour and a half of unwatchable nightmare trailers. Essentially like someone with a short attention span with a remote control flicking through a cable box of 900 channels. I told him I'd never seen anything like it, and I wasn't lying about that. Then I was faced with that terrible thing when somebody shows you their work and everything about it is shit. [21]

Here we find the limit of what is art stated as bluntly as possible by someone who has himself pushed the limits of the concept to the breaking point by taking art out of the galleries and into the streets. For Banksy, the renowned street artist who had let this "filmmaker" into his life and creative process admits he was duped. We all have been duped, and not just by Guetta, but by Banksy too, and not just because the whole thing might have been a hoax.

Some of what we call art today is not art by the definition of any other time or place. There is, despite all postmodern claims, such a thing as a true artist. Much of what passes for art is the product of juveniles in the wealthy First World having the time and money to run around and vandalize things in the name of art, anarchy, revolution, you name it. But here we find someone, Banksy, who has strong artistic elements to his work, including planning, structure, and intent, who finally gave up the pretense of making art beyond art and frankly says that there are "rules" to art too.

But, in his mea culpa documentary, Banksy presses the point of the object lesson of Guetta, for the story only begins with Guetta's "documentary" of street art. Banksy's U.S. gallery sponsored a show of his work in Los Angeles in 2005. In the spirit of his avant-garde image it was not held in a fancy gallery but in a warehouse in a poor part of town. This show, called "Barely Legal," made street art a "white-hot commodity." No serious collector could be without some street art. It was a roaring success with people from all walks of life including film stars and industrialists who like to collect his art in attendance.

After this, Guetta realized that anyone could do this "art." While the rock star's roadie cannot simply pick up a guitar and in six months have a hit, Guetta proved that one can now with the proper hype become a renowned artist with dealers across the globe clamoring for your work within just a few weeks. Having dutifully documented Banksy's "Barely Legal" show, Guetta decided to have his own, very similar, show. He got Banksy and Fairey to give him two short quotable blurbs promoting his show, which were published everywhere in Los Angeles, something they both later regretted, because thanks to lending their authority to Guetta's show, it too was a booming success. Guetta sold over one million dollars' worth of "art" in one weekend. As the cultural anthropologist Jules Henry noted, truth has become what sells. [22] In the modern world validation is reduced to money. So why the regrets?

The problem was the art was horrible, most of it bad imitations of optical and pop art Guetta had seen in books. And worse than that, Guetta did not actually make any of the items himself. He did not even select any of the items for the show because he was consumed with promoting it. The objects had been manufactured by prop builders and computer photo people from Hollywood whom he hired on a per-day rate.

Guetta literally became an overnight success, a celebrity in the art world with some of "his" works appearing in galleries in Europe and Japan. What he did was hire not just prop builders but also people to scan images of other artists' works into computers and then Photoshop them into grotesque parodies. What may have taken the original artist years to achieve, Guetta took no time at all to modify and print. It is not unlike the disco-ization or hip-hop-ization of earlier famous tunes via computer sampling and synthesized sound alteration. It is not the deconstruction but the destruction of prior ages of art, something akin to what happened to classical art during the Dark Ages. Guetta's art was to deface art.

Within six months of the start of his self-promotion effort as the artist "Mr. Brainwash," which he literally plastered all over Los Angeles buildings, Guetta was launching his big show. He leased the abandoned former CBS headquarters in Hollywood for the venue. Guetta proved that through enough promotion one can debut at the top. As he put it himself, he became "an artist overnight, that is what happened to me." [23] Then, while rushing to finish everything for the opening, Guetta broke his foot. Being his friend, and unaware of what was about to transpire, Banksy intervened and contacted someone to step in and rescue Guetta's "little" show. Banksy sent in professional art promoters and exposition directors, the lead one Roger Gastman (Banksy's friend) finally, in the last desperate around-the-clock effort for

Guetta's show, called Guetta "retarded."[24] In reality, Guetta bankrolled the show, but all the contents were created by others, including the logistics of the show itself.

Now recall that Guetta's inspiration for this show was a huge show Banksy himself had put on in Los Angles a year earlier. In Banksy's show, he had painted a live elephant in a wallpaper pattern. The elephant represented things we know but don't talk about, the "elephant in the room." Banksy's documentary is just that. Guetta's instant artistic success exposed something wrong with art in the late-modern world. Commercialization has over-whelmed art. The promoters and directors Banksy sent to the rescue arrived in the nick of time to make the entire effort possible.

The blurb that Banksy lent to validate Guetta's show stated, "Mr. Brainwash is a force of Nature, he's a phenomenon. And I don't mean that in a good way."[25] Guetta's exploitation of his friends Shepard Fairey and Banksy worked. Their endorsements helped to legitimize his show. Part of the promotion was that Guetta told the *L.A. Weekly* that the first two hundred people to his show would receive a free, one-of-a-kind poster. No one could invent such irony. Nothing in his show was made by him. None of it was one-of-a-kind. The props were all imitations of other artists' ideas. With the premier approaching, Guetta hastily took two hundred identical copies of the same poster and turned them into unique Mr. Brainwash originals by laying them out in a row on the floor and, as his wheelchair was pushed along past them, he randomly splattered paint on them.

His show became a buzz of hype. Banksy, claiming to regret it all, re-sponded:

> Most artists spend years perfecting their craft, finding their style . . . Thierry really made [iconic artworks] meaningless . . . Maybe it means art is a bit of a joke. I didn't think Thierry played by the rules in some ways. But then there aren't supposed to be any rules. So I don't really know what art is, I mean I always used to encourage everyone I met to make art. I used to think that everyone should do it [pause] I don't really do that so much anymore.[26]

In the end, the fact that street art does not last had been one of the essential aspects of its particular allure. But then, the street artists themselves wanted to enhance the permanence of their work. They, like most people, wanted to preserve their efforts and share them. They wanted to be documented for the sake of egoism and posterity. The incredibly ironic twist to this rather hypo-critical stance of the artists is that when their chosen documentarian turned out to be a fake, they were upset.

After Guetta's super successful (by any standards) show in Los Angeles, Banksy's art dealer at the time, Steve Lazarides, said something very pre-scient and honest: "I don't know who the joke is on, or even if there is one."[27] This is the state of confusion about art and artists we see today.

As Banksy observed, just because Guetta didn't know how to make a film didn't stop him. In the preindustrial age juveniles were nurtured as apprentices with lengthy mentorships. They were taught how to do the craft, and consequently how to appreciate it. One must master the medium and the conventions before breaking them. Jackson Pollack had spent years studying art with various master teachers before making his own works. They may look chaotic and random at first but when one studies them, it become clear that he was not painting by accident. The execution of works by trained artists is as different when compared to untrained hacks as a piano sonata played by a master versus a novice. It is obvious. But then why are we so gullible? It is not the issue of the quality of the art. It is all about the potential return on investment.

Ironically, in the age of democratic comportment when every person can be an art critic, the expert art critic is king and that is largely due to the modern process of branding and seeing art as an investment alongside pork bellies, heavy crude, and orange juice.

Guetta's example proved, not only to Banksy, but to all of us that money and promotion can completely render quality irrelevant. Art has succumbed to pure quantification as dollar value. Genuine skill and years of artistic development are displaced by the rhetoric of sales, marketing, and promotion. Hans-George Gadamer argued that art, along with science, still has truths to teach us; this shows that Gadamer may have been naïve.[28] Art and science both are now subject to economic imperatives. What sells has become truth. And so we reproduce the art that sells just like we avoid research into medications that do not promise a hefty margin on investment. Artists are still working away but increasingly even "high art" is imitative.

In the end, even the avant-garde cannot hold their tongues. When Guetta equates art with "brainwashing" he exposes a profound failure to understand either process. And so Banksy himself stepped forward, like Dr. Frankenstein, to kill the creature he had inadvertently created. Not just art, but the "artist" had become an accident. By being friendly with a crazy man, Banksy had created a monster. Perhaps that was his intent all along.

As Malcolm Gladwell demonstrates in his book' *Outliers: The Story of Success*, it takes ten thousand hours of hard concentrated effort to become good at anything, from bricklaying to chess, from violin to basketball.[29] But in a world where young people are decreasingly exposed to handcrafted music and art, but instead mass-produced knock-offs and computer-sampled "music" and drum machines, they can't develop a sophisticated aesthetic sense. In other words, it does not just take ten thousand hours to produce something with extraordinary quality in a world overwhelmed with quantitative thinking, but it takes hours of exposure to also develop an old notion— taste.

While this may seem "highbrow," it actually involves humility: the ability to appreciate the efforts of others and to objectively assess one's own efforts. Guetta's delusion of grandeur is the essence of hubris, an attitude that pretends to be democratic and progressive but which merely says "anyone can be an artist" (scientist, doctor, singer . . .). The problem is anyone can try and if they are willing to put in ten thousand hours they may well achieve the status they aim for. But along such a long and arduous effort they come to new realizations not about the status they sought from the beginning but, through experience and maturation, they come to an appreciation of the medium, the tools, and others who went before.

In an unskilled world, people cannot appreciate truly extraordinary skill because they cannot empathize. If one is a pretty good stonecutter and understands the medium and skill necessary to make something, then when one confronts Michelangelo's *Pietà* (1498–1499) one gets it; one understands implicitly what an accomplishment it is. Sadly, as music and art are cut from our public-school curricula, our people become retarded in such sensibilities. If one has practiced piano for five years and can play so-so, then one can really appreciate a virtuoso performance. Taking away the opportunity to practice such things is robbing our society of the ability to appreciate.

This ability to appreciate is an essential part of what the ancient Greeks called the "good life." It is what they meant by being civil, by being civilized, by participating in collective life. It is not the smugness that came out of industrial class inequality. Rather, it is a humility, an ability to recognize fully and enjoy effort and accomplishment in the work of others and to realistically access one's own accomplishments. Because American children do not sincerely strive hard at mathematics and science they typically score well below children from other cultures and yet consistently assess their own abilities far higher than children from other countries. They score lowest but think they are the best. How is this possible? Because they do not accurately understand what it takes to be good because they have not been compelled to sincerely dedicate themselves to the effort necessary to become outstanding in math and science. They are deluded.

Appreciation also kindles something more. A consequence of appreciation is gratitude. Creativity is thus greeted with gratitude. Each handcrafted item has an emotional dimension that connects people, one to another in a collective way. To appreciate also means the ability to recognize quality and significance, phenomenon rejected in our modern fragmented world of indiscriminate quantification. To be able to appreciate others and their efforts makes their products and life more meaningful. But meaning too, we are told by measurers, is not real unless it can be expressed as a quantity.

Giving someone the ability to appreciate is profound. It is the ability to enjoy life more, to appreciate rather than depreciate. In ancient wars people pillaged. In modern wars entire cities are incinerated. When Alexander the

Great defeated Darius III he celebrated, became drunk, and burned the great Persian Palace of Xerxes at Persepolis. After sobering up he was remorseful because he did appreciate the beauty of the place and it is this act that gave his generals and historians the first clue to his general madness and alcohol-induced mania, a failing so concerning that it has been suggested that Aristotle himself, in his trepidation, requested that his pupil be poisoned lest he return to Greece an irrational megalomaniac and visit upon it his unbalanced brutality.

A failure to appreciate the creativity of others was considered not merely uncivilized but insane. And many wars were not campaigns of destruction but of theft. In this sense, to be targeted for attack was in an odd way a complement. Rome was repeatedly plundered because the "barbarians" appreciated its stuff.

Creativity itself, *sui generis*, is a virtue. Today, creativity is seen as a mere tool and is pursued to be exploited. Being creative itself is of little value. We are a culture that is product oriented. Process is merely something to be managed and made faster. In a world where art is mass produced, where "talent" is hired and fired and expected to come into an organization and generate profits right away, it is hard to appreciate it, even from the point of view of the talented person him/herself. Teaching art and music become "wastes of time and money." Why? Because anyone can enjoy recorded master musicians anytime, anyplace, and cheaply.

You can stop a great singer in mid-note with impunity by simply clicking a button. You can switch from an intensely effortful dramatic moment in a performance on your screen with a switch of the channel. What is manifested in such "minor" actions is disrespect and depreciation. And that is so because it is not real. It is a virtual recording and so people of minimal musical ability, with little rigor or discipline, can exploit electronics that brilliant engineers have created to sample masterpieces and play with them in ways that would mortify their creators.

We call such acts of disrespect and careless brutality to other peoples' efforts "taking liberties" with other peoples' art, and so it is for it heralds the hypertrophic state of late-modern egocentrism. This condition is described by Jean Gebser thusly:

> The current situation manifests . . . an egocentric individualism exaggerated to extremes and desirous of possessing everything . . . a hyper-valuation of the individual who, despite his limitations, is permitted everything. [30]

This is a "deficient" and "destructive" modality that affects "all areas of human endeavor."[31] This is the illness of a parasitic culture. The robust host, the heritage of creativity, of art and music, like declining Rome, has been set upon to be digested with bits regurgitated by bovine mentalities.

These are vandals who disrespect and disregard the effort and discipline it took to build the world they have inherited and feed upon. They have not built any structure. They just exploit what others have built. Who are they? Michael Medved, Rush Limbaugh, Rupert Murdoch, Banksy, Andy Warhol, Sean Hannity, and the like. They are limited. They cannot and do not even understand how, let alone have the capacity to, build anything from the electronics they exploit to the buildings they operate in. They cannot build their own house.

They too are part of the world and this is the grand self-contradiction that Karl Marx studied; a deficient modality is one that creates within itself the seeds of its own destruction. The displacement of organic community with instrumental society based on vicious "take no prisoners" competition and anonymity has manifested as an environment that neglects large segments of its population. In a world where value is measured only insofar as someone or something can be exploited (use-value versus being useless to an exploit-er), you end up with a self-destructive population and society: a self-abusive population and society that spawns musical lyrics, radio talk, politics, work environments, a financial system that is not only ugly, but brutal and uncivil, where even children's games are brutal, but a society that embraces ugly hideousness and brutality and seeks to be repulsive, where such qualities actually make individuals wealthy.

In a generation, we went from singers such as Frank Sinatra, Tony Bennett, Judy Garland, Bing Crosby, Rosemary Clooney, and Doris Day crooning gentle love songs written by the likes of Jerome Kern, Johnny Mercer, Sammy Cahn, Jimmy Van Heusen, the Gershwin brothers, and Cole Porter to death metal and rage rock with lyrics celebrating rape, gun violence, and drug abuse. The singing cowboy lamenting lonely trails and serenading his horse and sunset skies has been replaced with the angry specter of *Kiss* (with the s's imitating the Nazi death squad's insignia and Gene Simmons' sexual-ly explicit blood spitting "tongue action"), Alice Cooper and his imitator Marilyn Manson, *Black Sabbath* featuring Ozzy Osbourne biting the heads off of live animals on stage, and so forth. The new Ozzie and Harriet of this age were showcased on reality shows about people who used to be seen as fringe elements to a segment of our preteen and teenage market pop culture. The new family shows feature as the new standards of parental wisdom Ozzy Osbourne, the professional wrestler Hulk Hogan, and Gene Simmons. Just a century separates Simmons' *Kiss* and Rodin's sculpture *The Kiss* (1889), of a couple in warm embrace. What was once considered freakish today is main-stream. Even dancing is now called "grind" and "break."

Our schools now require armed guards to enforce minimal civility where gangs, Goths, and drug abuse are rampant. Escapism is the opposite of flow. Flow is joyous and addicting but to be able to achieve such a state, basic competencies must first be mastered so that one can control the tools and medium one is working with rather than the opposite. When a musician has become so familiar with his/her instrument that it no longer gets in his/her way, then s/he can begin to express through it. The instrument becomes transparent. But this takes discipline, effort, and respect for the instrument and those who teach it.

"Conservatives" who make political and talk-show kudos by endlessly attacking teachers, the teaching profession, and the institution of education itself form a massive self-contradiction in our current society. They are destructive because they attack the core principle of authority, which was institutionalized in the guilds and brotherhoods of past times that built the world we inherited. As skill was taken from workers, the guild degenerated into the unions we see today that do little education or training and mostly just fight for more money and benefits. Some even degenerated into revenue streams for organized crime. Workers became victimized from all angles.

Because they have lost their basic ability to withhold expertise, workers can be easily replaced by lower-wage, unskilled workers. And this, as Marx understood, was the *coup de grâce* delivered by managerial "genius." Management dehumanized work and made it mind-numbingly stupid and repetitive and/or brutal. The rise of the "super" visor taskmaster who used to have "over" sight of slaves became the model for all direct administration of other humans as workers. Hierarchy was imposed upon production and workers lost control of the process.

Modernity, with its separation of mind and body, was manifested pragmatically in what Max Horkheimer and Theodor Adorno called the "dialectic of Enlightenment," which means that the brains, the skills, and knowhow of creative production was separated from the hands.[32] This, as we have known for a very long time, is a profound move to dominate. You can give a starving man a fish that will feed him for one day, or teach him how to fish so he can feed himself for decades. This is the essence of empowerment, of personal freedom. When skills and competencies are lost the individual suffers and entire societies risk collapse. Despite its size and potential, after centuries of keeping intellectuals on a short leash and periodically burning all books, the empire of China found itself hopelessly backward and impotent to confront Western powers (technologies).

Education seeks to reunite the body and mind and this is why "conservatives" from the ancient emperors of China to the modern shop floor dictator are suspicious of education. The United States today is declining because it has a massive population of under- and unskilled people who also have not been cultivated or socialized to appreciate creativity and work enough to demand it. How can they? The old guilds have been destroyed. The amassing of fortunes that would make the old kings green with envy required mass consumption and mass production. Craftsmen were transformed into armies of workers. Work has been stripped of its creativity, joy, and humanity. Work has become drudgery to be avoided at all costs. People troll. They "look for work" and jobs. Too many are dependent and desperate.

Publishers of textbooks have consistently simplified textbooks and since the Korean War, the armed forces have had to steadily simplify their tests and manuals until today many are literally written in comic book format and still a sizable percentage of young people attempting to enlist cannot pass the exams demonstrating minimal competencies in reading, writing, arithmetic, and increasingly, physical condition. Ironically, corporate leaders decry the lousy "product" the public educational system is turning out. The quality of worker is so low now that many cannot function well in menial tasks let alone execute an artistic craft. Corporate leaders and "conservatives" decry the decline of the American family, linking it to poorly socialized children. But consistent declines in wages forced women into the workforce and so no one is home to raise the kids. The de-skilling of jobs in an effort to take control of the production process is having horrific consequences at all levels from individual freedom to national competitiveness. Under- and unemployment has become structural in entire communities while jobs and careers requiring highly skilled workers go begging with recruiters increasingly tapping foreign labor pools to fill such careers as computer programming and even medicine.

We have "conservatives" who failed miserably at the tasks of self-discipline, humility, and rigor such as Limbaugh, Glenn Beck, Hannity, and George W. Bush, who then openly denigrate teachers (although Bush tempered that, probably because of his wife's influence), especially research professionals, and disrespect all intellectual products including science. Disrespect for teachers is not "conservative." It is fascist.

Without a need for discipline, sustained effort, the experience of failure, one cannot appreciate greatness and so it vanishes from our world and the world becomes dull and boring, and we become desensitized and uncultivated. There is such a thing as putting love and care into production. Even though my mother's color scheme is not to my taste, and the knitted weave is not perfectly uniform, the afghan blanket she made for me herself is priceless. This is the magic associative dimension of care we find in all handcrafted products. This is why we value originals over even the best, sometimes hard-to-detect, copies. We know that Rembrandt's own hands crafted this painting. It matters. That is also why religious relics are so important to secular scholars and the faithful alike. If I am holding in my hand a piece of the actual cross upon which Jesus of Nazareth, whom some call the Christ, was crucified, then it is far more significant than a fake mundane piece of old wood. The actual retains powerful emotions (care) while virtual digital copies that can be replicated endlessly are neither valuable nor inspiring. When there is only one, it is rare and we take care; we are humble and grateful—we appreciate. And the deviation, the brush hair, or smudged fingerprint embedded on the canvas makes it unique. The fact that the artist had to mix her own paints creates uniqueness. Vermeer's ocher is warmer and more complimentary to cyan than the reds Gauguin concocted. Does pigment matter? Of course. That is why we have an academic field called colorimetry, and why shades of colors and scents are fiercely protected by armies of corporate lawyers defending right-protected brands of automobile paint and shampoo manufacturers.

Artists often make their own canvases, paints, brushes, and tools. They master all there is to the process. Many famous guitarists such as George Harrison and Jeff Beck either made or were directly involved with the specifications of their instruments. This agency is an exercise in productive power. This is so well understood and the more one can be involved the more powerful one is. Modern corporations try to offer a version of this in the form of options to customers from houses and automobiles, to college curricula and television cable service. Industrialization and clock time standardizes the world and it is even exhibited in the very names of the great manufacturing enterprises from *General* Electric and *Standard* Oil, to *General* Foods and *General* Motors. Processing from food to medicine is artificial while the organic farmers' market carries only what is in season and no two apples are as alike as much as a Big Mac from Vancouver and one from Miami. Standardization involves quantity—mass production. Organic reality is contingent.

In the modern world stressed by time, predictability or the defeat of uncertainty allays some anxiety. Knowing, being familiar with a thing, calms frazzled nerves. That is because the temporally stressed modern person perceives uncertainty only as anxiety. But if one is not frazzled, then surprise is welcome. It punctuates the normal with wonder and amazement. Only difference can generate meaning and ecstasy or bliss (*jouissance*).[33] The joy of discovery presumes the unknown. If you see a punch line coming, then it is not a punch line and the joke does not work.

We can appreciate *only* difference. Endless redundancy becomes boring. Much contemporary art like Warhol's soup cans and portraits are redundant and not a few art critics have labeled his work commercially viable logos, not art. And that is not surprising as Warhol, who was, like so many artists today, trained in commercial illustration, was mostly interested in becoming a celebrity, not creating art. Art for him was an instrument, a means to celebrity. In fact, in *Exit Through the Gift Shop*, Banksy says that Warhol repeated great works of art until they became meaningless.[34] *Campbell's Soup Can* (1964), *Brillo Boxes* (1964), and repetitions of soup cans (*100 Soup Cans*, 1962) collapsed commercial illustration with art but without satire.

While Roy Lichtenstein was using Ben-Day dot type of pointillism to create parodies of comic strip art, Warhol craved to be, and believed himself to be, a great artist, creating great art. Warhol's "radical" pop art is totally redundant to the real issue raised by Marcel Duchamp, who had established himself as a great artist with his *Nude Descending a Stair, No. 2* (1912) before placing a urinal in a museum as "art." The object (*Fountain*, 1917), one of his "readymades" or "found art" objects, disappeared, probably removed by a janitor of the museum and thrown away, which Duchamp's did not regret because it had served *not his artistic purposes but had made his satirical and philosophical point*. Duchamp "made" replicas and in 2000, two performance artists (Yuan Chai and Jian Jun Xi) took the whole thing to its illogical conclusion by urinating on one at the Tate Museum, London. But even this childish act was nothing but mimicry for the Swedish artist Björn Kjelltoft, who urinated in the Fountain at Moderna Museet in Stockholm in 1999. Nevertheless, one of the eight 1964 "editions" sold for $1.7 million at Sotheby's in 1999.

Not just the art but the market itself has become surreal. To our knowledge, never before in history anywhere has urinating on something been considered an act of artistic expression. Rather, it seems to express contempt for art in general as a joke. Western art is in a crisis precisely because it became words, philosophemes, arguments when, as Niklas Luhmann puts it:

> Art can exist only when there is language—this is less trivial than it sounds. Art is unique in that it makes possible a type of communication that, in the strict sense of the work, avoids language along with the routines involved in language use. The forms of art are understood as communications, but without language, without argumentation . . . Art permits a circumvention of language—of language as the form of structural coupling between consciousness and communication. Even when employing linguistic means, art engenders different effects . . . Art communicates by *using perceptions contrary to their primary purpose* . . . Art . . . defies normality.[35]

In this sense much of what we call art definitely defies normality but art is more than that. Anything abnormal, unusual, is, by definition, not normal. But art is not normal in a specific way. It takes our expectations and transcends them and us by uncommon vision (insight and outsight). It shows us what we as human beings can achieve but rarely do. Urinating is not a transcending accomplishment few can achieve. Taking a commercial illustration of a soap can and putting it in a gallery is also not a difficult accomplishment.

As for redundancy, only when redundancy forms a pattern that is itself unique, such as fractal art or an installation such as Christo and Jeanne-Claude's *Umbrellas* (1991) do we enjoy it. Wow, look. This has never been seen before. An entire valley filled with giant umbrellas. This is also not easy to do.

As we saw, even among practitioners of "lowly" street art,[36] if something is too easy, then the art itself cannot be fully appreciated and the artist is devalued as a producer. Expertise and authority are denigrated. The result is that others' efforts become depreciated. This is what mass production of art and music does. For instance, many dedicated photographers are lamenting the invention of high-quality digital cameras because now anyone can shoot indiscriminately, literally thousands of pictures, and find one or two that, by accident, are really good. So the art, the craft—the experience, knowledge, diligence, and effort—is eliminated. Some say that with the Internet being flooded with great pictures the art of photography is dead. Anyone can play great music—on their portable media device.

Via increasing dissociation, the world is becoming depersonalized. This famously occurred with art at the Wedgewood ceramic factories and to portrait painters with the invention of photography. To run a newspaper used to require not just the ability to write stories but the ability to set up, run, and maintain a print shop with a press and with understanding of inks and different stocks of paper. Soon anyone with a camera could render a likeness without years of practice and without individual style.

The change in the mode of art and production was part of a larger change in the world toward fragmentation, atomization, and division and subdivision. Occam's razor was brought to bear on all things so that a worker no longer built a car but just put the door handles on, over and over and over. Even the small art of expressing one's personal and often private sentiments was taken over by mass-produced greeting cards and companies such as Hallmark cloaked themselves in images of the "good old days" they were helping to destroy.

Today, with all our advances, Americans work longer hours than any people anywhere before. The same is true in places like China. While child labor and horrible working conditions have improved in the industrial West that is because the work has been shipped overseas. Methamphetamine addiction is rampant throughout Asia where workers use it to keep up with production quotas. Out of sight out of mind. But not for those who are informed such as intellectuals and artists.

The horrible working conditions in places like Vietnam, Thailand, India, and China with their workers' dormitories and subsistence wages is well known. But what of the shiny prosperous successes? Singapore, for instance, seems to be idyllic until one realizes that it is only a wealthy city-state. The wealth is not produced in the city. That is where the finance and accounting occurs. Rather, the secret to Singapore's success are the factories only miles away across the border in Malaysia where young girls go blind by age fifteen or sixteen using stereoscopic microscopes to assemble high-tech electronic components. Once they lose their depth of vision it is gone for good and so too is their high-tech job. They are unceremoniously fired and replaced by another ten- or twelve-year old girl. Artists reflect reality.

Keep in mind that Bacon regarded Velázquez as one of the greatest paint-ers ever and was obsessed with his portrait of Innocent X. So this is not Bacon criticizing Velazquez's work but taking a nightmarish turn in vision itself and of vision, a turn already underscored by the surrealists in their shocking 1929 short film *Un Chien Andalou* in which a man slices a wom-an's eye open with a straight razor in the opening scene. Luis Buñuel and Salvador Dalí force the initially unsuspecting captive audience sitting in rows of seats bolted to the floor in the dark to watch a close-up of the horrific act as one hand forces her to open her eye wide while the other slices it. We have an unblinking, unflinching look.

Modern realism attacks vision itself, turning back upon itself like a Möbius form of grotesque contradiction suggesting that the viewer be blinded by what they see. One is dared to look. The act of the gaze becomes self-destructive along with so many other mundane acts in late modernity. Perhaps more than a footnote, both leading actors in the film ended up committed suicide. In 1932 Pierre Batcheff overdosed on Veronal in a hotel in Paris, and Simone Mareuil committed self-immolation on October 24, 1954, by dousing herself in gasoline and burning herself to death in a public square in Périgueux, Dordogne. The French government banned the film for many years because of its content. Today, it is common fair in every under-graduate film class in the world and available to all on YouTube. The vio-lence of many films and video games makes *Un Chien Andalou* seem almost quaint.

The turn in art may be called the embrace of life as terror, the emergence of the age of the scream. We see it in the Edvard Munch's *The Scream* (1893) or shriek of not just man but of the world (all of nature) where the entire world is portrayed as throbbing with horrific emotion.

Art today is, like all art, part of a larger sociocultural and economic world. Twentieth-century art not only breached the question "what is art?" but "what is an artist?" Much of art today is self-parody, which is what the art critic for the *Guardian* Adrian Searle concluded in his article "Painted Screams" about Francis Bacon's career.[37] He argues that by the end of his career, not unlike Picasso, Bacon had started to produce, or reproduce "fake Bacons."

Art, in the twentieth century, like philosophy, fell into crisis because, with the rise of modernity art became increasingly philosophical and ideological and there was no turning back to authentic mytho-religious sensibility. Art became social critique. Everything became critical. Instead of giving us respite from suffering, art sought to underscore human misery tenfold. Eventually, it lost purpose. A mirror becomes just a reflection of the same, a sort of metaphysical redundancy. Art moved from inspiring and educating illiterate masses about the religious universe to accurately re-presenting spatial and temporal relationships, and finally to accurately extending modern alienation. It became uninspiring, miserable to behold—meaningless.

The subject had been separated out from the whole leaving it to starkly confront a dead and vacuous object universe. Art became impressions and commentary on violence, loss of self, relentless exploitation, inhumane machine warfare and industrial production. Art was responding to the Twilight of the Idols, the advancing pall of nihilism. The universe had been cleared of ancient mystery only to reveal the *horror vacui*, which the church had warned against in its own way. Here was the gape of human misery—a void surrounded by grimy broken teeth emitting a sound that is prelinguistic but universally understood. Grunge was born a century before an alienated kid from a trailer park picked up a guitar in Aberdeen, Washington to found the "flagship band of Generation X," achieving all that was the promise of modern super-celebrity status: wealth and accolades as a rock star only to end it with a self-inflected shotgun wound to the head. Kurt Cobain's suicide note was addressed to his imaginary childhood friend "Boddah" stating that he could no longer feel anything for his music.[38] His band, beyond irony, was called "Nirvana."

This is a world marked by Mary Shelley's *Frankenstein*, where the doctor is the monster, not his pathetic creation, where her husband Percy Shelly and friend John Keats sought solace in suicide despite their status as great poets and writers. The idealism of Shelly, Keats, Byron, and other romantic utopians of the early nineteenth century was dashed on the reality of rising globalism and power politics. It was at this time that we begin to see the looming crisis that would haunt the technological successes of modernity. Perhaps a way to understand the mood was one of disappointment in ourselves. For instance, a great fan of Napoleon and his promise to spread Enlightenment and the Napoleonic Code, Beethoven wrote his Third Symphony in 1804. But once Napoleon's mania for power and imperial ambition became clear to him, Beethoven so violently scratched out the name "Bonaparte" on the title page that it tore a hole in the work. He retitled the piece and rededicated it to his patron.

At the same time Edvard Munch was capturing the ethos with *The Scream* (1893), social science was born as a reaction to the growing alienation observed by writers such as Karl Marx, Ferdinand Toennies, Emile Durkheim, Edmund Husserl, and Max Weber. After his son was killed on the French side during World War I Durkheim would never write again. And after his son was killed on the German side in the same conflict, Husserl stopped writing for a long period, finally to explode with his work *The Crisis of the European Sciences and Transcendental Philosophy*[39] in which he decried the elevated value of free action and disinterested observation to the status of virtues. He regarded such "objectivity" as merely a rationale for irresponsible technological catastrophe in the interest of "the great powers." Organization was depersonalizing the world. Individuals, as Jean Gebser explains, became social atoms aggregated and yoked for production.[40] Franz Kafka (1883–1924) would reflect a world on fire and without sense; senseless pain despite the fact that it comes in the form of writing, carved into the flesh.

The initial new positivist religion with its utopian dreams had failed, gassed to death in the bosom of Europe itself in the "no man's land" between the trenches of World War I, dualism taken to horrific levels of efficiency and the scorched silhouettes of children in Hiroshima just a generation later—a kind of luciferous photography with walls catching the negative power of modern technology. Finally, mass production visited art as technique itself with "artists" who are as much or more marketers than skilled and innovative creators.

NOTES

1. Interview with Shepard Fairey in Bansky, *Exit Through the Gift Shop: A Banksy Film*, VHS, directed by Banksy. USA: Paranoid Pictures, 2010.

2. Harold Bloom, *Anxiety of Influence: A Theory of Poetry* (New York: Oxford University Press).

3. *Summa de Arithmetica, Geometria, Proportioni et Proportionalita*, published in Venice 1494 using techniques that had migrated into Italy developed by Johannes Gutenberg decades earlier.

4. Jeremy Bentham, *An Introduction to the Principles of Morals and Legislation* (Oxford: Clarendon Press, 1823).

5. George Homans, *Social Behavior* (New York: Harcourt, Brace and World, 1961).

6. Eric Kramer, "The Body in Communication," in *The Body in Human Inquiry: Interdisciplinary Explorations of Embodiment*, ed. Vincent Berdayes, Luigi Esposito, and John Murphy (Cresskill, NJ: Hampton Press, 2004), 51–86.

7. Werner Sombart, "Medieval and Modern Commercial Enterprise," in *Enterprise and Secular Change: Readings in Economic History*, ed. Frederick Lane and Jelle Riemnersma (New York: R. D. Irwin, 1953), 38.

8. E. P. Thompson, *The Making of the English Working Class* (New York: Penguin, 1980).

9. Leslie Perlow, "The Time Famine: Toward a Sociology of Work Time," *Administrative Science Quarterly* 44 (1999): 57–81.

10. Ellen Wood, *Democracy Against Capitalism* (Cambridge: Cambridge University Press, 1995) and Ellen Wood, *The Origin of Capitalism* (New York: Verso, 2002).

11. Perlow, "The Time Famine."

12. Jacques Ellul, *The Technological Society*, trans. K. Wilkinson (New York: Knopf, 1964).

13. Perlow, "The Time Famine."

14. Wood, *The Origin of Capitalism*.

15. Mihaly Csikszentmihalyi, *Flow: The Psychology of Optimal Experience* (New York: Harper & Row, 1990), 90.

16. Robert Levine, *A Geography of Time: On Tempo, Culture, and the Pace of Life* (New York: Basic, 1998).

17. Edward Hall, *The Silent Language* (New York: Doubleday, 1959) and Edward Hall, *The Dance of Life* (New York, Doubleday, 1983).

18. Csikszentmihalyi, *Flow.*

19. Bansky, *Exit Through the Gift Shop: A Banksy Film*, VHS, directed by Banksy. USA: Paranoid Pictures, 2010.

20. Bansky, *Exit Through the Gift Shop.*

21. Bansky, *Exit Through the Gift Shop.*

22. Jules Henry, *Culture Against Man* (New York: Vintage, 1963).

23. Thierry Guetta in Bansky, *Exit Through the Gift Shop.*

24. Roger Gastman in Bansky, *Exit Through the Gift Shop.*

25. Bansky, *Exit Through the Gift Shop.*

26. Bansky, *Exit Through the Gift Shop.*

27. Steve Lazarides in Bansky, *Exit Through the Gift Shop.*

28. Hans-Georg Gadamer, *Truth and Method*, trans. J. Weinsheimer and D. Marshall (New York: Crossroad, 2004).

29. Malcolm Gladwell, *Outliers: The Story of Success* (New York: Little Brown, 2008).

30. Jean Gebser, *The Ever-Present Origin*, trans. Noel Barstad and Algis Mickunas (Athens: Ohio University Press, 1985), 3.

31. Gebser, *The Ever-Present Origin*, 3.

32. Max Horkheimer and Theodor Adorno, *Dialectic of Enlightenment*, trans. E. Jephcott (Palo Alto, CA: Stanford University Press, 2007).

33. Roland Barthes, *S/Z*, trans. Richard Miller (New York: Hill and Wang, 1974) and Roland Barthes, *The Pleasure of the Text*, trans. Richard Miller (New York: Hill and Wang, 1975).

34. Bansky, *Exit Through the Gift Shop: A Banksy Film.*

35. Niklas Luhmann, *Art as a Social System*, trans. E. Knodt (Palo Alto, CA: Stanford University Press, 2000), 22.

36. Street art is sometimes referred to as postgraffiti art to distinguish it from vandalism, public-space official art, or corporate decorative art.

37. Adrian Searle, "Painted Screams," *Guardian*, September 9, 2009, www.guardian.co.uk/artanddesign/2008/sep/09/bacon.art.

38. Marian Liu, "Kurt Cobain's Death, 15 Years Later, Being Marked with Friday Tribute," *Seattle Times*, April 6, 2009, seattletimes.nwsource.com/html/musicnightlife/2008993909_zmus06dispatchcobain.html.

39. Edmund Husserl, *The Crisis of the European Sciences and Transcendental Phoenomenology*, trans. D. Carr (Evanston, IL: Northwestern University Press, 1970).

40. Gebser, *The Ever-Present Origin.*

Chapter Six

Postdenominational Christianity and Coarseness

How is it possible that society should escape destruction if the moral tie be not strengthened in proportion as the political tie is relaxed?

—Alexis DeToqueville, 1835, *Democracy in America*[1]

Addressing religion in a discussion about public coarseness seems counterintuitive. After all, religion is a private matter and isn't coarse, right? Considering the definition of coarseness used in this book, we ask the reader to reconsider the relationship between contemporary faith and coarseness, market logic, and hypertrophic individualism. Our goal here isn't to indict religion in general or any specific denomination. Instead, we ask the reader to consider with us where religion is headed. The most successful Christian worship model today is the megachurch. A good example is the extremely successful and popular Lakewood Church, headed by Joel Osteen, known more affectionately as The Smiling Preacher. Megachurches like Lakewood exist either with ambiguous Protestant alignments or as nondenominationals (collectively referred to as postdenominationals throughout this chapter). Megachurches have been extremely successful and have shown tremendous growth over the past decade.[2] Megachurches, which fail to draw in the unfaithful "seekers" they claim to pursue, simply trade believers with traditional and mainline worshippers. That which makes these churches more attractive, we contend, are theological elements that fail to contradict the disturbing trends that we outline in this book.

By no means have churches *caused* the adoption of free-market logic. Nor are churches making people more publicly coarse. Our argument about religion is far more nuanced than to hurl criticism at faith traditions with thousands of years of history, near-countless manifestations, and that have been credited with being central to the success of this nation. Instead, we make two arguments that focus almost exclusively on postdenominational Christianity. First, we contend that religions have been subjected to the same marketplace realities (e.g., pressure for attendance, growth, margins, solvency) that have given rise to public coarseness. Second, we maintain that by adjusting to these realities, in many of the ways that postdenominational megachurches have, they have inadvertently become complicit in the rise of coarseness. These fast-growing elements of Christianity are losing their ability, compulsion, and doctrinal charge to work as a cultural counterweight to the siren song of selfishness.

The most noteworthy and troubling trend in Christianity of late is that the combination of postdenominational customer-oriented Christianity (i.e., the adoption of market logic) with popular Southern/rural faith traditions is helping to foster and justify hypertrophic individualism. James Twitchell, a scholar who has published noted books on megachurches and branding, explains that the new megachurches thrive on anonymity,[3] what we believe fosters hypertrophic individualism. According to Religious Studies Professor Scott McKnight, "There's an unwritten code involved in this . . . You can enter into the church to the degree that you want. There's a guaranteed anonymity, if you want it."[4] Scott Thumma, Hartford Institute professor and coauthor of *Megachurches Today 2005* describes the megachurch experience this way:

> They find the megachurch to be "home." They are willing to drive past dozens of other congregations, fight to find a parking space, follow the signs to get to the nursery, and worship in a communal setting with five thousand other relatively anonymous persons, just like they do every day of their lives.[5]

These new churches are alluring, in part, by virtue of the fact that one can attend and never know another soul in the church. Hypertrophic individualism is fostered by anonymity because with anonymity, responsibility declines; self becomes paramount. One's relationship with God becomes, oddly in the midst of so many people, private. Gone are channeled confession, public confirmation, public statements of faith, and witnessing. The sacrament of baptism remains, perhaps only because the Bible, it is believed by many, mandates it. Charity, as postdenominational Christianity would have it, is performed to grow the flock. The postdenominational faith-equation is reduced to just two principle agents—God and self. The other is reduced to an object whose compliance is to be gained. The success of the God-self dyad is determined by metrics alone: church attendance and wealth accrual—pure modernity.

Recently, many Christian churches have come to function in the ways corporations and their employees have operated for quite a while. While churches embrace the corporate ethos, it is unclear what they do to avoid many of the coarsening elements of free-market logic. When, like corporations, churches gauge their success according to measureable ends, other than for efficacy, little consideration is given to the means. Unlike corporations, Christian churches attribute their success less to the means and more to the approval of the Holy Spirit. Thus, numbers function not only as a measure of success, but as a metaphysical sanctioning of the means—signs of God's approval.

We draw a distinction between both traditional and mainline churches (that have struggled within and between themselves for centuries over matters of metaphysical truth) and postdenominational megachurches (a growth-oriented or megachurch that eschews or downplays denomination).[6] For hundreds of years, the histories of traditional and mainline churches have evidenced their pursuit of truth. Their splits and schisms emerged over matters of what is true, and the stakes were their eternal souls. How is God properly worshipped? If His gift is eternal life, how is it properly obtained? How is grace lost? How does one achieve grace? Must sacraments be performed? Must confession be shared? What constitutes a priest? Does God continue to reveal Himself? What was meant when Christ said *this*? What did Paul really mean when he said *that*? Different traditional and mainline denominations are distinguished according to their varying answers to questions like these. If one church is right, then the other one is wrong. By virtue of one faith's incorrectness, its followers are denied grace. For centuries, Protestant faiths have maintained that Catholics have been led astray. Martin Luther went so far as to claim that the Pope was the anti-Christ ("See the Pope is the Antichrist, I believe that he is a devil incarnate"[7]) in part because the Pope was alienating people from God's good word of his salvific sacrifice. These questions of metaphysical truth have resulted in reformations, counterreformations, inquisitions, sectarianism, nationalism, and Klans.

Few people in the West fight about these truths anymore, nothing on the scale of a St. Bartholomew's Day Massacre. That's because today we live comfortably with and among contradictions. Today a Lutheran can be the best friend of a Catholic, and it fazes neither. Jews marry Catholics despite the fact that the Catholic Church makes clear that without baptism Jews will suffer eternity in hell.[8] We are at a moment of postmodern liminality, as many people are increasingly aware that being on the "right" or "wrong" side of religious arguments is a role of the dice. Knowledge about the eternal death sentences bound to be issued to their friends and neighbors is rarely taught to kids anyway, and is often learned by listening to grownups discuss these topics in a light-hearted or dismissive fashion. Increasingly aware of the capriciousness with which souls are vetted for heaven, it is more attractive for many to just back off from the entire act of splitting the hairs of truth. An amazingly effective way to satisfy one's spiritual needs in such a milieu is to worship postdenominationally.

Adapting to this new attitude toward dogma, "pastorpreneurs" have adapted their messages to be less offensive, easily digested, and positive.[9] Pastorpreneurs are pastors who seek to grow the flock by applying generic business and marketing principles to the management of their churches. The *Time* magazine description of Saddleback Church pastor Rick Warren fits this definition:

> For Purpose-Driven church leaders, he has developed an 'evangelism strategy' that includes a casual dress code, convenient parking, bright lights, live bands, short prayers and simple sermons that accentuate the positive.[10]

According to *Congressional Quarterly Researcher*, students studying to be tomorrow's pastors are often required to take business courses. The same article cites social scientist Os Guinness, author of *The Case for Civility*,[11] "[Pastors] have used, for better or worse, the best modern ideas in terms of messages and marketing and so on."[12] And growth-oriented or megachurch model successes have been had at the *expense* of the traditional and mainline churches. According to Philip Goff, director of the Center for the Study of Religion and American Culture,

> The megachurch story is not really about growth, it's about shifting allegiances. People want to feel good about who they already are . . . If a church is too challenging or not entertaining, they'll move one.[13]

Twitchell points out that 50 percent of U.S. Christians worship at 12 percent of U.S. churches. The other half spread themselves out among the remaining 88 percent. Of this, he states that, "The suppliers are redundant, and church space is oversupplied."[14] Catholics have enjoyed growth simply because of the immigration of Central and South Americans. The only mainline Protestant denomination to consistently show growth in recent years, Twitchell points out, has been the Unitarian-Universalists, far more liberal institutions.[15] Thus, how successful these modern marketing efforts have been in *spreading* the faith, as opposed to shifting it, is highly questionable. Mark Chaves in his statistical study of the growth of megachurches argues:

The increasing concentration of people in the very largest churches is *not* a consequence of megachurches tapping into a previously uninvolved population. Increased concentration is occurring mainly because people are shifting from smaller to larger churches, not because people are shifting from uninvolvement to involvement in big churches.[16]

What can't be questioned is that they are growing.

A CRITIQUE OF POSTDENOMINATIONAL MEGACHURCHES

Our contention is that as churches become less "truth" oriented and more "growth" oriented, the church changes from a tool that reforms the individual, functioning as a conduit to an eternal afterlife, to an institution that serves his/her earthly needs. God and church/community are no longer at the center of religious life. The self is. Church becomes, in essence, psychologized. From this standpoint, participating in a church is healthy because, like owning a dog or watching an aquarium, it lowers your blood pressure. Our argument is much different than simply maintaining that churches should become more dogmatic. Instead, we are critiquing a *specific* though *implicit* dogma, not the absence of a dogma. It is, we argue, a dogma of the self that is reified by the emerging pastorpreneurial outlook directing today's most successful churches.

We need to distinguish this argument from a lamentation that traditional and mainline churches are shrinking or that megachurches are too big. Having attended services at several postdenominational megachurches, it must be said that the experiences were uplifting, inviting, and inspiring. Our criticism lies in that the "rebranding," as Twitchell puts it, or the "pastorpreneurship," a term Dr. John Jackson has coined, has been accompanied by substantive theological change. Religious discipline and sacrifice seems supplanted by a raw celebration of God's grace. You've been saved, now let's rock!

It seems that we are entering an age of Rorschach religion; like the marketing language that Jules Henry warned of, the churchgoer sees what s/he wants or needs to see in it. That's not to say that all people who attend growth-oriented postdenominational churches aren't disciplined people who sacrifice. However, people raised in a selfish, corporatist, and materialistic society will find little that contradicts the values of the larger culture. In some instances, the very values of the player and his/her market logic are reinforced. Joel Osteen's Lakewood Church in Houston, Texas, for instance, includes among its statements of belief that God intends to reward his followers with an "abundant life." "Abundance" is a popular word in Osteen's ministry and his abundance message is consistent with the theology of the Prosperity Gospel. Osteen's Facebook "Ministry Notes" posted the following after the 2009 New Year:

> Do you see this year as being crowned with a bountiful harvest? Notice, God didn't say He would crown with a "barely-get-by" harvest or a "just-let-me-survive" harvest. No, He blesses His people with an overflow harvest. Even the hard places overflow with abundance. Our attitude should be "2009 is going to be a great year. I can already sense it! Favor is coming my way. Blessings, good ideas, promotions already have my name on them!" As long as you stay faithful and keep sowing good seeds, eventually that harvest will find its way into your hands.[17]

What "sowing good seeds" means is as vague as "abundance" or "favor," but we propose that in the language of money, it means return on Christian investment. If I give, then I'll get. In this equation, I can put the power of God to work for me. I activate God by having strong faith. In essence, God is waiting for his orders. And if I have faith enough, God will move my mountains. The hierarchy on which the entire Christian cosmology has long been based has been turned upside down. Man is at the top. God serves him.

THE CHURCH AS BUSINESS MODEL

> The market model views churches and their clergy as religious producers who choose the characteristics of their product and the means of marketing it. Consumers in turn choose what religion, if any, they will accept and how extensively they will participate in it. In a competitive environment, a particular religious firm will flourish only if it provides a product at least as attractive as its competitors.
>
> —Finke and Iannaccone, 1993[18]

Evidence that churches have adopted a business model abound. Stephen Ellingson points out in *Megachurch and the Mainline* that mainline churches have been struggling with the pull toward evangelical-style worship.[19] If they do it, they sacrifice theological integrity for growth. But with their numbers dropping and the costs of operating traditional small churches increasing annually, they are facing a crisis. Churches will either have to adapt to growing costs, churchgoer demands, and spirited marketing-driven competition or they will likely suffer bankruptcy.

Large postdenominational churches are an ingenious way to counter the costs of running a church. Small churches, though intimate, are shrinking and are running out of money. In his study of church finances, Robert Stonebraker noted in 1993 that, "The national and synodical bodies of many mainline protestant churches are broke."[20] Examining the relationship between size and finances, he concluded:

> Increased size lowers unit costs per member faster than free-rider effects lower unit revenues. The study suggests that a denomination comprised of large congregations will produce more total ministry than a similar-sized denomination comprised of smaller congregations.[21]

"Free-riders" are people who attend church but who contribute little. It is found that as the anonymity that accompanies church size grows, free-riders increase as average contributions decline. Nevertheless, the overall gain in efficiency far outweighs the loss in average contribution. The lower cost per worshipper increases the overall margin.

Couple the inherent cost challenges of remaining a small traditional or mainline church with the changing demands of churchgoers, and the mainline problem magnifies. According to a 2006 study published by the Barna Group, people are decreasingly committed to congregations:

> Fewer than one out of every five adults firmly believes that a congregational church is a critical element in their spiritual growth and just as few strongly contend that participation in some type of community of faith is required for them to achieve their full potential.[22]

In the same study, only 18 percent said that "spiritual maturity" requires involvement in a community of faith. Increasingly, Christians are noncommittal free agents. That someone is baptized and confirmed in a particular denomination doesn't necessarily mean that they will continue their involvement in that faith. This is consistent with Barna's 2007 finding that in the hierarchy of their own identities, respondents ranked religious affiliation very low.[23]

If a large number of individuals are uncommitted and yet predisposed to Christianity, a church capable of providing a church experience that is unthreatening, anonymous, and light on doctrine is likely to succeed. And they are succeeding, some argue, because of the enthusiastic embrace and application of modern marketing principles and strategy. According to *Forbes* magazine in 2009, since their numbers counted fifty in 1970, megachurches (customarily defined as churches with two thousand congregants) have increased to more than 1,300 today.[24] These new churches are termed "seeker sensitive" because their services are designed not to offend the newly initiated. Dr. John Jackson, author of *PastorPreneur*, explains that such changes need to be made in order to attain growth.[25] Within the semiotic universe of Christianity, growth is inherently positive, and positive signs are attributed to the Holy Spirit (even if new members are really just being shifted from

church to church). So, doing what one can in as innovative a way as possible
to grow the church is a good thing—it is the work of God himself. Jackson
justifies this approach citing 1 Corinthians 9:19–23:

> Though I am free and belong to no man, I make myself a slave to everyone, to
> win as many as possible. To the Jews I became like a Jew, to win the Jews . . .
> To the weak I became weak, to win the weak. I have become all things to all
> men so that by all possible means I might save some. I do all this for the sake
> of the Gospel, that I may share in its blessings.

From this, he argues that, "a fresh Spirit-led burst of entrepreneurial activity
will lead the church to greater cultural impact than ever before." As such,
large churches now provide a growing number of tax-free services including
fitness centers, daycare, and auto repair[26] and recruit corporate sponsors like
McDonalds, Coca-Cola, and Bank of America to sponsor their outreach
events.[27]

THEOLOGICAL UNDERPINNINGS OF THE GROWING POSTDENOMINATIONAL CHURCHES

There is a tendency to assume that megachurches are very light on theology.
Their seeker sensitivity discourages much explicit theological discussion, it
seems, with the intention of easing people into the new church. Joel Osteen,
for instance, explained to *Forbes* magazine that he didn't want to appear "too
religious" in hopes of reaching the "everyday person."[28] Despite this impression fostered by the nature of their message, Thumma, Travis, and Bird have
produced survey data demonstrating that megachurch-goers have firm theological beliefs. Seventy-eight percent of respondents in his study reported
having "strong beliefs and values."[29] Looking beyond the inherent flaws in a
self-report of weak or strong values, we believe that there are clear theological foundations on which many of these churches rest. These foundations just
aren't often talked about. For instance, Rick Warren's Saddleback Church
does little to discuss its Southern Baptist affiliation; its own "History" or
"What We Believe" links at its website don't mention this.[30] The vast majority of these large churches *are* affiliated—only between 35 percent and 40
percent are postdenominational. Most of these churches are Southern Baptist,
United Methodist, and Assemblies of God.[31] Many that are postdenominational have Pentecostal and Evangelical ties.

These growing postdenominational churches are perceived by many as
authentic or as possessing genuine Christian heft. There probably are a number of factors contributing to this. Perhaps it is the product of raising an entire
generation of young people on rock-and-roll style services. Perhaps it is the

striking difference from the grotesque televangelist-style of worship disgraced in the 1980s and 1990s. The weaving together of scripture with the virtual absence of dogma strikes a palatable balance between hard and soft homiletics. More than anything else, however, is that postdenominational churches didn't just pop out of nowhere. They brought populations of believers with them. Various theological elements of Osteen's Prosperity Gospel are by no means new. In the late nineteenth century Russell Conwell preached his famous speech "Acres of Diamonds" in which he preached that men could find their riches right where they lived, that men didn't need to go out and search for their wealth. Of the poor, Conwell preached:

> I sympathize with the poor, but the number of poor who are to be sympathised with is very small. To sympathize with a man whom God has punished for his sins . . . is to do wrong. . . . let us remember there is not a poor person in the United States who was not made poor by his own shortcomings.[32]

Thus, if poverty is punishment for wrongdoing, then wealth (abundance) is God's reward for righteousness. Conwell was a celebrated Baptist preacher, and his own beliefs reflected an interpretation of the Baptist's theological underpinnings. People delighted in Conwell's message, and he later became the first president of what is today known as Temple University. His message fit the times. Likewise, the entire package that the large postdenominationals offer today fits the moment: anonymity, material gain, minimal sacrifice, all wrapped up in an unimposing and common vernacular.

We identify what we believe are three basic characteristics shared by many of the large growth-oriented churches. First, they are person-centered, as opposed to community-oriented. Second, they are anti-intellectual. Third, they are antinomian, indirectly freeing churchgoers from moral obligations.

PERSON-CENTRISM

A person-centric church is really little more than the pure democratization of the church. Imagine trying to sell a car by insisting that your car is the right car. Your car may maximize aesthetics, towing capacity, storage, comfort, size, and fuel efficiency. At the end of the day, your lot is crammed with unsold cars. Who is right? The manufacturer or the buyer? Marketers teach us that the customer is always right. Design and sell what they want, and they will buy it. While that may not be the case when it comes to the veracity of theology, it is proving numerically successful. And if the buyer is enculturated in a society valuing the self, this outcome should be predictable. Churches certainly aren't going to want to alienate "shoppers" by condemning their sin or avarice.

In early American small Puritanical hamlets, condemning behavior and employing hot brimstone rhetoric worked because there were few options for worship. There were no Universalist/Unitarian alternative churches just up the way. To be anybody in town, you attended THE church. The churches at that time also functioned as de facto governments, offering schooling, welfare, and coordinating public efforts. Nearly everyone you knew and dealt with subscribed to the same brand of "truth." Today, few people know the people in their own towns, and are unlikely to know the names of their neighbors. The average person in the United States moves every five years. Few remain in the towns in which they were raised. Anonymity is the norm. Robert Putnam thoroughly evidences that what he terms "social capital" has declined considerably since the 1960s.[33] It is into this culture of atomized people with shallow community roots that traditional and mainline faiths sit and await the faithful. Their congregations are relatively small, shrinking, and characterized by uncomfortable intimacy (by today's standards).

Traditional and mainline churches are competing with three theological threads and their present-day manifestation, which considering the culture, are proving far more attractive. First, much of the ethos of these growth-oriented churches emerges from the historical experience and evolution of post-Awakening faiths emerging out of the South, including Methodists, Evangelicals, Baptists, and Pentecostals. These faiths stem from the Protestant split from the Roman Catholic Church during the Reformation. Martin Luther and John Calvin both placed a significant stamp on the direction of Protestant faiths. Here, we highlight the Calvinistic notion of preordination, which, though rarely considered today, continues to influence Protestant thinking, *writ large*. Preordination is the idea that God, due to his omniscience, knew at creation who would spend eternity with him in heaven. As such, the saved have already been chosen. This removes agency from the individual Christian; there is nothing that I can do to save myself. I can only look for signs of my election. I might have an epiphany while out in the fields or while driving my car. I may also live a life of grace and refinement, demonstrating that I'd transcended the *status naturae*, as evidence of God's election. I might also be fabulously wealthy. As the Great Awakening of 1720 triggered the movement of more populist faiths through the South and out of the Northeast, the notion of refinement-as-sign-of-grace was largely shed but not the ideas of material blessing. So, the faith systems emerging out of the Great Awakening do not challenge the idea of wealth-as-blessing and they preclude almost all acts (barring baptism) from helping an individual attain grace.

It is little surprise, then, that today we see the growing popularity of the Prosperity Gospel and Word of Faith movements—both movements that emphasize God's material blessings. The Prosperity Gospel is often cited as starting with Russell Conwell's "Acres of Diamonds" in which he preached:

How many of my pious brethren say to me, "Do you, a Christian minister, spend your time going up and down the country advising young people to get rich, to get money?" "Yes, of course I do." They say, "Isn't that awful! Why don't you preach the gospel instead of preaching about man's making money?" "Because to make money honestly is to preach the gospel."[34]

But in that period of time others promoted similar ideas. In 1886 Andrew Carnegie published *The Gospel of Wealth* in which he maintained that accumulation wasn't a sin, but a social responsibility to uplift others. E. W. Kenyon introduced his ideas that later became the ground on which the Word of Faith movement was built. Kenyon preached, "Here is the foundation for faith, the living word of God. What God says, is. What man says, may be."[35] In short, to say and believe the contents of the Bible is to make them so. For instance, man's sickness, according to the New Testament's Matthew, was borne by Christ. Thus, man has no right to sickness, according to Kenyon. One only needs to believe in God's sacrifice in order to relieve him or herself from illness. In his sermon "Do You Believe in Miracles," Kenyon laments the loss of miracles in the modern church, explaining that this loss of faith has chased successful and intelligent people from God's church. He explains that miracles do exist, and that we fail to realize them because of a lack of faith. We can will them; he says, "You cannot think God's Thoughts after Him without God following His Thoughts into your life; and changing your thoughts into Reality."[36]

For over a thousand years, Christians had perceived the self as profane and transitory, inherently tainted by sin and needing redemption. Catholics earned expedited entry into heaven through selfless acts of charity. Protestants demonstrated their faith in Christ's redemption by acts of charity. Initially, asceticism and pietism were at the core of both ways of showing unity with God. Later, among some, wealth and success were to become ways of demonstrating one's good standing with God. With Conwell, Kenyon, Carnegie, and others from the late nineteenth century, the trend shifts to put the individual at the center of the relationship between self and God—displacing the other and community. To be fair, Carnegie's message was one of responsibility for one's wealth; he argued that to *die* with wealth or to live ostentatiously was sinful. Wealth, he explained, was placed in the hands of the able and industrious in order to raise up others. Similarly, Conwell explained that wealth was intended for the operation of the church.

Today, the Pentecostal, Charismatic, and Word of Faith approaches to Christianity have helped complete the separation of man from community in the equations of grace. Ken Hagin, the de facto head of the Word of Faith movement, more or less teaches that believers can have whatever they want. They just have to have faith enough to get it. He's quoted saying:

> The Lord said, "I'll have to correct your theology a little" (I'd been indoctri-
> nated with all that "religious" thinking, and unconsciously I still thought that
> maybe it was wrong to have the things of this world.) "In the first place—and
> this will help you—don't pray about money anymore; that is, the way you've
> been praying. Claim whatever you need.[37]

Joel Osteen preaches a version of the Hagin-esque Prosperity Gospel—that what one wants one can have by virtue of willing it. Osteen's Lakewood Church is a postdenominational megachurch seating sixteen thousand per service in the former home of the Houston Rockets. His books have sold millions of copies, and his Sunday services are broadcast weekly to over seven million U.S. viewers and others in over one hundred countries.[38]

Whereas Hagin, Osteen, and others tailor a message by which individuals can receive what they want by way of faith, word, and prayer, other churches are doing the same in a more literal way—by making churches into service-delivery institutions. Twitchell argues that large postdenominational churches, those relying on "purposeful identity ambiguity" facilitated by church names with no historical or community bases, provide venues for shopping, financial counseling, dating services, weight-loss programs, self-help/12 step, daycare, hiking, and entertainment all in an anonymous mall-like environment that encourages browsing and happy consumption. A visit to the Willow Creek megachurch will show no Christian iconography throughout the campus. According to Gregory Pritchard, Willow Creeks' services make almost no references to scripture; he found 167 references to scripture compared with six thousand references to "I."[39] This is further evidence of the shift in the relationship between church and churchgoer. The purpose of the church is no longer to re-form the individual to a state of grace. The church's purpose has been revised to teach the individual how to reform his/her situation, family and culture to better fit his/her needs.

ANTI-INTELLECTUALISM OF THE POSTDENOMINATIONAL MOVEMENT

Many of today's postdenominational churches emerge from the Southern faith traditions that split from the Northeastern religions during the first Great Awakening. At that time Baptist, Evangelical, and Methodist faiths were faith systems that were far more appealing to masses of people outside the relatively more urbane Northeast. Richard Hofstadter notes that before 1720 getting qualified clergy to venture into these areas was as difficult as was making their message appealing. He writes of the Northeastern faiths, "Abstract and highly intellectual in their traditions, they had lost the power to grip simple people."[40] Particularly in the southern colonies Baptists, Evangelicals, and Methodists were appealing. There was a populist element to this appeal, as the "established" Anglican churches were "classed," or perceived as churches for people with money and education. Placing far less emphasis on educated ministry, these faiths found fertile ground. Other than stodgy versus revivalist or class orientations distinguishing these faiths, however, there are real theological differences that matter.

There are two specific theological characteristics that we believe contribute to the kind of anti-intellectualism we've criticized elsewhere and believe is fostered by today's growing churches. First, the feeling-centered approach to worship countered the intellectual orientation of the Northeastern churches. Second, the Protestant notions of the "priesthood of all believers" and the *sola scriptura* concept further challenge the importance of the intellect. We will be clear that there is nothing necessarily wrong with any of these approaches to worship. Instead, our point is that when combined and taken to their logical end, they contribute to the phenomena we are discussing in this book.

FEELING-CENTERED FAITH

Reformation splinters from the Roman Catholic Church extinguished the church's magic, at least for those who became Protestants. Phenomenologically, the Roman Catholic Church performs magic, manipulating the unseen: turning water to wine, releasing souls from purgatory, giving grace through confession, wedding souls together for eternity. New churches didn't attempt to take this authority, but they undermined it by claiming it was unnecessary, distracting, and even unholy. The only magic necessary, to grossly oversimplify the early-Protestant argument, was Christ's sacrifice. Once that was done, all a person needed to do was accept it. Nothing else was necessary for salvation (*sola gratia)*. Certainly there are biblical laws that these faiths insist people follow, but none of them are necessary for salvation. Postdenominationals, by contrast, have brought back the magic and dispensed with reason. Theology is largely ignored and personal magical experience is made paramount. The magic is different, however. The individual performs today's magic by opening him/herself to the Holy Spirit, experiencing ecstasy, speaking unknown tongues, healing, and making wealth. This power is evidenced through feeling. One *feels* the Holy Spirit and channels its power.

Pejoratively, some refer to the distinction between Roman Catholic/Anglican styles of worship and those more liberalized as high and low church, respectively. High church or high liturgy involves formula, tradition, vestments, incense, hierarchy, and a focus on continuity. The latter means engaging in a long-term historical exploration for how to properly worship God, and trusting that God would not have misled those who preceded the current cohort of worshippers. Historic liturgy links the church of old with the present and the future, and theoretically ties those living with those who have passed and are praising God in proper form in heaven. This practice of being Christian is highly intellectualized. Plato, whose works many believe influenced the budding Christian church, described in his dialogue *The Phaedrus* his allegory of the chariot. According to it, each man is a charioteer who must control his chariot's two horses: the white horse representing reason and the dark horse representing passions. In his circuit, the charioteer's purpose is to climb higher, which necessitates the control of one's passions. As one climbs, one comes closer to the knowledge of the gods. Applied to Christianity, refinement, reason, repression of passion, and discipline were signs of closeness to God. The goal of the early church was to execute God's will on earth. Knowing God's will was the challenge, and helps explain the pursuit of timeless form and order in the church and the control of profane and earthly passions.

By contrast, famous Great Awakening preachers like George Whitefield, John Wesley, and Jonathan Edwards were distinguished by their emotional rhetoric and moving services. The emotional turn in worship was further advanced during the second Great Awakening, when Pentecostals emerged in Los Angeles. Placing the need to save souls over the adherence to form, these preachers brought the Gospel to the masses. Initially, little of the theology changed, just the tenor of the homiletics and the manner with which worship was performed. The theology, or abandonment of it by some, has come to mimic the manner. Baptists and Evangelicals, for instance, have only a few shared core beliefs including, but not limited to *sola scriptura, sola gratia*, and the sacrament of baptism. The rest is left up to the believer. True to the Enlightenment values out of which Protestantism emerged, the individual, not the community, became the central actor in worship; this is evidenced by the Baptist insistence that only adults be baptized so that the action is a result of individual choice. Each worshipper and pastor is a free agent who will understand the Bible as she or he sees fit. There is no central governing body, and church funds are not pooled (setting the stage for the reasoning that God blesses those with the right message). During their early ecumenical efforts with Pentecostals, Father Juan Usma Gomez found Pentecostals to have little or no theology at all:

> At the beginning of the International Catholic-Pentecostal Dialogue in 1972, the group of Pentecostal representatives had no theological formation, nor did they desire any. In fact, as a consequence of the emphasis on the experience of faith and on witness as a source of the community's faith life, a distrust developed regarding theology, which was considered a purely speculative exercise that in a certain sense replaces the faith professed and lived. [41]

Instead of theology, truth, for many, is realized at the moment of worship or during personal revelation. Pentecostals experience the outpouring of the Holy Spirit in the forms of healing and emotional outbursts. Whereas the Roman Catholic Church understood the Holy Spirit to give inspiration and force to the church (the community body), thus enabling it to interpret scripture and bring people to faith, post–Great Awakening Protestants believed that the Holy Spirit acted also through the individual (the Holy Spirit indwelled). Such outbursts were believed to be the result of ecstasy brought on by the Holy Spirit's inspiration, His indwelling, something akin to that experienced by Great Awakening predecessors the Shakers and Quakers.

PRIESTHOOD OF ALL BELIEVERS AND *SOLA SCRIPTURA*

Just as the Great Awakening helped make widespread the idea that Spirit-inspired feeling was a legitimate and desired religious experience, it was made possible by the Protestant theology that clergy need not intervene in a believer's relationship with God. The doctrine of the priesthood of all believers equips any believer, properly inspired, to preach the Gospel. The Northeast's Anglican, Presbyterian, and Congregationalists clergy valued specialization and extensive education. Such specialization was also consistent with their theology: the idea that the transitory and profane world was to be transcended. Max Weber points out in *The Protestant Ethic and the Spirit of Capitalism* that the ultimate pursuit of Calvinist Protestants was a rational life:

> It had developed a systematic method of rational conduct with the purpose of overcoming the *status naturae*, to free man from the power of irrational impulses and his dependence on the world and on nature. It attempted to subject man to the supremacy of a purposeful will, to bring his actions under constant self-control with a careful consideration of their ethical consequences. [42]

Such refinement was a sign of election.

Baptist, Evangelical, and Methodist faiths, on the other hand, differed with their beliefs that anyone could access God's word. The priesthood of all believers presupposes that anyone can access the word of God and perform sacraments regardless of their knowledge or intellect. Theoretically, a man could just be inspired to begin preaching who has no formal training whatsoever (e.g., Ken Hagin, Joel Osteen, former baseball player Billy Holiday). That inspiration would be derived from the Holy Spirit. The faiths of the Great Awakening, fully embracing the Protestant notion of the priesthood of all believers, helped to reduce the value placed on proper training and education (though not necessarily intentionally).

Additionally, *sola scriptura* functions to undermine any authority other than that of the Bible. *Sola scriptura* helps clearly define the separation of Protestants from the Roman Catholic Church, perceived by many as having abused authority and having placed itself on God's pedestal. The problem remains that once authority is entirely undermined, no one can claim to be right or wrong. How can I claim that your interpretation is incorrect? How can you defend your own? Only belief in the inerrancy of the Bible can help the faithful break from this hermeneutical trap. If the Bible says it is so, then it is so. If it doesn't, then it doesn't. Keith Mathison explains rather nicely that this reasoning, however, spirals into relativism:

> If one asks a dispensationalist pastor, for example, why he teaches premillennialism, the answer will be, "Because the Bible teaches premillennialism." If one asks the conservative Presbyterian pastor across the street why he teaches amillennialism (or postmillennialism), the answer will likely be, "Because that is what the Bible teaches." Each man will claim that the other is in error, but by what ultimate authority do they typically make such a judgment? Each man will claim that he bases his judgment on the authority of the Bible, but since each man's interpretation is mutually exclusive of the other's, both interpretations cannot be correct. How then do we discern which interpretation is correct? . . . The typical modern Evangelical solution to this problem is to tell the inquirer to examine the arguments on both sides and decide which of them is closest to the teaching of Scripture. He is told that this is what *sola scriptura* means—to individually evaluate all doctrines according to the only authority, the Scripture. Yet in reality, all that occurs is that one Christian measures the scriptural interpretations of other Christians against the standard of his own scriptural interpretation. Rather than placing the final authority in Scripture as it intends to do, this concept of Scripture places the final authority in the reason and judgment of each individual believer. The result is the relativism, subjectivism, and theological chaos. [43]

Thus, each individual is vested with final authority on the matters, Christians would argue, that matter most—eternal life and redemption. But, without a final authority, the only empirical measure remaining with which to gauge Biblical validity is church membership and collection plates. None would claim to subscribe to that reasoning, but it stands to reason, many would agree, that the Holy Spirit wouldn't bless a ministry if it didn't agree with its content. *Sola scriptura* helps seed Christianity with the possibility for the hyperindividualistic relativism and wealth as a measure of authoritativeness.

ANTINOMIANISM

There is no significant Christian faith that doesn't maintain that the individual has a responsibility to others and community. Responsibility to others is the charity prescribed by Christ in several passages of the New Testament. According to Roman Catholics, one must be charitable for his/her faith to have meaning. This is supported by their interpretation of James 2:14–17:

> What good is it, my brothers, if a man claims to have faith but has no deeds? Can such faith save him? Suppose a brother or sister is without clothes and daily food. If one of you says to him, "Go, I wish you well; keep warm and well fed," but does nothing about his physical needs, what good is it? In the same way, faith by itself, if it is not accompanied by action, is dead.

Out of its frustration with Roman Catholic abuse of indulgences and the legalism of confession, Martin Luther proposed the notion of *sola fide*, or the idea that individuals are saved by faith alone in Christ's sacrifice for their salvation. What to do with James? Luther wanted to remove the Epistle of James from the Bible altogether, though he ultimately did not.

Luther and other reformers saw the Bible as God's law, separating the law from the Gospel. Souls that accepted the Gospel were saved. All were to follow God's law. Those failing to follow God's law were saved anyway. After all, no one is perfect and humans were tainted by original sin anyway. So, where is the imperative to be charitable? To be generous and kind? Christ instructs people to be generous, but is it necessary for salvation? By virtue of their evangelical imperative, all churches need to reach out in order to bring others to accept the Gospel. However, whereas the Roman Catholic Church maintained that the individual necessitated acts of charity, Protestant faiths make no such demand. No works, the Protestant is reminded, will bring a person closer to grace, for it is by faith alone that one is saved—*sola fide*. Likewise, no sin can alienate a believer from God. According to Protestants, works are evidence of one's relationship with the Holy Spirit. One with a strong relationship with God will have love for others, and will consequently be charitable.

To sum, these churches are growing and are permanent fixtures. They are likely to shape mainline reform if or when that occurs. What can't be missed, however, once the mainlines get to adapting, is what has caused these larger churches to be successful. It's not just the size. It is an appeal to people who've been enculturated to be atomistic and self-involved. In a marketplace where everything is personalized, postdenominationals are providing a make-your-own religion. This encourages and, worse, justifies the hypertrophic individualism we are criticizing.

A growing number of people are being raised to think that: (1) they are saved solely by their faith in and acceptance of Christ's sacrifice; (2) they are to rely on his/her own interpretation of scripture; (3) and are taught that truth is better accessed through personal feeling as opposed to reason. Thus, we contend that the groundwork for major religious and sociological change is being laid. This arrangement of ideas being promoted by today's growing churches portends a coarser social environment where appeal to intersubjective realities is supplanted by pecuniary logic and individual feeling. My desires are warranted if they are fulfilled, no matter how grotesque. The world beyond me functions as an arena for acquisition. There is little valid ground for public scrutiny of ideas and action when final judgment is left to God and his decision whether or not to bless their purveyors.

NOTES

1. Alexis DeToqueville, *Democracy in America* (New Providence, NJ: Barnes and Noble Publishing, 2003), 280.

2. Scott Thumma and Warren Bird, "Changes in American Megachurches: Tracing Eight Years of Growth and Innovation in the Nation's Largest-Attendance Congregations," Hartford Institute for Religion Research, accessed March 25, 2011, hirr.hartsem.edu/megachurch/Changes%20in%20American%20Megachurches%20Sept%2012%202008.pdf.

3. James Twitchell, *Lead Us into Temptation: The Triumph of American Capitalism* (New York: Columbia University Press, 2000).

4. Alan Greenblatt and Tracie Powell, "Rise of Megachurches," *CQ Researcher*, September 21, 2007, www.library.cqpress.com, 15.

5. Scott Thumma, "Exploring the Megachurch Phenomena," Hartford Institute for Religion Research, accessed March 25, 2011, hirr.hartsem.edu/bookshelf/thumma_article2.html.

6. Twitchell, *Lead Us into Temptation*.

7. Martin Luther, *The Familiar Discourses of Dr Martin Luther*, trans. Henry Bell (London: Sussex Press, 1818), 252.

8. Pope Paul VI, "Dogmatic Constitution of the Church—Lumen Gentium," Christus Rex at Redemptor Mundi, November 21 1964, accessed March 26, 2011, www.christusrex.org/www1/CDHN/v3.html. This document states, "[Jesus] himself explicitly asserted the necessity of faith and baptism (cf. Mk. 16:16; Jn. 3:5), and thereby affirmed at the same time the necessity of the Church which men enter through baptism as through a door. Hence they could not be saved who, knowing that the Catholic Church was founded as necessary by God through Christ, would refuse either to enter it, or to remain in it." *Catechism of the Catholic Church* (London: Burnes & Oates, 1999), 285. Catechism in section 1257 states, "The Lord himself affirms that Baptism is necessary for salvation. He also commands his disciples to proclaim the Gospel to all nations and to baptize them. Baptism is necessary for salvation for those to whom the Gospel has been proclaimed and who have had the possibility of asking for this sacrament. The Church does not know of any means other than Baptism that assures entry into eternal beatitude; this is why she takes care not to neglect the mission she has received from the Lord to see that all who can be baptized are 'reborn of water and the Spirit.'"

9. John Jackson, *PastorPreneur* (Friendswood, TX: Baxter Press, 2003).

10. Sonja Steptoe, "The Man with the Purpose," *Time*, March 29, 2004, 54.

11. Os Guinness, *The Case for Civility* (New York: Harper One, 2008).

12. Greenblatt and Powell, "Rise of Megachurches," 15.

13. Cathy Lynn Grossman, "As Their Numbers Stall, Megachurches Seek 'Seekers,'" *USA Today*, September 9, 2008, www.usatoday.com/news/religion/2008-09-08-megachurches-numbers_N.htm.

14. James Twitchell, *Branded Nation: The Marketing of Megachurch* (New York: Simon & Schuster, 2004), 65.

15. Twitchell, *Branded Nation*, 71.

16. Mark Chaves, "All Creatures Great and Small: Megachurches in Context," *Review of Religious Research* 47 (2006): 337.

17. Joel Osteen, "Choose to Bless Your Future," Joel Osteen Ministries Notes, January 27, 2009, accessed August 11, 2009, www.facebook.com/note.php?note_id=46479064421.

18. Roger Finke and Laurence Iannaccone, "Supply-Side Explanation for Religious Change," *Annals of the American Academy of Political and Social Science* 527 (1993): 29.

19. Stephen Ellingson, *Megachurch and the Mainline: Remaking Religious Tradition in the Twenty-First Century* (Chicago: University of Chicago Press, 2007).

20. Robert Stonebraker, "Optimal Church Size: The Bigger the Better," *Journal for the Scientific Study of Religion* 32 (1993): 231.

21. Stonebraker, "Optimal Church Size," 239.

22. "Americans Have Commitment Issues," Barna Group, accessed August 12, 2009, www.barna.org/barna-update/article/13-culture/155-americans-have-commitment-issues-new-survey-shows.

23. "American Individualism Shines Through in People's Self Image," Barna Group, accessed August 12, 2009, www.barna.org/culture-articles/99-american-individualism-shines-through-in-peoples-self-image.

24. Jesse Bogan, "America's Biggest Megachurches," *Forbes*, June 26, 2009, www.forbes.com/2009/06/26/americas-biggest-megachurches-business-megachurches.html.

25. Jackson, *PastorPreneur*.

26. Bogan, "America's Biggest Megachurches."

27. Greenblatt and Powell, "Rise of Megachurches."

28. Bogan, "America's Biggest Megachurches."

29. Scott Thumma, Dave Travis, and Warren Bird, "Megachurches Today 2005: Summary of Research Findings," Hartford Institute for Religion Research, accessed March 26, 2011, hirr.hartsem.edu/megachurch/megastody2005summaryreport.pdf.

30. "History," Saddleback Church, accessed August 11, 2009, www.saddleback.com/, and "What We Believe," Saddleback Church, accessed August 11, 2009, www.saddleback.com/.

31. Thumma, Travis, and Bird, "Megachurches Today 2005."

32. Russell Conwell, "Acres of Diamonds," American Rhetoric, accessed August 22, 2009, www.americanrhetoric.com/speeches/rconwellacresofdiamonds.htm.

33. Robert Putnam, *Bowling Alone: The Collapse and Revival of American Community* (New York: Simon & Schuster, 2000).

34. Conwell, "Acres of Diamonds."

35. Essek William Kenyon, "Jesus the Healer," scribd, accessed March 26, 2011, www.scribd.com/doc/31209152/Jesus-the-Healer.

36. Kenyon, "Jesus the Healer."

37. Ken E. Hagin, "How God Taught Me About Prosperity," Law of Abundance Living, accessed March 26, 2011, www.law-of-abundance-living.com/faith-and-finances.html.

38. Bogan, "America's Biggest Megachurches."

39. Gregory Pritchard, *Willow Creek Seeker Services: Evaluating a New Way of Doing Church* (Grand Rapids, MI: Baker, 1996).

40. Richard Hofstradter, *Anti-Intellectualism in American Life* (New York: Vintage, 1966), 65.

41. Juan Usma Gomez, "Dialogue with Pentecostals," Eternal Word Television Network, accessed March 26, 2011, www.ewtn.com/library/CURIA/PCCUPENT.HTM.

42. Max Weber, *The Protestant Ethic and the Spirit of Capitalism* (Mineola, NY: Dover, 2003), 118–19.

43. Keith Mathison, *The Shape of Sola Scriptura* (Moscow, ID: Canon Press, 2001).

Chapter Seven

Entertainment and the Entertainment Market-as-Democracy Meme

.

I'm a great fan of freedom of speech, but are Howard Stern and Larry Flynt worthy of that protection? Yes, they are in the broader picture—but worth listening to? . . . I thought that Steve Allen's heart was in the right place when he was trying so hard to get TV to clean up its act in the years before he died.

—Dick Smothers, 2004, *Press-Telegram*[1]

People don't seem to defend the content of the entertainment industry so much as defend the right to produce it. Those who criticize it are pitted by the industry's defenders as either prudes or opponents of free speech. We are neither prudes nor are we proponents of censorship. Freedom of speech provides plenty of space for criticism of expression, and thus we are confident that the public sphere can accommodate our arguments. In this chapter, we contend that the general arguments used to defend much popular entertainment betray an unwillingness to outline its merits—an implicit concession to its questionable quality. What have *Jersey Shore*, Rihanna music videos, or *Call of Duty* video games done for our culture? One is hard-pressed to find people in the industry willing to outline the virtues of these products. Instead, the trend in coarse entertainment is defended behind a firewall of free-choice mythology, or what we term the "entertainment market-as-democracy meme:" the ideas that entertainment selection is democratic, more choice is better, and free choice is sacred.

Entertainment and the criticism it engenders are two parts of a molecule. If one ever exists without the other, the physics of entertainment will be all wrong. They'll both always coexist. No entertainment criticism, nor any amount of attention to it, will "remedy" entertainment's supposed problems. Entertainment will always violate someone's expectations, moral codes, and cultural mores. We should expect it to. Through entertainment we encounter different perspectives, ideas, and cultures. To be clear, our argument in this chapter isn't that coarseness in our entertainment is the cause of any one problem in particular. Nor do we argue against any particular shows, genres, or media. Our point has more to do with the *general* effects of entertainment on our society; that mass-consumed entertainment helps shape our culture, for better or worse (we believe that, at present, it's generally worse). In *Democracy and Education*, John Dewey states,

> Society not only continues to exist by transmission, by communication, but it may fairly be said to exist in transmission, in communication. There is more than a verbal tie between the words common, community, and communication. Men live in a community in virtue of the things which they have in common; and communication is the way in which they come to possess things in common. [2]

We agree with this, but suspect we'll offer nothing new to change the minds of those inclined to disagree. Instead, we argue that our entertainment industry, the entire array of products produced to entertain paying audiences, is the vehicle through which people are acculturated to marketplace ideology, to its freedoms, inventiveness, excesses, its limitations, and its defenses.

People in the United States are generally dismissive of entertainment criticism, except to the degree that it tells us whether a film is worth the cost of admission. There's a positivistic underpinning to this attitude that holds that one's opinion is just one's opinion; all opinions are equally subjective. You have a right to yours and she has a right to hers. In the end, they are all equally meaningful—or meaningless. Far more influential in determining the "value" of entertainment is the authority of objective measures—earnings. So, does criticism of media products even "work" in a society inclined to reject opinions? It seems the condemnation of media products simply draws more attention to their existence—free media it's called. The public relations adage goes that "there's no such thing as bad press." Commenting on network disdain for FCC oversight, then-FCC Chairman Michael Powell observed:

> It would seem to me that while we get a lot of broadcasting companies complaining about indecency enforcement, they seem . . . willing to keep the issue at the forefront, keep it hot and steamy in order to get financial gains and the free advertising it provides. [3]

The Catholic Church's condemnation of *Monty Python's The Life of Brian* or *The Last Temptation of Christ*, for instance, probably did more to boost ticket sales than the quality of the films themselves.

This cultural attitude toward entertainment criticism, we argue, is a function of a horizon shaped by a deep-seated distrust of authority. This distrust is a part of our history. It's part of our nation's founding narrative—both in terms of our roots in religious diaspora and our origins in revolt against monarchy. But like most cultural attitudes, we maintain that these go widely unexamined and uncriticized. To what extent do our reflexes against kings and religious tyrants serve us when they get mapped onto our evaluations of entertainment products? Are we to tolerate anything? Is condemnation of gratuitous violence marketed to children (e.g., WWE wrestling) or to adults (e.g., Ultimate Fighting Championship) the path to a slippery slope (a fallacy) leading ultimately to some destructive end where the culture's prigs tell us what we can and can't watch? Does criticism of Baby Einstein videos as potentially harmful open the door to Big Brother telling us how to raise our children? Is it out of line to question whether reality television's depiction of an inebriated woman (Nicole "Snooki" Polizzi) flashing her digitally blurred vagina on an Italian dance floor deserved airing? Not only did MTV air that content, but it evidently was so culturally valuable that it warranted further discussion on MTV's *Jersey Shore "After-Show"* so viewers could get deeper inside the reality of the "reality program." As obvious as the latter example is of entertainment pandering, there was no outcry.

The line between entertainment criticism and censorship is *not* a fine one. If the grounds for avoiding censorship are found either in the belief in the absolute sanctity of free expression or in our shared faith that the marketplace of ideas exercises its own remedies, then our system should be able to more than endure criticism—even ours. The point of this chapter isn't to argue that our entertainment industry is coarse. Nor do we develop an argument against the "mirror" perspective, which holds that our entertainment merely *reflects* our culture or the market's demands. Instead, we proceed from the assumption that entertainment *is* coarse and that it *doesn't* merely reflect society. Our central argument here is rhetorical in nature. We argue that the "defenses" given for media content by its producers and broadcasters employ a democracy rhetoric and rhetorics of choice; these defenses reveal that the calculus used to determine what entertainment is produced and marketed is simply what sells, or pays. Democracy, a means of legitimizing the use of political power, functions ironically in the entertainment marketplace to limit power. The entertainment market-as-democracy meme engenders the idea that the only legitimate way to exercise power over the industry is through spending: not through criticism, and *certainly* not through regulation. While this may empower us to limit our own exposure to entertainment content, it delegitimizes the idea that the citizenry has either an interest in or the authority to judge or limit its content.

Our point here is not to advocate censorship—though we are fully aware that entertainment producers and distributors censor material all the time. Instead, we investigate what cultural attitudes have brought us to a place where there's so much coarse entertainment content to fret over. In short, the entertainment market-as-democracy meme has been so fully adopted into our cultural horizon that it's like the air we breathe. We aren't even aware of it anymore. It is an attitude. The widespread hold of this meme on public discourse about entertainment helps explain both the decisions of entertainment producers and widespread indifference to and complicity with this system on the part of consumers. As consumers, we often function unquestioningly within its paradigm by turning off shows we don't like (if in fact we do) while shrugging off critics as old-fashioned hacks. Likewise, those inside the entertainment industry operate within the paradigm by producing coarser and coarser products while also condemning those who criticize. Their sentiments aren't unlike those voiced by Frank Zappa in his testimony to the Parents Musical Resource Center (PMRC) in 1985.

> No one has forced Mrs. [Susan] Baker or Mrs. [Tipper] Gore to bring Prince or Sheena Easton into their homes. Thanks to the Constitution, they are free to buy other forms of music for their children. [4]

It's a procedural defense that asserts the right to produce and market the content. It's also a concession that little more can be said on the content's behalf.

COARSENESS IN ENTERTAINMENT

If one looks at mass mediated comedy, for instance from the 1930s up through the 1960s, and compares it with the comedy regularly available on television and radio today there is a marked difference in wit, style, tenor, and vulgarity. The same can be said for popular music, films, news, sports, theatre, and television. Sticking with comedy, a long list that is very demonstrative and consistently so proves the point. Stan Laurel and Oliver Hardy, Buster Keaton, Will Rogers, Charlie Chaplin, the Marx Brothers, Mae West, W. C. Fields, Bud Abbott and Lou Costello, George Burns, Gracie Allen, George Jessel, Jack Benny, Bob Hope, Jimmy Durante, Sid Caesar, Imogene Coca, Phyllis Diller, Dean Martin and Jerry Lewis, Shelley Berman, George Gobel, Bob Newhart, Morey Amsterdam, Danny Thomas, Peter Ustinov, Dick Van Dyke, Woody Allen, Bill Cosby, Carol Burnett, Tim Conway, the

Smothers Brothers, Joey Bishop, Flip Wilson, and many other giants of comedy created humor with wit, pantomime, impersonations, slapstick, and more to the point here, complex, intelligent narrative and behavioral scenarios (like the "fixes" the Little Tramp often found himself in).

It may not be an overstatement to say that these comedians *never* stooped to juvenile toilet or drug abuse jokes for laughs. Why? No doubt, in part because the audience would not have reacted well to such humor. Something has changed. Lisa Lampanelli is as different from Gracie Allen as Chris Rock is from Phil Silvers. Comedy Central's celebrity roasts make Dean Martin's roasts of the 1970s look like children's PBS fare. Allen Funt has nothing on Daniel Tosh's Web Redemptions and occasional "Dick of the Week" segment. Lewis Black's humor makes Steve Martin look like a man from another era, and maybe he is. Today much comedy (not all of course, that is, generally speaking the comedy of Billy Crystal or Jerry Seinfeld, for example) is "edgy," meaning crass, mean, sensationally vulgar, and stupid. Many, such as Jackie Gleason, Hope, Van Dyke, Burns, and Cosby have noted this change in our collective sense of humor. Andrew "Dice" Clay and Howard Stern are a far cry from Lenny Bruce or Don Rickels, let alone Red Skelton or Art Carney. While Bruce was no "Mork" of *Mork and Mindy*, which always ended with a sympathetic soliloquy by Mork, an almost reverent homily about humanity's condition that had a touch of consideration similar to Skelton's "God Bless," and Durante's "Good night Mrs. Calabash—wherever you are," Bruce was not vulgar on television. Neither was Richard Pryor.

Bruce's nightclub routine would be considered tame by today's standards. And yet the shift in attitudes is evident in the reaction Bruce received for his jokes from community leaders, audiences, and authorities. The meanest jokes used to be in the form of self-deprecation as masterfully stylized by Martha Raye, Red Buttons, Woody Allen, George Gobel, Dom Deluise, Don Knotts, and Rodney Dangerfield. Even Red Foxx would be hard pressed to keep up with the typical banter today. By contrast, Dan Whitney, or Larry the Cable Guy, is well known for bigoted, ageist, sexist humor. Fellow comedian David Cross criticized Whitney in *Rolling Stone:*

> It's a lot of anti-gay, racist humor—which people like in America—all couched in "I'm telling it like it is." He's in the right place at the right time for that gee-shucks, proud-to-be-a-redneck, I'm-just-a-straight-shooter-multimillionaire-in-cutoff-flannel-selling-ring-tones act. [5]

Whitney responded in his book *Git-R-Done* by accusing *Rolling Stone* of running a hit piece.

Can't anybody even go to a comedy show anymore without havin' to worry
about the PC police attackin' ya for doing nothin' except drinkin' a few beers
with some friends and havin' a few laughs?[6]

He terms this humor "blue collar," which is to say it refuses to accommodate
the "elitists"—critics—who find his humor easy and pandering. Cross later
clarified his criticism in an open letter to Whitney. In it, Cross insisted he
could match Whitney's "un-P.C.ness" any day of the week, but that he refused to stoop to biased insults for easy laughs, noting Whitney's line: "Mad-
der than a queer with lockjaw on Valentine's Day."[7] Still, the networks
saddle up to Whitney, tapping him as a temporary cohost with former *CBS
Evening News* anchor Katie Couric on ABC's *Live! With Regis and Kelly.*
The History Channel, part-owned by Disney-ABC Television Group, cast
Whitney in his very own show titled *Only in America.* Indeed.

To be sure, comedians of past generations could tell saucy jokes and
stories but if and when they did they were reserved for specific types of
small, usually live adult audiences, a fact that seems utterly passé today with
all ages being lumped together into one giant mass.[8] A change in humor
occurred when a new venue opened and another closed. When the Borscht
Belt faded and Las Vegas expanded, a new stage that invited ever more edgy
comedy opened. But still, television and radio were spared. Home viewing
families were protected because there was a sense that children are different
from adults. Foxx, aka the widower junkman Fred Sanford, became famous
not for his adult humor but for feigning an endless wave of "big ones" (heart
attacks) to make his son "Lamont" feel guilty, clutching his heart while
looking heavenward and crying, "I'm comin' Elizabeth," sparring with
"Aunt Ester," and plotting shenanigans with "Grady." It was the role of
Foxx's career. Fred Sanford, not his bawdy routine, gave Foxx his first and
only financial stability. His nightclub standup routine was never very successful in large part because its coarseness found a very small audience.

The word "coarse" is a very good term to describe much contemporary
popular entertainment in the United States. One can look at the demise of the
retail environment as it is increasingly "Wal-Martized," or to the churches
that actually use old Wal-Mart stores for their sanctuaries, and services that
are not uncommonly led by "reverends" and "bishops," with little or no
theological training. One could look at the debased level of discourse on talk
radio, or to "reality TV" (including Universal's *Jerry Springer* with show
titles like "Battle of the Broken" and "Battling Babes"), which specializes in
humiliating poor people before a national audience. Today's music is filled
with racial epithets and misogynist and homophobic lyrics. Once-*Monday
Night Football* pitchman Hank Williams Jr., sporting a confederate flag,
sings in his 1988 hit song *If the South Woulda Won*, "If the South woulda
won we'd a had it made. I'd put the capital back in Alabama. We'd put

Florida on the right track 'cause, we'd take Miami back. If the South woulda won we'da had it made (spoken) I'd be better off!" And in his 1995 song *New South*, he sings, "The New South is still the same and I'm so glad of it." The irony here is that Williams Jr. was commissioned by Disney's ABC Sports the same year his song "If the South Woulda Won" came out to write and perform the opening for *Monday Night Football*. Williams Jr. won an Emmy for *Are You Ready for Some Football?* The illogical paradox comes into vision when it is understood that 90 percent of wide receivers and more than 60 percent of the overall NFL roster of players are made up of African Americans, who make up only 14 percent of the overall population, and who are of course glad the South lost.[9]

Meanwhile, megastars like Michael Jackson, M. C. Hammer, and Will Smith fall out of favor with music audiences because they are not authentically mean enough. The light-hearted images of a smiling Elvis and the Beatles wearing matching suits and ties would not cut it now. Preteens spend millions to see child artists prance and lip sync more than play instruments and sing in extravaganzas that resemble burlesque shows of the past more than musical concerts. The differences cause one to wonder if fifty or even thirty years ago were more conservative times or eras that just knew how to have fun? So much public discourse today seems genuinely angry. The "Rat Pack," or "Clan" as Shirley MacLaine[10] claims the group really called itself, consisted of Humphrey Bogart, Frank Sinatra, Dean Martin, Sammy Davis Jr., Peter Lawford, and Joey Bishop. They were *hardly* conservative. So what changed?

DEMOCRATIZATION OF CULTURE IS NOT THE LIBERALIZATION OF CULTURE

Often, those who criticize culture are accused of ignoring the liberalizing influence of popular entertainment: specifically, entertainment's ability to expand the horizons of the privileged and to give alternative ideas and perspectives access to mainstream marketplace of ideas. We don't deny the progressive influences that popular entertainment has had and still has on our culture, albeit largely inadvertent. Instead of denying this, we seek to balance those considerations by looking at how the mythos of entertainment's liberalizing effects is used to cast entertainment's coarseness as good, innocuous, or necessary. The widely held notion that entertainment exposes us to the diversity of the so-called global village, we maintain, is exploited by the entertainment industry in order to rationalize the dissemination of cheap, unscripted, voyeuristic, and violent product.

It wasn't until the last half century that anything other than the now pejoratively termed "high" culture was considered culture at all. This view of culture was classical in nature; it was akin to refinement or civilization. Today, people possess a more anthropological understanding of the term, accepting that just about anything intentionally made by humans is reflective of the standpoint of the group. Thus, what people make, regardless of who they are, is reflective of culture. The high and low cultural distinction evinces its origin in phrenology, and phrenology's contention that the height (either high or low) of one's brow ridge was indicative of a person's intelligence.

The success of erasing the hierarchical distinctions between low and high culture has been celebrated by those seeking to deconstruct the barriers to equal access to the public sphere, to mass communication, to opportunity, to justice and to wealth. The history of the development of the mass media is one largely marked by a struggle between promoters of high culture against purveyors of popular culture—or entertainment crafted to appeal to the widest audience. Barnouw documented how early radio was viewed by many at the time as a vehicle with which to introduce the masses to classical music and college instruction. The failure of these advocates to shape the future of radio was a harbinger to the direction in which mass media was headed. Its future and its content would be largely determined, almost exclusively,[11] by what attracted audiences. Inasmuch as car wrecks turn more heads than cellos and the Federal Radio Commission (FRC), precursor to the FCC, was staffed with friends of the broadcasting industry, radio's future as a profit center was determined. What would be broadcast would be governed by profit and audience size.[12] It was "democratized."

Surrendering control over what is broadcast to the individual choices of consumers is the democratization of entertainment. Consumers, like voters, "vote" for their preferences by tuning in—or so we are told. Programs that aren't preferred get cancelled, while those with profitable audiences survive. *My So Called Life* dies and *Jersey Shore* thrives. With kids, learning-oriented programs lose out to violent cartoons, "tween" dramas, and situation comedies. While PBS, with its orchestras, plays, and history programs, averages a 1.7 primetime rating (and declining),[13] the major broadcasting networks (FOX, CBS, ABC, and NBC) together averaged between a 5.0 and a 7.0 primetime rating.[14] In our entertainment democracy edification seems a perpetually bad candidate.

Democratizing popular culture is the process of handing regulatory control of broadcasting policy to the free market's invisible hand. Those seeking to legitimize dubious entertainment products, such as programs, film, news talk, and music with violent, vulgar, hateful, and sexual themes, like to compare democracy as a system of governance to marketplace selection. Doing so links the legitimizing powers of democratic majority preferences to market preferences. This makes the practice of selling socially damaging products seem less repugnant because responsibility for its existence is shifted from the producers to the consumers. "Nobody would make the stuff it people didn't want it," some might defend. While one's entertainment choices may be private, the effects of these products are not contained to our individual relationships with our televisions and iPads. Novel public communication alters everyone's communication environment.

There are glaring problems with the democratic marketplace metaphor. First, the entertainment marketplace ignores democratic theorists' concerns with majority tyranny: a matter of concern for numerous democratic theorists.[15] In fact, those utilizing the metaphor claim to celebrate majority rule. Madisonian democracy, in contrast, was tailored to "balance" the interests of the majority and minority, for fear that the majority—poor agrarians—would take the property of the upper class.[16] Madison wrote in Federalist #10 that the goals of pure democracy can prevent the "public good" from being acknowledged and realized. He claimed that pure democracy is "found incompatible with personal security or the rights of property; and have been as short in their lives as they have been violent in their deaths."[17] Evidently, Madison and the vast majority of wealthy men who ratified our own constitution were no fans of pure democracy.[18] Yet, today's wealthy owners of our entertainment industry appear to be big proponents of a marketplace that enables and encourages individuals to pursue their personal viewing interests, no matter what. The aggregate of their voices is heard and listened to by producers who reward the majority with more of what they want. The majority rules in our marketplace (or so we are made to believe). Such attitudes are evident in the comments Mel Karmazin, former CEO of Viacom, makes when asked by Charlie Rose in 2007 if he would have fired Don Imus after his infamous "nappy headed ho's" comment. He replied, "No, no chance. I mean, I found the comments offensive, but you know what? It's free speech . . . don't listen to him."[19] Don't listen to him, and he'll go away, so the mythology goes. Karmazin went on to explain how big Imus' audience was. Ironically, audience size could have been a measure of the number of people affected by Imus' bigoted statement. Instead, audience size vindicates bigotry. The logic goes, if you have the audience, you have the public's vote of confidence.

Second, the majority doesn't actually rule in our entertainment "democracy." Unlike a candidate, ignoring a show *doesn't* make it go away. If enough of a sellable audience can be gathered for a show, and the program is produced cheaply enough to make it profitable, it will survive. The key word here is "enough," which, with respect to audience size, doesn't mean majority. Dean Batali, writer for *That 70s Show,* said of broadcasting decisions,

The success of a show is not measured by how good it is, or who says they loved it, or even how many people watch. A show is a success if the people who watched it go and buy the products that were advertised during the commercials. It is all about what is being sold and (just as important) who is doing the buying. [20]

For instance, per week *Pawn Stars* is among the top-rated cable shows with audiences around three million,[21] a number dwarfed by broadcast television numbers. Additionally, the "ballots" for every viewer are not counted equally; advertisers prefer younger viewers. Explaining the early success of the *Arsenio Hall Show* against Johnny Carson in the 1990s, Michael Norman of the *New York Times* explained, "Hall has been building ratings steadily throughout the year. His show has been especially popular with viewers 12 to 34 years old, the ratings cohort that buys high-volume items such as blue jeans, soft drinks, records and cosmetics."[22] Unless an older audience can be distilled down to Buick-purchasing golf aficionados during a time of day when the more coveted audience is out skateboarding, people over thirty-five have few viewing options. This highlights the fact that the viewing decisions, or "votes," of people under thirty-five are weighted more than those who are older. Brian Lowry of *Variety* magazine discussed this phenomenon of appealing to the youth audience. Specifically, Lowry notes that networks pursue strong eighteen to thirty-four numbers to the neglect of viewership aged fifty-five or older. Lowry warns, "The imperative to get younger [audiences] increasingly comes at the expense of substance, and requires pushing older viewers away rather than trying to drag them along for the ride. Blame it to some extent on the divisive nature of reality TV as well as a lockstep emphasis on young-adult demographics as television's principal currency." He terms content aimed at this audience "loud, garish and dumb."[23]

While Herbert Gans defended popular culture with his classic mirror argument, stating it must "meet the standards of form and substance which grow out of the values of the society,"[24] his writing presupposed that the cultural products were targeted at the entire population. Writing in 1974, when there were three major broadcasting companies, this was a safer assumption. Today, many cultural products are being shaped by the values of the least mature spenders in society. To claim that there is no qualitative or substantive difference between these populations would be, on its face, very difficult to defend.

In his book *The Ethics of Voting*, Jason Brennan writes:

> From a moral point of view, voting is not like ordering food off of a menu. When you order salad at a restaurant, you alone bear the consequences of your decision. No one else gets stuck with a salad. If you make a bad choice, at least you are hurting only yourself. For the most part, you internalize all of the costs and benefits of your decision. [25]

While your choice of salad may have little or no consequences for others, like voting your selection of entertainment *does*. This brings us to our third point; the idea that people would vote their individual interests was long believed by many, and still today by some (conservatives), to be democracy's greatest flaw. In *The Social Contract* Jean-Jacques Rousseau explained that majority rule is predicated on the notion that the majority will act in the interest of the many.

> [Democracy] presupposes, indeed, that all the qualities of the general will still reside in the majority; when they cease to do so, whatever side a man may take, liberty is no longer possible. [26]

In the realm of politics, this democratic ethic is used to discourage people from voting in favor of their own self-interests. It's an attitude that's implicit in conservative condemnation of political messages that encourage voters to consider their material well-being. For these folks, voting one's own interests is believed by some to be anathema to "real" democracy; it's argued that doing so harms others. The relationship between consumption and self-interest causes Randian conservatives to do an about-face with respect to the harms of self-centric decision making. According to this line of "logic," buying, viewing, downloading, or listening to whatever you want actually promotes public welfare. The point is that this is a glaring contradiction that, bizarrely, appears to cause no dissonance among contemporary conservatives. It is itself stupid—coarse.

More than anything else, the entertainment market-as-democracy meme masks over the potential harms of abandoning a public interest ethic in exchange for free market guidance is that it grafts the positive metaphorical entailments of the "democracy" meme onto our consumption decisions. Buying is good, and buying in one's self-interest is right. Just as the principles of democracy are sacrosanct and thus largely unquestioned in our society, criticizing the tenets of free and unfettered markets evokes similarly resistant responses.

But is democratizing culture a bad thing? As noted, many have celebrated the move. People on the political left and right have both praised and condemned this phenomenon. Gans describes it as, at worst, innocuous, noting that none of the concerns expressed by critics or academics have been supported. [27] Barnouw noted the role of early radio broadcasting in exposing large, white, American audiences to music created and recorded by African Americans, an ethnicity that has brought an immeasurable richness to U.S. culture. This has significantly helped lift the economic profile of that community. Meanwhile, the mainstream condemned exposing American audiences to such music because, some claimed, it aroused people sexually and was influenced by the devil himself. The popular outreach of broadcasting enabled radio personalities to grow enormous audiences. Fr. Charles Cough-lin and Dr. John Brinkley developed large bases of listeners that enabled them to branch from their original stated missions of evangelizing and shar-ing medical advice, respectively. Both became politically involved and even-tually vocally sympathetic toward the Nazis. [28] Both revealed the persuasive powers of the mass media and the influence that radio-demagogues could have behind a microphone. Today, as in the 1940s, the political left quite often condemns the content of talk radio as demagoguery and has, in recent years, entertained the reintroduction of the Fairness Doctrine: an FCC gov-erning doctrine, repealed by the FCC during the Reagan administration, that required contrasting views be presented in broadcast forums. It should be noted that in 2000, the FCC also repealed the "personal attack" doctrine, which required broadcasters to notify those publicly attacked on their air-waves of what had been said, and to provide those individuals with an oppor-tunity to respond. [29]

While democratizing entertainment culture is often credited, quite rightly, with the growth of political access and influence for various ethnicities and underprivileged communities, the companies that brought us these develop-ments shouldn't be confused for altruistic organizations. Corporations don't champion social causes unless there is money in it. That's not as much a criticism as it is a statement of fact. Audience-attracting transgression has no point but to attract audiences. Sure, ABC broadcast the coming-out episode of *Ellen* with Ellen DeGeneres, but it also cancelled the show under contin-ued pressure from antigay groups. Entertainers are in the business of provid-ing spectacles, and *Ellen* delivered. Airing the episode, though, threatened to affect the network's branding. What is evident is that broadcasters' boun-dary-pushing can't be confused with activism. For further evidence, look to MSNBC's on-again, off-again relationship with conservative commentator Ann Coulter; the network both loved her and hated her for the various TV crowds she attracted by calling Arabs "swarthy men." [30] With some excep-tions, just about every controversial public issue had been "boldly" addressed by the major networks by the time *Maude* was cancelled in 1978, but the inertia of transgression continued. Around that time, dealing with issues like abortion and race-hate *was* considered a matter of taste—bad taste. Whites didn't drag contentious political matters into each other's homes. But doing so drew an audience. *The Smothers Brothers Comedy Hour* taught people that a controversial show will deliver strong ratings, desirable audiences of significant size and Emmy awards. The lesson further instructed that if the show is too political, it will still get cancelled, just as *The Smothers Brothers Comedy Hours* was in 1969. The lesson learned was to avoid politics, or to guarantee plausible deniability through subtext.

Today, programs depicting homosexuals as main characters don't receive the credit that shows in the 1970s received for featuring racial and ethnic minorities, perhaps because we now have a better sense of what the networks were, and are, actually up to—*gaysploitation*. The fact that nonwhites played any central characters on television forty years ago was so novel that it obscured the fact that the storylines were hardly transgressive in any political way. Still, casting nonwhites was groundbreaking. Ultimately, many of the sitcoms of the period were marked by the implicit argument that racial epithets and stereotyping aren't nice. Viewers laughed at Archie Bunker's racial paranoia while George Jefferson was rewarded with money and entree into an exclusive New York penthouse in exchange for cleaning the clothing of white folks. The 1970s certainly grew the population of minorities on television, but the programs often dealt with political matters by cushioning them, advocating little, or providing opposing hyperbolic perspectives (e.g., Archie Bunker and Michael Stivic, Chico Rodriguez and Ed Brown). In the 1980s the "socially conscious" sitcom morphed into apolitical family-oriented programs with didactic themes, designed to raise awareness of topics such as racism, sexism, ableism, and drug and alcohol abuse while exploring the various facets of teen angst (e.g., *Diff'rent Strokes*, *Family Ties*, *Blossom*, *Charles in Charge*). Competition heated up with the introduction of the FOX network and the ubiquity of cable. Networks saw the need to launch shows with built-in audiences, and so plucked comedians straight out of nightclubs to host half-hour evening comedies (e.g., Drew Carey, Chris Rock, Jerry Seinfeld, Gary Shandling, Robert Klein, Rosanne Barr, Steve Harvey, Ellen DeGeneres, Brett Butler, Martin Lawrence, Ray Romano). On its face, this phenomenon may appear to parallel early-broadcasting's employment of former-Vaudeville entertainers. While the wholesomeness of Vaudevillians varied, once they moved to television and radio, public discourse standards applied. When radio first made the scene, the U.S. government built into its free-market broadcasting model the requirement that broadcasters uphold the public's interest. Standards and Practices boards were developed by broadcasters early on, with dump-buttons and the charge to keep the airwaves clear of both gratuitous advertising and indecent content. Standards of decency seemed governed by what wouldn't be considered acceptable to say in a stranger's home. So, words like "damn" were dumped; unfortunately, so were mentions of birth control.[31] While early broadcasting successes were driven by Vaudeville talents like Fred Gwynn and Red Skelton, they were careful programs. Just as prohibitions against advertising have today become laughingly anachronistic, so have standards of decency. Increasingly what is seen on television seems fit for a crowd at a nightclub—Jerry Seinfeld completely blurred these distinctions by weaving standup into his program famously billed as "a show about nothing."

Our entertainment programs consistently seem to push the boundaries of vulgarity. George Carlin's "Seven Dirty Words You Can't Say on Television" was a comedy bit highlighting the absurdities of censorship. It seemed to have perfectly fit the ethos of the early 1970s. Though certainly gratuitous, it can be argued that he had a point; his humor instantiated contestation. Thirty years later having a point is a distraction. When Howard Stern took his radio show from "terrestrial radio" to XM/Sirius satellite, many of his fans questioned his ability to maintain the quality of his comedy after moving from a context in which he was always battling lawsuits over his content. At Sirius, he became part of the ownership and the FCC had no oversight. His fans were worried that there'd be no friction. There'd be no one with whom to do battle. Stern rejected that idea, arguing that the old format just limited him.[32] With the move, he'd be free to produce contextless and apolitical shtick without limits. The fruits of his labor have included a penis shoved into the eye socket of a man with a luxated eyeball (in exchange for a television), games involving guessing what is wrapped in someone's foreskin, and police tasers attached to testicles and labias. Though with no cause but audience growth at XM/Sirius radio, Stern brands himself a rebel, thieving in his marketing materials the semiotic qualities of protest and disenfranchisement embodied in the image of the upraised black fist. Being transparently provocative and irreverent for no purpose, he even employed on his website a passion image of himself wearing a crown of thorns. He casts himself in the victim role, harmed by those who'd dare criticize him. His rebellion is symbolic only. Clever but cynical marketing.

UNDERSERVING THE PUBLIC INTEREST

Soon after his appointment to chair the FCC in 1961 Newton Minow delivered his famous "vast wasteland" speech. Many of its specifics are dated, but its push for broadcasters to consider public interest in addition to profitability when producing and airing entertainment are still very relevant. In it he stated:

> We all know that people would more often prefer to be entertained than stimulated or informed. But your obligations are not satisfied if you look only to popularity as a test of what to broadcast.[33]

The first part of the quotation is an overgeneralization, but the exhortation in the second part is as relevant today as it was then. Broadcasters, or producers of entertainment, need balance in their decision making. If the industry is guided exclusively by profit, then we can expect content to become more coarse as producers seek novel ways to turn heads.

Unfortunately, the industry's pursuit of profit is the reason that entertainment criticism misses the mark when it condemns the entertainment industry for having no values. Capital gain *is* a value, and its importance to the industry is both implicit and explicit in much of what the industry produces. And the value of profit isn't always consonant with the public interest. While today's entertainment seeker has more variety than anyone in 1961 could have imagined people wanting, with some cable systems delivering well over five hundred channels to people's homes to compete with limitless websites and multi-player 3D video games, it is easy to confuse a plurality of options with a plurality of values.

A good way to start to understand the spirit of today's entertainment industry is to consider a representative controversy. What is going on is very well illustrated in an argument between *Friday Night Lights* author Buzz Bissinger and former Deadspin.com blogger Will Leitch that took place on HBO's *Costas Now*. During a roundtable discussion about the effects of blogging on sports journalism two positions emerged, with one side arguing in favor of traditional journalistic conventions and standards and a blogger who implicitly characterized his opponents as old fashioned. Bob Costas, the show's host, described the criticism of sports blogs this way, "The reasonable criticism is of the tone, of the gratuitous potshots and mean-spirited abuse." Bissinger added, "I think blogs are dedicated to cruelty, journalistic dishonestly, they're dedicated to speed." Blogs as sources of news are very new to the news scene. Their publics have grown accustomed to free, edgy, instantaneous, and interactive news over the Internet. The vast majority of these blogs is not run by trained journalists and so, ostensibly, are unfamiliar with and/or dismissive of the traditions and conventions of news writing. In fact, many define themselves in contradistinction to traditional sources of information (or mainstream media). Their blogs have no editorial policies, there are no ombudsmen, and in very many cases readers get to post anonymous reactions that are quite often vulgar and entirely irresponsible.

The statements made by Will Leitch are standard democracy tropes often used by those defending the media's coarse content; he defends the content of his own blog, the motto of which is "Sports without access, favor or discretion," by professing his faith in audiences, a propaganda technique whereby the speaker flatters the audience and awkwardly situates the opponent in the position of appearing to distrust the very people s/he is trying to entertain, inform, or persuade. Leitch also suggests that the defenders of the mainstream journalistic institution are old fashioned, drawing on the rhetorical power of the accusation that journalistic stalwarts are old, mature, and inflexible—a cardinal sin in a youth-worshiping culture. Audience flattery is almost universally effective, especially in our own culture. Though not fully articulated by Leitch, it doesn't really need to be. It's an enthymematic line of argument with populist-seeming premises. Major premise: elitists don't trust the preferences of the masses. Minor premise: so-and-so doesn't trust the preferences of the masses. Conclusion: so-and-so is an elitist. In this scenario, "elitist" functions as a devil-term—rhetorical kryptonite. This is also made operative in the discussion when Leitch claims, "The nice thing about the web is that it's a meritocracy." He's not given the time to fully develop this thought, but it seems reasonable to assume he means that only the best blogs become profitable and survive. This begs the question, however, what is the best blog? Considering Leitch's penchant for upsetting journalistic conventions, one can only surmise that the best blog is the one with the biggest or most profitable audience. Further support for our assessment can be found in the following statement by Leitch, "Every time someone does something new or something a little different everyone is like, 'that's not really journalism, that's not really what we do, but it's no, it's just not what *you* do.'" Here, quite clearly, Leitch is relying on *ad hominem*, intimating that his opponent is old fashioned. Meanwhile, he positions himself as the maverick, the only voice in the room willing to forge past the dusty, old practices of journalism. Meanwhile, he reveals his ignorance of the profession, stating, "One of the fundamental principles of journalism is honesty and forthrightness, and I think if I pretended that I did not have my own viewpoints or my own biases, I'm not sure that's being more truthful to the reader." This suggests that his audiences are interested in who he is, what he thinks, and his authenticity. And while he may be right about his audience, he's wrong about journalism.

These sentiments are employed in former NBC CEO Jeffrey Zucker's defense of contemporary news:

> Look, I think, ultimately the viewer decides here and the viewer is smart enough to make their own decisions and I think that there is more access to news and information today than there's ever been. And the fact is if you go back 25 years, you know when you basically had three evening news programs that were being programmed by, uh, you know, ivy educated graduates, that were all, you know, delivering the same kind of program. I think the fact is today there's much more varied choice than there's ever been and I think that's in the best interest of the consumer. Just because it's loud and noisy doesn't mean you have to watch it. [34]

Better than a defense of the status quo, he argues the virtues of our present trajectory. This "blogosphere world," as Zucker termed it, allows everybody to be heard today who has a blog and a Flip Cam. In such an environment, the line between entertainment and information is blurred, and must be if you want an audience and you want to remain relevant.

The future of "infotainment," that which many suspect is supplanting traditional journalism, appears to look something much more like *TMZ* and less like a newspaper. *TMZ* is difficult to define because it isn't just a magazine-style celebrity-news television show or website, though it is news according to the FCC.[35] It is both those things, but it also communicates celebrity updates via your mobile phone. Moreover, it is interactive, encouraging its viewers/readers to submit stories and to comment anonymously about front-page items. This program emerged from the ethos of the Internet long before *TMZ* came to television. The result is an entity that provides titillating and voyeuristic stories, images and video with snarky and abusive commentary—all necessary to provide spectacle enough to distract viewers from more familiar and established programs. Brian Steinberg of *Advertising Age* describes the show this way, "Where most gossip media present a glorified view of celebrity—even stars with problems seem glamorous and cool—TMZ goes for the jugular, airing clips of famous folk using profanity and swaying around while intoxicated; it even named one alleged sex-abuse victim." This edginess helps explain a recent story featuring tennis professional Rafael Nadal playing golf and swimming with a female titled, "Nadal Plays 19 Holes." While newspapers struggle, *TMZ* posted significant gains in key demographics.[36]

The content is not what matters from the perspective of today's online news "innovators." From the standpoint of a television executive, it is safe to say that it doesn't matter what a television program's content is provided it gathers viewers. Most important is the audience reaction. If a cultural product garners an audience reaction—good *or bad*—it is a success. Liberal documentarian Michael Moore addressed this very phenomenon when explaining why major studios produce and distribute his films:

> You know, I've often thought it's very ironic that I'm able to do all this and yet what am I on? I'm on networks. I'm distributed by studios that are owned by large corporate entities. Now, why would they put me out there when I am opposed to everything that they stand for? And I spend my time on their dime opposing what they believe in. Well, it's because they don't believe in anything. They put me on there because they know that there's millions of people that want to see my film or watch the TV show, and so they're gonna make money. And I've been able to get my stuff out there because I'm driving my truck through this incredible flaw in capitalism, the greed flaw.[37]

Moore gets produced and distributed because he makes money for himself and corporations. Today, broadcasters granted licenses by the FCC are no longer under any obligation to provide for the public interest in any specific sense. Mark Fowler chaired the commission during the Reagan administration, and in 1984 he led the FCC in its change of standards by which broadcast license holders were determined to have met the public interest. The public interest, up to that point, had been deemed served by diversifying viewpoints shared by broadcasters. This was predicated on the scarcity of broadcast channels, a publicly owned commodity. Much like instructing a child to eat good food while defining "good" as anything the child feels like eating, Fowler dismissed the scarcity assumption and replaced it with a "marketplace" assumption that deemed public interest met if the market could bear its content.[38] This effectively ended the public interest mandate. Broadcasters no longer produce news as a public-service obligation. Released from these obligations corporate charters don't require broadcasters to disseminate information. The job of broadcasters is to maximize profit for stockholders.

Today, our great information infrastructures have little that is meaningful to say. Endless channels repeat the same twenty minutes of news and television in an endless search for content. Reruns perpetually recycle and nations borrow and copy formats of shows like *Who Wants to be a Millionaire* and *Wheel of Fortune* from each other. There is too much signal, which leads to audience fragmentation and as audiences shrink the shows get cheaper and cheaper. No one wants to invest a huge budget in a show that is unlikely to garner much of an audience share. So we get shows without scripts or actors. Complex narrative drama is replaced by cheap thrills on reality shows and gross talk formats. Reflection and ideas give way to crass impulses, to efforts to assuage macabre curiosity about fighting families, drug addicts, hoarders, pregnant teens, Roseanne Barr's macadamia nut farm (on the not-so-subtly named *Roseanne's Nuts*), people drinking concoctions of blended worms and cockroaches, and svelte, barely clad youths trying to unlock themselves before they drown in submerged Plexiglas coffins. Even if a profound statement should be made on one of the channels, it is likely to be lost in the clutter of sensational visuals. As the world gives way to capitalism and multiplying channels launched by the profit motive, success breeds endless imitation.

The homogenization of culture globally has left no corner of the world untouched by marketplace values. The world is shrinking not just in communicative distance, but in creative breadth. Initially, wiring the world brought people in touch with a plenitude of different cultures. But as the system matures, cultures are going extinct as commodity culture spreads with global marketing. The world's communication infrastructure is being built by and for commercial messaging. All of the various experiments that have solved the common survival needs of people around the world, all of the different solutions or cultures are being reduced to a handful of types. The consequence is a drastic collapse in the semantic richness of cultural diversity, a dramatic decrease in linguistic, religious, political, pedagogical, aesthetic, and economic systems.[39] The communicative sphere of humanity is being reduced, which, on one hand, makes communication more uniform and easy, but on the other involves the vanquishing of entire cosmologies, value systems, languages, epistemologies, spiritual faiths, and the like. In 1999, the last television-free nation, Bhutan, entered the television age after introducing Rupert Murdoch's Star TV network, enabling people to watch Western programs like *Baywatch*. Following this, *Kuensel* Editor Kinley Dorji (Bhutan's only newspaper) lamented:

> Bhutan has always been an oral society, therefore especially vulnerable to the media. This is a society where the family depended on the grandfather's stories, the oral tradition of communication. Suddenly this family has 24 channels to watch. . . . television is having a direct impact on our culture, which is the basis of Bhutan's identity. I mean the impact on the language, the impact on the dress . . . consumerism coming in, the materialistic value coming in.[40]

This kind of cultural exposure is often celebrated, until one realizes that it's direction is almost entirely one way unless the local population intervenes somehow. No one is watching Bhutanese shows—not even the Bhutanese. The colonial ambition begins at its origin in various European variants from Spain to Great Britain, and today finds its greatest proponent in their progeny, the United States of America. From the extermination of hundreds of indigenous cultures to the institutionalization of slavery, the New World continues as a cultural and linguistic "steamroller"[41] on its march of manifest destiny.

NOTES

1. "Smothers Feels 'A Lot of Pain' Over FCC Skirmish," *Chattanooga Times Free Press*, April 24, 2004.

2. John Dewey, *Democracy and Education* (New York: Macmillan, 1916), 5.

3. Doug Halonen, "'MNF' Next Indecency Target," *Television Week*, November 22, 2004, 1.

4. "Part 1—Frank Zappa at PMRC Senate Hearing on Rock Lyrics," video, 1985, YouTube, accessed November 26, 2011, www.youtube.com/watch?v=lxB-ZePpS7E.

5. Gavin Edwards, "Larry the Cable Guy Bared," *Rolling Stone*, March 11, 2008.

6. Larry the Cable Guy, *Git-R-Done* (New York: Three Rivers Press, 2006), 87.

7. David Cross, "David Cross—On Open Letter to Larry the Cable Guy (1 of 2)," video, 2009, accessed November 26, 2011, www.youtube.com/watch?v=DDimQTJMjB0.

8. Josh Meyrowtz, *No Sense of Place: The Impact of Electronic Media on Social Behavior* (New York: Oxford University Press, 1985).

9. Travis Reed, "Study: NFL Has Slightly More Latino, Asian Players," *USA Today*, August 27, 2008.

10. Shirley MacLaine, *My Lucky Stars: A Hollywood Memoir* (New York: Bantam, 1996).

11. Other advertiser considerations are also taken into consideration, such as excluding information from broadcast that may alienate advertisers.

12. Erik Barnouw, *A Tower in Babel* (New York: Oxford University Press, 1966).

13. John Mitavalli, "PBS Facing Crisis," *Television Week*, October 20, 2003, 1.

14. "Nielsen Television (TV) Ratings: Network Primetime Averages," Zap2it, accessed November 26, 2011, mserv.zap2it.com/tv/ratings/network/.

15. Robert Dahl, *A Preface to Democratic Theory* (Chicago: University of Chicago Press 2006).

16. Dahl, *A Preface to Democratic Theory*.

17. Alexander Hamilton, James Madison, and John Jay, *The Federalist Papers* (New York: SoHo Press, 2011).

18. Howard Zinn, *A People's History of the United States: 1492–Present* (New York: Harper Perennial Modern Classics, 2005), 90–91.

19. Charlie Rose, *An Hour with Mel Karmazin*, televised interview, recorded October 10, 2007.

20. Dean Batali, *Behind the Screen*, eds. Barbara Nicolosi and Spencer Lewerenz (Grand Rapids, MI: Baker Books, 2005), 13.

21. Robert Seidman, *Monday Cable*, August 16, 2011, accessed November 25, 2011, tvbythenumbers.zap2it.com/.

22. Michael Norman, "TV's Arsenio Hall: Late-Night Cool," *New York Times*, October 1, 1989.

23. Brian Lowry, "Tuning In," *Variety*, August 21, 2005, 14.

24. Herbert Gans, *Popular Culture and High Culture* (New York: Basic Books, 1999), 91.

25. Jason Brennan, *The Ethics of Voting* (Princeton NJ: Princeton University Press, 2011), 2.

26. Jean-Jacques Rousseau, *The Social Contract and Discourses by Jean-Jacques Rousseau*, trans. G. D. H. Cole (Toronto: J. M. Dent and Sons, 1923), 94.

27. Gans, *Popular Culture and High Culture*.

28. Erik Barnouw, *A Tower in Babel* (New York: Oxford University Press, 1966), 128–33.

29. See Christopher Stern, "Court Ends 'Fairness Doctrine,'" *Washington Post*, October 12, 2000.

30. John Cloud, "Ms. Right," *Time*, April 17, 2005.

31. Barnouw, *A Tower in Babel*, 86.

32. See Richard Huff "It's Howard, Raw and Ready" *New York Daily News*, December 11, 2005, and Joana Weiss "With Fewer Limits, Will Stern Still Have a Shtick?" *Boston Globe*, December 11, 2005.

33. Newton Minow, "Television and the Public Interest," American Rhetoric, accessed November 26, 2011, www.americanrhetoric.com/speeches/newtonminow.htm.

34. Charlie Rose, *An Hour with Jeff Zucker*, televised interview, recorded December 2, 2010.

35. John Eggerton, "FCC: Telepictures Productions' TMZ is a News Program," *Broadcasting & Cable*, May 2, 2008.

36. Eggerton, "FCC: Telepictures Productions' TMZ is a News Program."

37. *The Corporation*, DVD, directed by Jennifer Abbot and Mark Akbar (New York: Zeitgeist Films, 2005).

38. Mark Fowler and Daniel Brenner, "A Marketplace Approach to Broadcast Regulation," *Texas Law Review* 207 (60): 1–51.

39. E. Kramer, *The Emerging Monoculture: Assimilation and the "Model Minority"* (Westport, CT: Praeger, 2003).

40. "Bhutan—The Last Place," *Frontline*, aired May 1, 2002.

41. Jared Diamond, *The Third Chimpanzee* (New York: Perennial 1992).

Conclusion: Our Age of Cynicism

> The first man who, having enclosed a piece of ground, bethought himself of saying this is mine, and found people simple enough to believe him, was the real founder of civil society.

—Jean Jacques-Rousseau, 1754, *Discourse on Inequality*[1]

Landowners advocate for private-property rights, knowing full well their property was stolen from Native Americans. Many rich heirs perpetuate the myth that wealth is the product of hard work. Our government continues its charade of popular support, parading the president down Pennsylvania Avenue, for instance, while the road is lined shoulder-to-shoulder with police officers and the president is encased in an explosion-proof limousine with "five-inch thick bulletproof glass, ultra high strength ceramic armor and cellphone jammers."[2] We are awash in deception. In our present communication environment, facts have little currency. There seems to be agreement that what is true, what is evidenced, what is reasonable, particularly among those who inhabit the world's superstructure, doesn't entirely matter. Our elites function knowingly inside of paradigms or ideologies they know are incommensurable with reality—ideologies they don't even agree with. These people, including ourselves, exist throughout society: labor, leadership, ownership, secular, religious—everyone. Resigned to functioning inside of the ideological systems handed down to us, we cynically make them work. And in doing so, we allow nonsensical messages in advertising, politics, and radio and in other areas to permeate our communities. We believe that doing so is pragmatic, even economical. This version of pragmatism, which enables coarse expression to dominate our world, the symbolic field that is our culture, is the core of cynical regard.

We maintain that our communication has become coarse because the limits of what many of us are willing to express publicly lie at the boundary of what benefits the self. The attitude of cynicism is so prevalent that people find it difficult to voluntarily sacrifice the achievement of their own ends in order to comply with master narratives that are perceived as old fashioned, naively altruistic, or bogus. Meanwhile, they willingly and strategically propagate other master narratives in the marketplace of ideas if doing so enhances the bottom line. Our beliefs and passions have been reduced to mere chess pieces. People transcending the morals and ethics of our paradigms are the players. To them, rules no longer matter unless they get to write them. The rules elites have devised for governing our culture bear the stamp of Jeremy Bentham's "hedonic calculus," doing what is in our own best interest in pursuit of pleasure or pain avoidance. Our communication culture conditions us to pursue our self-interests, an imperative predicated on absolute private-property rights. Bentham termed community a "fictitious body" and relationships between people as "fictitious entities."[3] Politicians, artists, pastors, and entertainers are the tip of the iceberg as far as the cultural prevalence of egoistic hedonism is concerned, but each is central to our society's superstructure. These actors play a central role in shaping our culture, and in so doing have a tremendous impact on how U.S. citizens communicate.

Our culture's hedonism might cause one to ask what the liberals have done to us. We remarked at the start of this book that the folks running our entertainment industry are not among the liberal elite. They are corporatists. They are capitalists. They seek to make money, not smut and violence. It just so happens that many find that in order to make the former they must produce the latter. And the smut and the violence have to outdraw everything else in the marketplace. The changes in our society can hardly be attributed to our politically liberal elements. Yes, liberals are the ones who upset master narratives, criticizing religion, government, and stodgy conventions. But it's today's self-billed conservatives who've given a full embrace to this liberalization, in the spirit of free-market liberalization.

Bentham's hedonic calculus is a self-fulfilling prophecy that states if we all pursue our own interests somehow rationality will prevail; reasonability will spontaneously emerge as a synthetic outcome. This notion is repeated in George Homan's notion of Exchange Theory whereby every action and every decision we take is based on an intuitive cost-benefit analysis from our personal point of view.[4] As soon as I perceive that my marriage, my business partnership, or a friendship is costing me more than it benefits me, I dump it and move on. This is the Homanian version of pragmatic calculus. It also shows up in various versions of Social Darwinism or Spencerianism.

Though our culture conveys selfishness as a universal law of human behavior, we submit that these are expressions of a contingent time and place—us, right now: a modern, individualistic worldview that is culture-bound and that does not adequately explain all human behavior. It is cynicism perpetuated and reified by our coarseness. The hedonic calculus is less an explanation than an ideological justification for greed, a justification that seeks to naturalize greed and selfishness. That which is accepted as natural becomes universally true and beyond debate. It is senseless to argue with positive fact, with objective reality, with the nature of things. But this we argue is a rhetorical sleight of hand at the metaphysical level. The claim that greed is neither good nor bad but inevitable because it is our nature needs to be tested against the facts of altruistic acts and the widely recognized phenomenon of true sacrifice for a greater good.

Sometimes, in fact very often, it is better for a person to lose if a s/he can see things from a larger or different perspective. Sometimes people compromise and give up personal advantage even when it really does hurt because they believe it is the right thing to do. Humans, unlike any other animal, live in a semantic field. Culture is passed on from generation to generation via symbolic interaction. Culture, unlike instinct, can be lost and it must be interpreted. Unlike other animals we do not merely adapt to our environment but we project desires and needs and adapt the environment to those desires and needs. We dam rivers, move mountains, travel into the vacuum of outer space and to the bottom of oceans. We live in all environments and battle natural forces such as disease. We are the artifact maker. We are artificial in our efforts to bend nature to our wills.

The refusal to recognize that some people go out of their way to help others, that they choose to leave comfortable lives behind and travel to areas of great human suffering and that they do so not out of personal gain but as a sense of resolve and moral duty demonstrates to us a failure of the Benthamite's imagination. Just because he or she cannot imagine someone actually choosing to endure hardship that really does bring little pleasure or satisfaction is not an objective observation of that person, but instead a clear expression of the limits of the Benthamite's imagination. The Benthamite's description of the world tells me less about the "objective" world than it does about the Benthamite's ideology. Pragmatism of an egoistic variety has had great currency because it appeals to our darker nature but not our *entire* nature. And it utterly fails to explain our constant efforts to curb our appetites and discipline ourselves. It justifies our selfish tendencies with pseudo-scientific "Enlightenment" arguments. But it fails to accurately and adequately explain unselfish behavior that we see every day.

In fact, we agree with the primatologist and "human watcher" Desmond Morris that such an explanation for human interaction utterly fails to explain how we succeeded as a species.[5] We agree with Morris that it has been and continues to be our extraordinary ability to sacrifice for the group and to cooperate that has enabled each of us individuals to survive. The human capacity for complex communication has enabled us to coordinate and cooperate, thus enabling us to flourish. The notion of the "lone wolf" human who is so swift and strong as to be "self-made" and self-sufficient in all ways is the real myth here. Simply the fact that humans take so long to mature to a point where they might be viable on their own proves that community is necessary for our species' survival.

But this too is cynically interpreted as selfishness by the Benthamites. We care for our young so that they will carry our personal genes into the future, or so say population geneticists George Price and W. D. Hamilton. But what then of adoption? Cynical pragmatism literally regards altruism as a myth and so society is portrayed as a Hobbesian aggregate of individuals constantly elbowing each other for bits of wealth and status. To the Benthamite, sacrifice is not only stupid; it is regarded as being nonexistent. All behavior it is argued is actually self-centered egoism. Even when a soldier throws him/herself on a hand grenade to save his/her comrades, the Benthamite will argue that it is because s/he gets personal satisfaction from knowing s/he will be elevated to hero status and/or that s/he will feel good for knowing that s/he preserved lives s/he covets and cherishes. Or it's out of pure precognitive reaction due to military drilling—a war reflex. According to this hypertrophic individualism, all of society is held together and functions out of pure egoistic drives and competition. Cooperation, compromise, and sacrifice are all defined as either veiled manifestations of selfish interest pursued through deferred gratification or as nonexistent. Bentham's hedonic calculus emerged along with advanced capitalism. It is a facet of our particular time and place. Cynicism naturalizes inequality by arguing that it is either the inherent talent of some to be more able than others to accumulate wealth or that inequality is due to individual effort, that the rich simply work much harder than everyone else. But such naturalizing ideologies, mythmaking in the service of inequality, is cynical because we should all know better—and many elites do. We know the history of tyranny and of resistance to it. Facts may be inconvenient for the naturalizing justification for greed and inequality, but they stubbornly persist as the truth of many histories

CYNICISM AND SELF INTEREST

The abandonment of codes, creeds, or ideologies that prescribe selfless, altruistic behavior is cynicism. Perhaps what we know to be right and wrong is easily compartmentalized, dependent upon the various contexts in which we find ourselves during our day: work, home, in public. Maybe we can switch right and wrong off and on. Or we rationalize that what produces profit helps everyone with jobs and tax revenue. This attitude toward ideology Peter Sloterdijk terms "cynicism," describing it as inclining cynics toward being unaffected "by any critique of ideology."[6] In *The Critique of Cynical Reason* Sloterdijk argues that the enlightenment and critical theory once functioned to moderate the excesses of dominant ideologies, but that today even those who benefit most from our dominant ideologies are aware of the problems inherent in these ideologies. Instead of balking, however, we cynically participate in and perpetuate them. Harry Frankfurt terms this approach to truth "bullshit," writing:

> The contemporary proliferation of bullshit also has deeper sources, in various forms of skepticism which deny that we can have any reliable access to an objective reality and which therefore reject the possibility of knowing how things truly are. These "anti-realist" doctrines undermine confidence in the value of disinterested efforts to determine what is true and what is false, and even in the intelligibility of the notion of objective inquiry. One response to this loss of confidence has been a retreat from the discipline required by dedication to the ideal of *correctness.*[7]

Capitalists know, for instance, that unrestrained industrialism is harming the planet. Few of these capitalists counter Glenn Beck, who provides for them a wonderfully cynical service for industry with his obfuscations about global warming, for instance. About global-warming science, Beck argues God "created the rules. He is the ultimate scientist. He will play by his rules."[8] Precisely what that means is unclear, but it provides solace for those who find human culpability regarding climate change difficult to accept. Beck is rewarded as a member of the plutocracy's mindguard, an agent of refeudalization. Other examples of bullshit, puffery, and cynicism abound throughout this book. If Sloterdijk is right about our willing complicity in the cynical perpetuation of problematic ideologies, how do we find the limits of our participation? If we collectively agree that spinning bullshit is how the world goes around, then when do we tell the truth? What's the limit?

Today's cynicism instructs us that there are no limits. The ego is the measure of all things, and we've been led to believe it is boundless. Egoism has even co-opted sacrifice and altruism. "Sacrifice," we are taught today, is what one does to earn money and to someday enter the community of the rich that that will be set free of obligation once it "arrives." If I sacrifice now by demanding little, I'll have to give little when I get there. But it is cynical because the "sacrifice," the willingness to endure hardship and fight one's way to the top while not "punishing" those who have already made it, is pure egoism. It suggests that, "when I make it to the top, I don't want proportional obligation." It is hypertrophic individualism posited as human nature. Expect no help. Give none to others. And when you achieve unequal power and wealth expect freedom . . . freedom from obligation and duty to others. This is the essence of the dog-eat-dog culture. But as we notice if we care to be honest, in fact, dog packs and wolf packs are very communicative, very cooperative, and socially supportive. They do *not* eat each other. And it is the natural role and responsibility of their elites, their Alphas, to protect the pack, to lead the charge against external threats and to defend the weak from undue and excessive abuse by other stronger dogs, not languish behind in luxury. The appeal to dogs fails utterly to justify human upon human abuse. It is a cynical trope. Rather, dogs, which have coevolved with humans for thousands of years, reflect our truer nature of cooperation and social support. The hedonic calculus of the Benthamites and Randians is a narrow ideology popular only in postindustrial Western and Westernizing societies that stress affectively neutral instrumental relationships over expressive organic relationships that actually characterized human interaction for millions of years.

THE COMPLICITY OF CONTEMPORARY CONSERVATIVE ELITES

Rather than attribute public coarseness to a general breakdown of master narratives, we assert that the proliferation of coarseness is propelled by contemporary conservative hedonism that some have promoted as remedies to the "flawed" and "naïve" philosophies and theologies of the past (e.g., Christianity). Social Darwinism and Randianism are two philosophical perspectives that are implicitly and explicitly trumpeted by today's conservatives. Both are supposedly grounded in natural human tendencies, and place pursuit and fulfillment of the individuals' needs as desires above social and government correctives to inequities and human suffering. Social Darwinism valorizes survival of the weak over the strong. Randianism celebrates society's successful over those less so. Morality from the standpoints of both is gauged according to whether behaviors foster competition and accede to its outcomes. Ultimately, Randianism is a version of Social Darwinism that reduces success to measurable units—dollars. Truth equals financial winners over financial losers.

While it may be a bit simplistic to do so, we draw a distinction between what we term "contemporary conservatives" (including Randian conservatives and those leaning toward libertarianism) and "Christian conservatives" (those who believe government possesses a legitimate role in enforcing the wishes of a perceived moral majority). As we consider morality with regard to public coarseness, we draw a distinction between contemporary conservatives and both Christian and traditional conservatives (Burkean conservatives), suggesting that while each qualifies as conservative inasmuch as each views the roles of governments and citizens according to a transcendental truth, contemporary conservatives appear to take no moral stance with respect to truthful expression.

Plato argued for the existence and pursuit of transcendental truth in much the way contemporary U.S. conservatives do—or claim to. Plato believed that *true* reality was composed of forms that weren't readily available to mortals. Humans, limited to earthly knowledge and ways of knowing, couldn't perceive "true" reality. The material world humans experience is but an imperfect version of the true reality. Plato's distinction between material and nonmaterial reality (or forms) not only contributed to Christianity's heaven–earth duality, but it was the precursor for Rene Descartes' mind–body duality. Descartes explained that human perceptions were deceptive, and that truth could only be accessed by rational contemplation.

This theoretical division between the less perfect perceived material reality, and perfect form lays much of the ground for what is called conservatism today. There is a truth, so the perspective maintains, and political order should follow it, or at least not impede it. As noted in chapter 7, this truth is in many instances the so-called "general will." Edmund Burke, the father of modern conservatism, explains this distinction between subjective desires and the more objectively determined *true* general will:

> Parliament is not a *congress* of ambassadors from different and hostile interests, which interests each must maintain, as an agent and advocate, against other agents and advocates; Parliament is a *deliberative* assembly of *one* nation, with *one* interest—that of the whole—where not local purposes, not local prejudices, ought to guide, but the general good, resulting from the general reason of the whole. You choose a member, indeed; but when you have chosen him, he is not a member of Bristol, but he is a member of *Parliament*.[9]

According to Burke, those determining the general will were to be exceptional men. For Plato too, governing according to popular preference is harmful. Here, Plato has Socrates criticize Callicles in *The Gorgias*:

> When you say something in the assembly, if the Athenian populace denies that it's the case, you turn around and say what *it* wants [emphasis added].[10]

Philosopher kings, according to Plato, were the only ones familiar enough with the knowledge of proper forms to govern Plato's utopia, a prescriptive arrangement of the ideal society.[11]

Contemporary conservatives also brand themselves champions of moderate living. Look at the rhetoric of any GOP candidate for public office, and the notion that individuals as well as government should live within its means is prominent. It seems on its face that this firm principle is consistent with Plato's suggestion that people practice moderation, run from self-indulgence, and that discipline results in happiness. These ideas are also consistent with Christian conservatism. In important ways, however, today's conservatives break from Plato and with their own rhetoric of moderation. The only moderation today's conservatives promote is government moderation, as small government, they explain, should get out of the way of the free market. This, Ronald Reagan instructed, is what "unleash[es] the energy and individual genius of man."

When government gets out of the way, so far as contemporary conservative rhetoric goes, liberty thrives. Liberty is a term that is central in all conservative political rhetoric. Reagan preached that, "As government expands, liberty contracts." Former Massachusetts Governor Mitt Romney has said of liberty, "Americans acknowledge that liberty is a gift of God, not an indulgence of government."[12] But what does liberty mean? It's a word with significant ideographic meaning, but it's rare that people explain precisely what constitutes it. Richard Sennett defines liberty as "opposed to the idea of convention as public order."[13] He explains in *The Fall of Public Man* that as the principle of natural self-moderation is displaced, it is the individual personality that takes its place. The ego less restrained by convention and moderation becomes hypertrophic.

Yet, upholding convention is a centerpiece of traditional conservatism. Adherence to form, be it religious or traditional form, are from where we derive the virtues that Burke argued prevent folly, vice, and madness.[14] These traditional values include, but are not limited to marriage before sex, avoiding birth control, worship, eschewing divorce, and respect for various hierarchies. How can a political perspective that values liberty be the perspective that advocates adherence to traditional values? How are those two positions commensurable?

We don't intend to suggest that any major political party has a monolithic and consistent political philosophy. It's not possible, and it isn't necessarily desirable. Yet, we argue that a central, though all too unexamined, element of contemporary conservatism is a platonic universal that holds that the needs and desires of the self are the measure of all things good. It is always the case that what is in the interest of everybody is revealed in the self-interested consumption behaviors of an aggregate of the individuals, provided enough consumers make such consumption profitable. It has the appeal of being a platonic principle that is inductively grounded, though strangely situationally dependent. In the face of collapsing metanarratives, conservatives have adopted the hedonic calculus as an empirical-seeming moral, ethical, and legislative compass—Randian Objectivism (Randianism). Ayn Rand, author of *Atlas Shrugged*, describes her philosophy of objectivism this way:

> My philosophy, in essence, is the concept of man as a heroic being, with his own happiness as the moral purpose of his life, with productive achievement as his noblest activity, and reason as his only absolute.[15]

Rhetoric such as this, prevalent throughout conservatism today, functions to reconcile the values of liberty and tradition; doing whatever you want has become the tradition. With the founders elevated to flawless and god-like beings and the Declaration of Independence doubling as governing "scripture," conservatives cast today's United States as in a struggle between those who'd compromise the founders' true intent and those brave enough to return us to the halcyon days. The enemy of the traditional United States are billed as those who'd use and enlarge the public treasury (i.e., "tax . . .") to solve public problems (i.e., ". . . and spend").

Randian conservatism is more than that. Ayn Rand's books promote liberty through choice, free markets, and limited government. Kentucky Senator Rand Paul recently shared a synopsis of her book *Anthem*, which illustrates these themes, during a hearing of the House of Representatives' Energy and Natural Resource Committee, suggesting that government involvement in the energy industry would necessarily harm innovation.[16] Conservative Supreme Court Justice Clarence Thomas has cited it as one of his favorite books.[17] William F. Buckley Jr. included former Federal Reserve Chairman Allan Greenspan among Rand's devotees:

> Every Saturday in New York . . . she met with her collective, ha ha "collective," ha ha, she was very anti-collectivist, . . . and they included Allan Greenspan . . . he was a devotee, a young economist, just bullwhipped by this lady and her philosophy.[18]

Stephen Moore, *Wall Street Journal* columnist, wrote in 2009 that familiarity with *Atlas Shrugged* would help the Obama administration find our way out of our economic quagmire, perhaps, by encouraging it to abolish the income tax.[19]

Ayn Rand's philosophy, which she terms "objectivism," bears a striking resemblances to Karl Marx's historical materialism, only with important differences with regard to economic class. Harkening to the dualisms mentioned above, Rand maintains that there exists a distinction between reality and consciousness. Unlike Marx, who argued that consciousness blinded people to the inequitable realities of material distribution, Rand maintained that collectivist mythologies (e.g., socialism, altruism, communism, liberalism) obscure people's understanding of reality. To make sure that our perceptions are consistent with reality, one must accept that what one knows is known only through the senses. Behaviorally, this amounts to the prescription that one behave in his/her own rational self-interest. Government consistent with this imperative is nonintrusive. It is small and enables free choice. The economic system that ensures the exercise and reward for self-interested action, she instructs in *The Virtue of Selfishness*, is "full, pure, uncontrolled, unregulated laissez-faire capitalism."[20]

Randianism advocates the abandonment of the Hobbesian social contract, which necessitated self-interested *cooperation*. Hobbes maintained that any government was ideal to no government, or return to humanity's natural state. The natural state, or the "condition of mere nature," he explained in *Leviathan*, was atomistic; in it judgment is private, there is no authority, no means for resolving disputes or enforcing decision. He warned:

> Where every man is enemy to every man. . . . [there is] no arts; no letters; no
> society; and which is worst of all, continual fear, and danger of violent death,
> and the life of man, solitary, poor, nasty, brutish and short.[21]

Hobbes' vision of social atomism is in any way recognizable to traditional conservative appeals for adherence to convention, powerful central government, and moderation.

The centerpiece of Rand's ideas, rational self-interest, puts her in direct confrontation with traditional conservative values of moderation and self-sacrifice. These values, which for many align conservatism with Western history's archetypal self-sacrificing figure Jesus Christ, contrast starkly with Ayn Rand's. In 1957 Whittaker Chambers published his review in *The National Review* criticizing the book, "From almost any page of *Atlas Shrugged*, a voice can be heard, from painful necessity, commanding: "To a gas chamber—go!"[22] He goes on:

> Like any consistent materialism, this one begins by rejecting God, religion,
> original sin, etc. etc. (This book's aggressive atheism and rather unbuttoned
> "higher morality," which chiefly outrage some readers, are, in fact, secondary
> ripples, and result inevitably from its underpinning premises.) Thus, Randian
> Man, like Marxian Man, is made the center of a godless world.

Hardly the stuff of Christian conservatism. In her essay *Philosophy: Who Needs It* she states, "The purpose of morality is to teach you, not to suffer and die, but to enjoy yourself and live."[23] It's no surprise, then, that Christianity created dissonance for Rand. She couldn't reconcile the Christian notion of the soul's "inviolate sanctity" with Jesus's code for altruism.[24]

In addition to its problems with Christianity, Rand's rational self-interest has problems with reality. Instead of being objective, it is a metaphysic: a self-fulfilling prophecy little different than Bentham's hedonic calculus or Homan's Exchange Theory. And these ideas are being used for predictive and prescriptive purposes in public deliberation, instructing that the outcome of government action in the economy will necessarily produce harms—regardless of the circumstances or the action taken. Today, policy makers are evaluating elaborate policies based upon the moral of a fifty-year-old novel? Chambers fretted in his review of the use of such a story for this purpose:

It is when a system of materialist ideas presumes to give positive answers to real problems of our real life that mischief starts. In an age like ours, in which a highly complex technological society is everywhere in a high state of instability, such answers, however philosophic, translate quickly into political realities. [25]

Taken to its logical end, reliance on stories like this renders deliberative public argument meaningless and evidence-based decision making obsolete. The actual philosophy functions to short circuit careful consideration in democratic deliberative forums, in favor of rule by free-market exchange. Randianism fails to consider whether the unbounded pursuit of self-interest is rational in the first place or has consequences on a society's capacity overall capacity to reason well. The desire, capacity, and willingness to reason is not a constant. It is dependent upon a society's willingness to foster it.

THE THIRD SOPHISTIC

In November of 2011 Republican presidential candidate Mitt Romney ran an ad in New Hampshire quoting President Barack Obama saying, "If we keep talking about the economy, we're going to lose." The quotation was, in fact, clipped from a video of Obama quoting an operative of his *opponent* Senator John McCain in 2008. The defense of the ad was described in the online news website Politico:

> None of that bothers Romney media strategist Stuart Stevens, who needled the Obama camp for what he called an overreaction to "a small buy on one station in New Hampshire." "It is now my goal for every ad we make to so upset the White House that they will force Jay to go out with his light saber and do his thing," Stevens said in an email, pointing out that Democrats have been more than willing to target his candidate in harsh terms. [26]

There's no defense, just a rationale. The writer of the piece follows suit; Alexander Burns adds, "The ultimate judgment on attacks like this one comes from the voters, who will end up deciding whether they're more persuaded by Romney's economy-themed blast, or by Obama's sharp, character-focused retort." [27] Truth be damned. Crossroads GPS (Grassroots Policy Strategies), a 501(c)(4) nonprofit corporation not required to disclose donor information and advised by Karl Rove, recently had a political ad removed from the air for simply making up a bill out of thin air that, it claimed, its target voted for. [28] Alex Pareene responded in *Salon.com*,

> Rove has, it seems, realized that you don't even have to base your attacks ad
> on something that actually happened. You don't need to take something out of
> context. You can just make up whatever attack you want! [29]

What's right, wrong, good, bad boils down to aggregate response; a swarm of "me"s and "I"s expressing judgment through a marketplace exercise.

The problems that Plato and Augustine of Hippo had with sophistry are minor compared to what we outline in this book both in terms of its cavalier attitude toward truth and because of the potential severity of its consequences. The Third Sophistic, the age into which we propose we've entered, goes well beyond the embrace of contingent truths (relativism) and manipulative persuasion (the separation of eloquence from wisdom) that characterized other historic sophistical periods. We are in an age of coarseness, which consists of willful deception. It goes beyond Frankfurt's bullshit to flat out lying. This is hypertrophic egoism posing as democracy, and its consequences reach beyond Habermas's refeudalization. This disequilibriating period of overconsumption will prove to be a short phase of extravagant luxury affordable only in a time and place of unprecedented abundance, an abundance accompanied by population explosion and accomplished by industrial scale exploitation of natural resources, such as wild fish protein and aquifers of ancient fresh water, that are fast being depleted. The greed of today will run into the true natural barriers of scarcity tomorrow. A time of great conflict will occur as the exhausted and invalid ideology of hypertrophic individualism struggles to endure in the face of mounting inequality until equilibrium with the natural environment is reestablished and our true natural fit within the environment is resumed. Either we as a species will return to our true natural equilibrium or we will cease to be because the carrying capacity of the biosphere has real limits. The inertia of culture, the enduring quality of tradition and habit, in this case of a culture of hypertrophic individualism that, as Jean Gebser put it, "manifests on the one hand an egocentric individualism exaggerated to extremes and desirous of possessing everything . . . a hyper-valuation of the individual who, despite his [sic] limitations, is permitted everything,"[30] and on the other a "collectivism" distorted by individualism into a mere aggregate, a churning mass of competing individuals will run into the very real limits of sustainability that will make it absurd, utterly illogical given the actual parameters of reality. The bullshit of today is that this level of egocentrism is desirable and sustainable. Whether one ascribe to pure hedonic calculus or belief in altruism is irrelevant. The larger facticity is that the current culture of hypertrophic individualism is unsustainable and this is the ultimate absurdity of arguments that cynically claim otherwise.

When we know this but choose to ignore it then we are abusing ourselves with cynicism . . . we are denying our own awareness for purely affective (irrational) ends. Such willful ignoring is a form of self-imposed ignorance and it is often tolerated by punting, by, as Glenn Beck so ably demonstrated, fatalistically surrendering to imaginary supernatural powers. It is the height of bad conscience of refusing to take responsibility for one's self. It is the cynical side of individualism. This is the essence of the Third Sophistic. It is self-denial of the self and its authentic responsibility. It is the childish desire to be free but have no responsibility. And as we've demonstrated, it is a culture-wide belief and value system propagated through the most powerful systems of communication ever devised.

NOTES

1. Jean-Jacques Rousseau, *Discourse on Inequality*, trans. G. D. H. Cole (Whitefish, MT: Kessinger Publishing, 2004), 41.

2. Wes Siler, "Obama's New Cadillac Limo Officially Unveiled," Jalopnik, January 14, 2009, jalopnik.com/5131380/obamas-new-cadillac-limo-officially-unveiled.

3. Jeremy Bentham, *An Introduction to the Principles of Morals and Legislation* (Oxford: Oxford University Press, 2005).

4. George Homans, "Social Behavior as Exchange." *American Journal of Sociology* 63 (1958): 597–606.

5. Desmond Morris, *The Human Zoo* (New York: Kodansha International, 1969/1996).

6. Peter Sloterdijk, *Critique of Cynical Reason* (Minneapolis: University of Minnesota Press, 2001), 5.

7. Harry Frankfurt, *On Bullshit* (Princeton, NJ: Princeton University Press, 2005).

8. "Beck and Pat: Scientists May Be Wrong on Global Warming Because God 'Is the Ultimate Scientist,'" Media Matters, August 22, 2011, mediamatters.org/mmtv/201108220013.

9. Edmond Burke, *Select Works of Edmund Burke* (Indianapolis: Liberty Fund, 1999).

10. Plato, *Plato Gorgias and Aristotle Rhetoric*, trans. Joe Sachs (Newburyport, MA: Focus Publishing, 2009).

11. Plato, *Plato: Complete Works*, ed. John M. Cooper (Indianapolis: Hacket Publishing Company, 1997).

12. Mitt Romney, "Transcript: Mitt Romney's Faith Speech," National Public Radio, December 6, 2007, www.npr.org/templates/story/story.php?storyId=16969460.

13. Richard Sennett, *The Fall of Public Man* (New York: Alfred A Knopf, 1977), 105.

14. Burke, *Select Works of Edmund Burke*.

15. Ayn Rand, *Atlas Shrugged* (New York: Plume, 1999).

16. Eric Kleefeld, "Rand Paul Gives Lesson in Ayn Rand and Light Bulbs" TPM, April 12, 2011, tpmdc.talkingpointsmemo.com/2011/04/rand-paul-gives-senate-lesson-in-ayn-rand-and-light-bulbs-video.php.

17. Clarence Thomas, *My Grandfather's Son* (New York: HarperCollins, 2007).

18. "William Buckley on Ayn Rand & Atlas Shrugged," YouTube, accessed November 30, 2011, www.youtube.com/watch?v=5KmPLkiqnO8.

19. Stephen Moore, "'Atlas Shrugged': From Fiction to Fact in 52 Years," *Wall Street Journal*, January 9, 2009, online.wsj.com/article/SB123146363567166677.html.

20. Ayn Rand, *The Virtue of Selfishness* (New York: Signet, 1964).

21. Thomas Hobbes, *Leviathan* (London: Greed Dragon in St Paul's Church-yard, 1651), 78.

22. Whittaker Chambers, "Big Sister Is Watching You," *National Review*, October 12, 2007, www.nationalreview.com/articles/222482/big-sister-watching-you/flashback.

23. Ayn Rand, "A Defense of Ethical Egoism," in *Moral Philosophy*, ed. Louis Pojman (Indianapolis: Hacket Publishing Company, 2003), 74.

24. Ayn Rand, *Letters of Ayn Rand*, ed. Michael Berliner (New York: Plume, 1995), 287.

25. Chambers, "Big Sister is Watching You."

26. Alexander Burns, "Top Mitt Romney, Barack Obama Strategists Spar over Ad," Politico, November 23, 2011, www.politico.com/news/stories/1111/69047.html.

27. Burns, "Top Mitt Romney, Barack Obama Strategists Spar over Ad."

28. "Conservative Attack Ad Pulled Amid Concerns It Falsely Accuses Tester over EPA Farm Dust Rules," *The Republic*, last modified November 11, 2011, accessed December 5, 2011, www.therepublic.com/view/story/19478e87c8b44b2ea0f5e7e3ddbb8776/MT--Tester-Attack-Ad/.

29. Alex Pareene, "Karl Rove Spending Millions Lying About Everyone," Salon, last modified November 12, 2011, accessed December 5, 2011, www.salon.com/topic/crossroads_gps/.

30. Jean Gebser, *The Ever-Present Origin*, trans. Algis Mickunas (Athens: Ohio University Press, 1985).

Bibliography

Abrams v. U.S., 250 U.S. 616 (1919).

Alterman, Eric. "Out of Print: The Death and Life of the American Newspaper. *New Yorker*, March 2008, 48.

"American Democracy in an Age of Rising Inequality." Report by the American Political Science Association, 2004.

"Americans Have Commitment Issues." Barna Group. www.barna.org/barna-update/article/13-culture/155-americans-have-commitment-issues-new-survey-shows (accessed August 12, 2009).

"American Individualism Shines Through in People's Self Image." Barna Group. www.barna.org/culture-articles/99-american-individualism-shines-through-in-peoples-self-image (accessed August 12, 2009).

"Anderson Cooper 360." CNN. February 16, 2010. archives.cnn.com/TRANSCRIPTS/1002/16/acd/01/html (accessed February 18, 2012).

Anderson, Christopher. "I Love Lucy." Museum of Broadcast Communications. www.museum.tv/archives/etv/I/htmlI/ilovelucy/ilovelucy.htm (accessed February 2, 2011).

"Angry Patriots Confront Turncoat Senator Arlen Specter at Town Hall Meeting." YouTube. www.youtube.com/watch?v=jV1jmvMHsS0 (accessed February 21, 2011).

Appelbaum, Binyamin, and David Hilzenrath. "SEC Didn't Act on Madoff Tips." *Washington Post*, December 16, 2008. www.washingtonpost.com/wp-dyn/content/article/2008/12/15/AR2008121502971.html (accessed March 13, 2011).

Armstrong, Jerome, and Marcos Moulitsas. *Crashing the Gates: Netroots, Grassroots, and the Rise of People-Powered Politics*. White River Junction, VT: Chelsea Green Publishers, 2006.

ATK. "Our Values." ATK. www.atk.com/Values/values_ourvalues.asp (accessed April 18, 2011).

Austin v. Michigan Chamber of Commerce, 494 U.S. 652 (1990.

Bagdikian, Ben. *The Media Monopoly*. Boston: Beacon, 1987.

———. *The New Media Monopoly*. Boston: Beacon, 2004.

Bansky. *Exit Through the Gift Shop: A Banksy Film*. VHS, directed by Banksy. Paranoid Pictures, 2010.

Barber, Benjamin. *Strong Democracy: Participatory Politics for a New Age*. Berkeley: University of California Press, 1984.

"Barnie Frank Floored by Nazi Insult at Town Hall." YouTube. www.youtube.com/watch?v=OjF4YjvLJe4 (accessed February 21, 2011).

Barnouw, Erik. *A Tower in Babel*. New York: Oxford University Press, 1966.
Bartels, Larry. *Unequal Democracy*. Princeton, NJ: Princeton University Press, 2010.
Barthes, Roland. *The Pleasure of the Text*. Translated by Richard Miller. New York: Hill and Wang, 1975.
———. *S/Z*. Translated by Richard Miller. New York: Hill and Wang, 1974.
Batali, Dean. *Behind the Screen*. Edited by Barbara Nicolosi and Spencer Lewerenz. Grand Rapids, MI: Baker Books, 2005.
Bauerlein, Mark. *The Dumbest Generation*. New York: Penguin, 2008.
Baumann, Nick. "The House GOP's Plan to Redefine Rape." *Mother Jones*, January 28, 2011. motherjones.com/politics/2011/01/republican-plan-redefine-rape-abortion (accessed April 22, 2011).
Beck, Glenn. "What is Social Justice." FOX News. March 23, 2010. www.foxnews.com/story/0,2933,589832,00.html (accessed April 9, 2011).
"Beck and Pat: Scientists May Be Wrong on Global Warming Because God 'Is The Ultimate Scientist.'" Media Matters. August 22, 2011, mediamatters.org/mmtv/201108220013 (accessed November30, 2011).
Benen, Steve. "Not Intended to be a Factual Statement." *Washington Monthly*, April 9, 2011. www.washingtonmonthly.com/archives/individual/2011_04/028869.php (accessed April 18, 2011).
Benet, Lorenzo. "Kim Kardashian Sues Over Sex Tape." *People*, February 21, 2007. www.people.com/people/article/0,,20012494,00.html (accessed February 7, 2011).
Bennett, William. *The Death of Outrage: Bill Clinton and the Assault on American Ideals*. Florence, MA: Free Press, 1999.
Bentham, Jeremy. *An Introduction to the Principles of Morals and Legislation*. Oxford: Clarendon Press, 1823.
Bhatnagar, Parija. "Comcast's Roberts: Hungry for More." CNNMoney. February 11, 2004. money.cnn.com/2004/02/11/news/companies/comcast_robers/index.htm (accessed April 22, 2011).
"Bhutan—The Last Place." *Frontline*, aired May 1, 2002.
Bianco, Anthony. "The *New York Post*: Profitless Paper in Relentless Pursuit." *Bloomberg Businessweek*, February 21, 2005. www.businessweek.com/magazine/content/05_08/b3921114_mz016.htm (accessed March 13, 2011).
Blair, Jayson. "FCC to Waive Rules for Acquisition by Murdoch." *New York Times*, July 21, 2001.
Bloom, Harold. *Anxiety of Influence: A Theory of Poetry*. New York: Oxford University Press.
Bogan, Jesse. "America's Biggest Megachurches." *Forbes*, June 26, 2009. www.forbes.com/2009/06/26/americas-biggest-megachurches-business-megachurches.html (accessed March 26, 2011).
Bohmann, James. *Public Deliberation: Pluralism, Complexity, and Democracy*. Cambridge, MA: MIT Press, 2000.
Bookman, Jay. "Even Karl Rove, Wrong as He Is, Has a Right to be Heard." *Atlanta Journal Constitution*, March 30, 2010. blogs.ajc.com/jay-bookman-blog/2010/03/30/even-karl-rove-wrong-as-he-is-has-a-right-to-be-heard/?cxntfid=blogs_jay_bookman_blog (accessed February 21, 2011).
Breitbart, Andrew. "Breitbart: A Million Stories To Tell." *Washington Times*, January 5, 2009. www.washingtontimes.com/news/2009/jan/05/a-million-stories-to-tell/ (accessed April 10, 2011).
"Brief Time Out From Heated Discourse Has Ended." *Toledo Free Press*, February 14, 2011. www.toledofreepress.com/2011/02/14/brief-time-out-from-heated-discourse-has-ended/ (accessed April 22, 2011).
Brennan, Jason. *The Ethics of Voting*. Princeton NJ: Princeton University Press, 2011.
Brock, David. *Blinded by the Right: The Conscience of an Ex-Conservative*. New York: Crown, 2003.
———. *The Republican Noise Machine*. New York: Crown, 2004.
Brooks, David. "The Tea Party Teens." *New York Times*, January 5, 2010.

Bunch, Will. *Tear Down This Myth: The Right-Wing Distortion of the Reagan Legacy.* New York: Free Press, 2010.

Burke, Edmund. *Select Works of Edmund Burke.* Indianapolis: Liberty Fund, 1999.

Burns, Alexander. "Top Mitt Romney, Barack Obama Strategists Spar over Ad." Politico. November 23, 2011. www.politico.com/news/stories/1111/69047.html (accessed November 23, 2011).

Campbell, Joseph. *The Power of Myth.* New York: Doubleday, 1988.

Carlson, Margaret. "Getting Nasty." *Time,* June 19, 2001. www.time.com/time/magazine/article/0,9171,1101890619-152038,00.html (accessed March 13, 2011).

Carville, James. *. . . And The Horse He Rode In On: The People v. Kenneth Starr.* New York: Simon & Schuster, 1998.

Cassirer, Ernst. *An Essay On Man: An Introduction to a Philosophy of Human Culture.* Hamburg: Meiner Verlag, 2006.

Catechism of the Catholic Church. London: Burnes & Oates, 1999.

Chambers, Whittaker. "Big Sister Is Watching You." *National Review,* October 12, 2007. www.nationalreview.com/articles/222482/big-sister-watching-you/flashback (accessed November 30, 2011).

Chaves, Mark. "All Creatures Great and Small: Megachurches in Context." *Review of Religious Research* 47 (2006): 337.

Citizens United v. Federal Elections Commission. 558 U.S. 08-205 (2010).

Cloud, John. "Ms. Right." *Time,* April 17, 2005.

Colbert, Stephen. "Stephen Colbert's Blistering Performance Mocking Bush and the Press Goes Ignored by the Media." Democracy Now. May 3, 2006. www.democracynow.org/2006/5/3/stephen_colberts_blistering_performance_mocking_bush (accessed February 21, 2011).

Colford, Paul. *The Rush Limbaugh Story: Talent On Loan From God.* New York: St. Martin's Press, 1993.

Comcast Corporation. "Brian L. Roberts." Comcast. www.comcast.com/corporate/about/pressroom/corporateoverview/corporateexecutives/brianroberts.html (accessed April 22, 2011).

Condon, Stephanie. "FOX News' Roger Ailes: 'Tone It Down.'" CBS News. January 10, 2011. www.cbs.com/8301-503544_162-20028077-503544 (accessed April 22, 2011).

"Congresswoman Gabrielle Giffords Talks Palin Cross Hairs." MSNBC. YouTube. March 25, 2010. www.youtube.com/watch?v=R7046bo92a4&feature=player_embedded (accessed February 18, 2012).

"Conservative Attack Ad Pulled Amid Concerns It Falsely Accuses Tester over EPA Farm Dust Rules." *The Republic,* last modified November 11, 2011. www.therepublic.com/view/story/19478e87c8b44b2ea0f5e7e3ddbb8776/MT--Tester-Attack-Ad/ (accessed December 5, 2011).

Conwell, Russell. "Acres of Diamonds." American Rhetoric. www.americanrhetoric.com/speeches/rconwellacresofdiamonds.htm (accessed August 22, 2009).

Corporation, The. DVD. Directed by Jennifer Abbot and Mark Akbar. New York: Zeitgeist Films, 2005.

Costa, Robert. "Exclusive: House Minority Leader John Boehner on the Health-Care Vote." *National Review,* March 18, 2010. www.nationalreview.com/corner/196465/exclusive-house-minority-leader-john-boehner-health-care-vote/robert-costa (accessed April 22, 2011).

Cross, David. "David Cross—On Open Letter to Larry the Cable Guy (1 of 2)." YouTube. www.youtube.com/watch?v=DDimQTJMjB0 (accessed November 26, 2011).

Csikszentmihalyi, Mihaly. *Flow: The Psychology of Optimal Experience.* New York: Harper & Row, 1990.

Dahl, Robert. *A Preface to Democratic Theory.* Chicago: University of Chicago Press 2006.

"Dangerous Backlash," *The Daily Rundown,* MSNBC, March 25, 2010.

Davis, Karen, Cathy Schoen, and Kristof Stremkis. "Mirror, Mirror on the Wall: How the Performance of the US Health Care System Compares Internationally, 2010 Update." The Commonwealth Fund. June 2010. www.commonwealthfund.org/Content/Publications/Fund-Reports/2010/Jun/Mirror-Mirror-Update.aspx (accessed March 14, 2011).

Dean, John. *Conservatives Without Conscience.* New York: Penguin, 2006.

"'Democracy Uprising' in the U.S.A.? Noam Chomsky on Wisconsin's Resistance to Assault on Public Sector, the Obama-Sanctioned Crackdown on Activists, and the Distorted Legacy of Ronald Reagan." Democracy Now. February 17, 2011. www.democracynow.org/2011/2/17/democracy_uprising_in_the_usa_noam (accessed March 11, 2011).

DeNavas-Walt, Carmen, Bernadette Proctor, and Jessica Smith. *Income, Poverty and Health Insurance Coverage in the United States.* US Census Bureau, Washington, DC: US Government Printing Office, 2010.

Depaul, Jennifer. "David Stockman: US Is In 'Race to the Fiscal Bottom.'" *Fiscal Times,* October 6, 2010. www.thefiscaltimes.com/Articles/2010/10/06/David-Stockman-US-Is-in-Race-to-the-Fiscal-Bottom.aspx (accessed March 14, 2011).

DeToqueville, Alexis. *Democracy in America.* New Providence, NJ: Barnes and Noble Publishing, 2003.

Dewar, Helen, and Dana Milbank. "Cheney Dismisses Critic with Obscenity." *Washington Post,* June 25, 2004.

Dewey, John. *Democracy and Education.* New York: Macmillan, 1916.

Diamond, Jared. *The Third Chimpanzee.* New York: Perennial 1992.

"Doing the Devil's Work." *Columbia Journalism Review* 15 (Jan/Feb 1980): 22.

Donegan, Lawrence. "Serena Williams is Fined $10,500 for U.S. Open Line Judge Tirade." *Guardian,* September 9, 2009. www.guardian.co.uk/sport/2009/sep/13/serena-williams-tirade-us-open (accessed September 13, 2009).

Economist, The. "Murdoch's Revolving Door." July 18, 1992, 59.

Edsall, Thomas. "The Reinvention of Political Morality." *New York Times,* December 5, 2011. campaignstops.blogs.nytimes.com/2011/12/05/the-reinvention-of-political-morality/ (accessed December 5, 2011).

Edwards, Gavin. "Larry the Cable Guy Bared." *Rolling Stone,* March 11, 2008.

Eggerton, John. "FCC: Telepictures Productions' TMZ is a News Program." *Broadcasting & Cable,* May 2, 2008.

Ellingson, Stephen. *Megachurch and the Mainline: Remaking Religious Tradition in the Twenty-First Century.* Chicago: University of Chicago Press, 2007.

Ellul, Jacques. *The Technological Society.* Translated by K. Wilkinson. New York: Knopf, 1964.

Fang, Lee. "Pollutocrat David Koch Refuses to Answer Questions about Citizens United Secret Right-Wing Meetings." Think Progress. January 9, 2011. thinkprogress.org/romm/2011/01/09/207307/tea-party-pollutocrat-david-koch-climate-change-shrugs-off-his-carbon-pollution/ (accessed February 18, 2011).

Farhi, Paul. "How Low Can TV Go? Stay Tuned to Find Out." *Vancouver Sun,* March 14, 2000.

Federal Deposit Insurance Corporation. "History of the Eighties: Lessons for the Future." Federal Deposit Insurance Corporation, last updated June 5, 2000. www.fdic.gov/bank/historical/history/ (accessed March 13, 2011).

Finke, Roger, and Laurence Iannaccone. "Supply-Side Explanation for Religious Change." *Annals of the American Academy of Political and Social Science* 527 (1993): 29.

Fisher, Marc, and Jeff Leen. "A Church in Flux Is Flush With Cash; Moon Linked to Bewildering Array of Entities." *Washington Post,* November 23, 1997.

Fowler, Mark, and Daniel Brenner. "A Marketplace Approach to Broadcast Regulation." *Texas Law Review* 207 (60): 1–51.

Frank, Robert. *Falling Behind: How Rising Inequality Harms the Middle Class.* Berkeley, CA: University of California Press, 2007.

Frankfurt, Harry. *On Bullshit.* Princeton, NJ: Princeton University Press, 2005.

Fraser, Nancy. "Rethinking the Public Sphere: A Contribution to the Critique of Actual Existing Democracy." In *Habermas and the Public Sphere,* edited by C. Calhoun, 109–42. Cambridge, MA: MIT Press, 1999.

Frum, David. "When Did the GOP Lose Touch With Reality?" *New York,* November 20, 2011. nymag.com/print/?/news/politics/conservatives-david-fum-2011-11/index3.html (accessed December 5, 2011).

Fuller, Wayne Edison. *Morality and the Mail in Nineteenth-Century America.* Champaign: University of Illinois Press, 2003.

Furguson, Thomas, and Joel Rogers. *Right Turn.* New York: Hill and Wang, 1987.

Furman, Phyllis. "Cruise-ing to Top of Forbes' Celeb 100." *Daily News*, June 16, 2006.

Gadamer, Hans-Georg. *Philosophical Hermeneutics.* Berkeley, CA: University of California Press, 1977.

———. *Truth and Method.* Translated by J. Weinsheimer and D. Marshall. New York: Crossroad, 2004.

Gans, Herbert. *Deciding What's News: A Study of CBS Evening News, NBS Nightly News, Newsweek, and Time.* New York: Pantheon, 1979.

———. *Popular Culture and High Culture.* New York: Basic Books, 1999.

Gebser, Jean. *The Ever-Present Origin.* Translated by Noel Barstad and Algis Mickunas. Athens: Ohio University Press, 1985.

Gerber, George, and Larry Gross. "Living With Television: The Violence Profile." *Journal of Communication* 26 (1976): 172–99.

Gerth, Jeff. "A Savings and Loan Bailout, and Bush's Son Jeb." *New York Times*, October 14, 1990. www.nytimes.com/1990/10/14/us/a-savings-and-loan-bailout-and-bush-s-son-jeb.html?pagewanted=all&src=pm (accessed March 13, 2011).

Gewirtz, David. "Heated Rhetoric, Social Networks, and Armed Psychos: A Deadly Combination?" ZDNew Government. January 10, 2011. www.zdnet.com/blog/government/heated-rhetoric-social-networks-and-armed-psychos-a-deadly-combination/9845 (accessed April 18, 2011).

"Gingrich: Snub Causes Impasse—Treatment On Air Force One Blamed." *Seattle Times*, November 16, 1995. community.seattletimes.nwsource.com/archive/?date=19951116&slug=2152925 (accessed March 11, 2011).

Gladwell, Malcolm. *Outliers: The Story of Success.* New York: Little Brown, 2008.

"Glass-Steagall Act (1933)." *New York Times.* topics.nytimes.com/topics/reference/timestopics/subjects/g/glass_steagall_act_1933/index.html (accessed March 14, 2011).

Gomez, Juan Usma. "Dialogue with Pentecostals." Eternal Word Television Network. www.ewtn.com/library/CURIA/PCCUPENT.HTM (accessed March 26, 2011).

"Gravely Ill, Atwater Offers Apology." *New York Times*, January 13, 1991. www.nytimes.com/1991/01/13/us/gravely-ill-atwater-offers-apology.html (accessed March 13, 2011).

Greenblatt, Alan, and Tracie Powell. "Rise of Megachurches." *CQ Researcher*, September 21, 2007. www.library.cqpress.com.

Greider, William. *The Education of David Stockman.* New York: Signet, 1987.

Griffiths, Katherine. "Sir Howard Stringer, US Head of Sony: Sony's Knight Buys Tinseltown Dream." *Independent*, September 18, 2004. www.independent.co.uk/news/business/news/sir-howard-stringer-us-head-of-sony-sonys-knight-buys-tinseltown-dream-6161447.html (accessed April 22, 2011).

Grossman, Cathy Lynn. "As Their Numbers Stall, Megachurches Seek 'Seekers,'" *USA Today*, September 9, 2008. www.usatoday.com/news/religion/2008-09-08-megachurches-numbers_N.htm (accessed May 27, 2012).

Grynbaum, Michael, and Michael Barbaro. "Paladino Is Taunting in a Letter to Cuomo." *New York Times*, September 19, 2010. www.nytimes.com2010/09/20/nyregion/20paladino.html (accessed April 22, 2011).

Guinness, Os. *The Case for Civility.* New York: Harper One, 2008.

Habermas, Jurgen. *The Structural Transformation of the Public Sphere.* Translated by Thomas Burger and Frederick Lawrence. Cambridge, MA: MIT Press, 1991.

Hagin, Ken E. "How God Taught Me About Prosperity." Law of Abundance Living. www.law-of-abundance-living.com/faith-and-finances.html (accessed March 26, 2011).

Hall, Edward. *The Dance of Life.* New York, Doubleday, 1983.

———. *The Silent Language.* New York: Doubleday, 1959.

Halonen, Doug. "'MNF' Next Indecency Target." *Television Week*, November 22, 2004.

Hamilton, Alexander, James Madison, and John Jay. *The Federalist Papers.* New York: SoHo Press, 2011.

Hannity, Sean. "Hannity: Waking Up the 'Obama Zombies'" FOX News. March 25, 2010. www.foxnews.com/story/0,2933,590004,00.html (accessed February 18, 2012).

Harper, Jennifer. "Talk Radio Voices Bailout Anguish: Listeners Seek Calm From Hosts." *Washington Times*, September 30, 2008.

Hasson, Judi. "Welfare Enters Whole New World Rules Could Take Years to Settle In." *USA Today*, August 23, 1996.

"Heisman Trust Calls Report Inaccurate." ESPN. September 8, 2010. sports.espn.go.com/los-angeles/ncf/news/story?id=5542215 (accessed March 11, 2011).

Henry, Jules. *Culture Against Man*. New York: Vintage, 1963.

Herbst, Susan. *Rude Democracy*. Philadelphia, PA: Temple University Press, 2010.

Hobbes, Thomas. *Leviathan*. London: Greed Dragon in St Paul's Church-yard, 1651.

Hofstradter, Richard. *Anti-Intellectualism in American Life*. New York: Vintage, 1966.

Holmes, Oliver Wendell. "U.S. Supreme Court: Abrams vs. U.S., 250 U.S. 616 (1919)." Find-law. caselaw.lp.findlaw.com.

Holmes, Stephen. "Gun Control Bill Backed by Reagan in Appeal to Bush." *New York Times*, March 29, 1991.

Homans, George. *Social Behavior*. New York: Harcourt, Brace and World, 1961.

———. "Social Behavior as Exchange." *American Journal of Sociology* 63 (1958): 597–606.

Horkheimer, Max, and Theodor Adorno. *Dialectic of Enlightenment*. Translated by E. Jephcott. Palo Alto, CA: Stanford University Press, 2007.

Huff, Richard. "It's Howard, Raw and Ready." *New York Daily News*, December 11, 2005.

Hughes, William. "Ronald Reagan: B Film Actor, Ladies' Man and FBI Snitch." *American Chronicle*, November 12, 2008. www.americanchronicle.com/articles/view/81186 (accessed March 14, 2011).

Hulse, Carl. "Arlen Specter's Closing Argument." *New York Times*, December 21, 2010. the-caucus.blogs.nytimes.com/2010/12/21/arlen-specters-closing-argument/ (accessed March 14, 2011).

"Hunting Witches." *Washington Post*, July 23, 2005. www.washingtonpost.com/wp-dyn/con-tent/article/2005/07/22/AR2005072201658.html (accessed March 14, 2011).

Husserl, Edmund. *The Crisis of the European Sciences and Transcendental Phoenomenology*. Translated by D. Carr. Evanston, IL: Northwestern University Press, 1970.

Hutchinson, Bill. "Viagra Holds Up Limbaugh for Three Hours." *Daily News*, June 17, 2006.

"Immigration Issue Draws Thousands Into Streets." MSNBC. March 25, 2006. www.msnbc.msn.com/id/11442705/ns/politics/t/immigration-issue-draws-thousands-streets/ (accessed February 7, 2011).

Jackson, John. *PastorPreneur*. Friendswood, TX: Baxter Press, 2003.

Jackson, Maggie. *Distracted: The Erosion of Attention and the Coming Dark Age*. Amherst, NY: Prometheus, 2008.

James, Susan Donaldson. "J. Crew Ad With Boy's Pink Toenails Creates Stir." ABC News. April 13, 2011. abcnews.go.com/Health/crew-ad-boy-painting-toenails-pink-stirs-transgen-der/story?id=13358903 (accessed April 18, 2011).

Jamieson, Kathleen Hall, and Joseph Capella. *Echo Chamber*. New York: Oxford University Press, 2008.

Janis, Irving. *Groupthink*. Orlando, FL: Houghton Mifflin, 1982.

———. *Victims of Groupthink*. Boston, MA: Houghton Mifflin, 1972.

Jefferson, Thomas. *The Jefferson Cyclopedia*. Edited by John Foley. New York: Funk & Wagnalls, 1900.

Johnson, Allie. "Bill Would Force UI to Sell $140 Million Pollack Painting." *Daily Iowan*, February 10, 2011.

Johnson, Dennis. *Campaigning in the Twenty-First Century: A Whole New Ballgame*. New York: Routledge, 2010.

Johnson, Maggie. *Distracted*. Amherst, NY: Prometheus Books, 2009.

Kenyon, Essek William. "Jesus the Healer." scribd. www.scribd.com/doc/31209152/Jesus-the-Healer (accessed March 26, 2011).

Khan, Huma. "'Man Up Harry Reid': Sharron Angle Attacks, Questions How Reid Made Money." ABC News. October 15, 2010. abcnews.go.com/Politics/vote-2010-elections-sharron-angle-attacks-harry-reid/story?id=11886670 (accessed April 22, 2011).

Kleefeld, Eric. "Rand Paul Gives Lesson in Ayn Rand and Light Bulbs." TPM. April 12, 2011. tpmdc.talkingpointsmemo.com/2011/04/rand-paul-gives-senate-lesson-in-ayn-rand-and-light-bulbs-video.php (accessed November 30, 2011).

Klein, Joe. *Politics Lost.* New York: Broadway Books, 2007.

Knowlton, Brian. "Bush 'Satisfied' with Cheney Tale; Delay in Announcing Hunting Accident had Raised Questions." *International Herald*, February 17, 2006.

Koop, C Everett. *Koop: The Memoirs of America's Family Doctor.* New York: Zondervan, 1992.

Koop, C. Everett, and Timothy Johnson. *Let's Talk: An Honest Conversation on Critical Issues: Abortion, AIDS, Euthanasia, Health Care.* New York: Zondervan, 1992.

Kramarae, Cheris. *Woman and Men Speaking: Frameworks for Analysis.* Rowley, MA: Newbury House, 1981.

Kramer, Eric Mark. "The Body in Communication." In *The Body in Human Inquiry: Interdisciplinary Explorations of Embodiment*, edited by Vincent Berdayes, Luigi Esposito, and John Murphy. Cresskill, NJ: Hampton Press, 2004.

—. "Dimensional Accrual and Dissociation: An Introduction." In *Communication, Comparative Cultures, and Civilizations*, edited by Jeremy Grace, 156–242. Cresskill, NJ: Hampton, In Press.

The Emerging Monoculture: Assimilation and the "Model Minority." Westport, CT: Praeger, 2003.

———. *A Prolegomena to an Ethic for Digital Deception: Rationale for an Ethic for New Technologies of Ontogenesis: Modernity and Visiocentris.* Department of Defense, American Forces Information Services, The Pentagon.

———. "Videocentrism." *Proceedings for the Twenty-Fifth Annual Husserl Circle.* Chicago: DePaul University Press, 1993.

———. "Visiocentrism." *The Journal of the Bulgarian Journalist Association* 36 (1994): 37–40.

Kramer, Eric Mark, and Richiko Ikeda. "Defining Crime: Signs of Postmodern Murder and the 'Freeze' Case of Yoshihiro Hattori." *The American Journal of Semiotics* 17 (2001): 7–84.

Kramer, Eric Mark, and Tae-Sik Kim. "The Global Network of Players." In *Globalization and the Prospects for Critical Reflection*, edited by J. M. Choi and J. W. Murphy, 183–211. Delhi: Aakar Books, 2009.

Krugman, Paul. "Reagan Did It." *New York Times.* May 31, 2009. www.nytimes.com/2009/06/01/opinion/01krugman.html (accessed March 13, 2011).

Lakoff, George. *Don't Think of an Elephant: Know Your Values and Frame the Debate—The Essential Guide for Progressives.* White River Junction, VT: Chelsea Green Publishers, 2004.

Larry the Cable Guy, *Git-R-Done.* New York: Three Rivers Press, 2006.

Lattman, Peter. "Sumner Redstone's Longtime Lawyer is Viacom's New CEO." *Wall Street Journal*, September 5, 2006. blogs.wsj.com/law/2006/09/05/sumner-redstones-longtime-lawyer-is-viacoms-new-ceo/ (accessed April 22, 2011).

Lessig, Lawrence. "Forward." In *The Future of the Internet and How To Stop It*, by Jonathan Zittrain, vii–iix. New Haven, CT: Yale University Press, 2008.

Levine, Robert. *A Geography of Time: On Tempo, Culture, and the Pace of Life.* New York: Basic, 1998.

Lewis, Michael. *Liar's Poker.* New York: Penguin, 1990.

"Limbaugh Letter Fetches $2.1 Million on eBay." FOX News. October 21, 2007. www.foxnews.com/story/0,2933,303569,00.html (accessed March 14, 2011).

Limbaugh, Rush. "Rush Limbaugh." *Wikiquote.* en.wikiquote.org/wiki/Rush_Limbaugh (accessed September 9, 2009).

Linkins, Jason. "Obama Smoking Picture: Andrea Mitchell Investigates." *Huffington Post*, December 17, 2008. www.huffingtonpost.com/2008/12/17/obama-smoking-picture-and_n_151787.html (accessed January 31, 2011).

Lippmann, Walter. *The Public Philosophy.* New Brunswick, NJ: Transaction Publishers, 2009.

Liu, Marian. "Kurt Cobain's Death, 15 Years Later, Being Marked with Friday Tribute." *Seattle Times,* April 6, 2009. seattletimes.nwsource.com/html/musicnightlife/2008993909_zmus06dispatchcobain.html.

"The Long March of Newt Gingrich." PBS. January 1996. www.pbs.org/wgbh/pages/frontline/newt/newtchron.html (accessed March 11, 2011).

Los Angeles Times, The. "Gingrich's Daffy 'Insight.'" September 17, 2010.

Lowenstein, Roger. *When Genius Failed: The Rise and Fall of Long-Term Capital Management.* New York: Random House, 2001.

Lowry, Brian. "Tuning In." *Variety,* August 21, 2005, 14.

Luhmann, Niklas. *Art as a Social System.* Translated by E. Knodt. Palo Alto, CA: Stanford University Press, 2000.

Luther, Martin. *The Familiar Discourses of Dr Martin Luther.* Translated by Henry Bell. London: Sussex Press, 1818.

MacDorman, Marian, and T. J. Mathews. "Behind International Rankings of Infant Mortality: How the US Compares with Europe." Centers for Disease Control and Prevention. November 2009. www.cdc.gov/nchs/data/databriefs/db23.htm (accessed March 14, 2011).

MacLaine, Shirley. *My Lucky Stars: A Hollywood Memoir.* New York: Bantam, 1996.

Madoff, Bernard. "From Prison, Madoff Says Banks 'Had to Know' of Fraud." *New York Times,* February 15, 2011. www.nytimes.com/2011/02/16/business/madoff-prison-interview.html?pagewanted=all (accessed March 11, 2011).

Mahar, Karen Ward. *Women Filmmakers in Early Hollywood.* Baltimore, MD: Johns Hopkins University Press, 2006.

Mann, Bill. "Limbaugh's Dirty Little Secret of Radio 'Success'" *Huffington Post,* April 12, 2009. www.huffingtonpost.com/bill-mann/limbaughs-dirty-little-se_b_185965.html (accessed January 31, 2011).

Martens, Maggie. "Chart: Comparing Health Reform Bills: Democrats and Republicans 2009, Republicans 1993." *Kaiser Health News,* February 24, 2010. www.kaiserhealthnews.org/Graphics/2010/022310-Bill-comparison.aspx (accessed February 21, 2011).

Mathews, John Joseph. *Life and Death of an Oilman.* Norman: University of Oklahoma Press, 1951.

Mathison, Keith. *The Shape of Sola Scriptura.* Moscow, ID: Canon Press, 2001

Mattera, Jason. "Does Al Franken Even Know What Was in the Helath-Care Bill He Voted For? Um . . . Nope." YouTube. www.youtube.com/watch?v=VFXr3if_y1A&feature=player_embedded#at=37 (accessed February 21, 2011).

———. "Rep. Charlie Rangel Swears at Jason Mattera Over Scandal Questions." YouTube. www.youtube.com/watch?v=rdtFWCrCh0s&feature=related (accessed February 21, 2011).

Mayer, Jane. "Covert Operations: The Billionaire Brothers Who Are Waging a War Against Obama." *New Yorker,* August 30, 2010. www.newyorker.com/reporting/2010/08/30/100830fa_fact_mayer (accessed February 18, 2011).

McCarthy, Kate. "Wisconsin Governor Scott Walker: We're Broke and Can't Negotiate." ABC News. February 21, 2011. abcnews.go.com/blogs/politics/2011/02/wisconsin-governor-scott-walker-were-broke-and-cant-negotiate/ (accessed March 20, 2011).

McDougal, Susan. *The Woman Who Wouldn't Talk.* New York: Simon & Schuster, 2003.

McGrory, Mary. "Contra-Intuitive." *Washington Post,* July 8, 2001.

McMorris-Santoro, Evan. "Trump Warns Cantor Not to Give Up Birther Fight: 'People Love This Issue'" TPM. April 16, 2011. tpmdc.talkingpointsmemo.com/2011/04/the-donald-warns-republicans-not-to-give-up-the-birther-fight.php (accessed April 18, 2011).

Media Matters for America. "Savage: Obama 'Is a Neo-Marxist Fascist Dictator in the Making.'" Media Matters for America. March 6, 2009. mediamatters.org/mmtv/200903060012 (accessed April 22, 2011).

Medved, Michael. *The Five Big Lies About American Business: Combating Smears Against the Free Market Economy.* New York: Random House, 2009.

———. *Hollywood vs. America.* New York: Harper, 1993.

Messerli, Jonathan. *Horace Mann: A Biography.* New York: Knopf, 1972.

Meyrowtz, Josh. *No Sense of Place: The Impact of Electronic Media on Social Behavior.* New York: Oxford University Press, 1985.

Michaels, David. *Doubt Is Their Product: How Industry's Assault on Science Threatens Your Health.* New York: Oxford University Press, 2008.

Mill, John Stuart. *On Liberty.* London: John W. Parker and Son, 1959.

Miller Center of Public Affairs. *American President: A Reference Resource.* millercenter.org (accessed March 11, 2011).

Minow, Newton. "Television and the Public Interest." American Rhetoric. www.americanrhetoric.com/speeches/newtonminow.htm (accessed November 26, 2011).

Minutaglio, Bill. "Bush Buys Land Near Crawford: Town Expects Changes After 1,500-Acre Deal." *Dallas Morning News*, August 10, 1999.

Mitavalli, John. "PBS Facing Crisis." *Television Week*, October 20, 2003, 1.

Montopoli, Brian. "237 Millionaires in Congress." CBS News. November 6, 2009. www.cbsnews.com/8301-503544_162-5553408-503544.html (accessed February 16, 2011).

Moody, Nekesa Mumbi. "West Gives VMAs Rude Awakening." *Washington Post*, September 14, 2009.

Moore, Stephen. "'Atlas Shrugged': From Fiction to Fact in 52 Years." *Wall Street Journal*, January 9, 2009. online.wsj.com/article/SB123146363567166677.html (accessed November 30, 2011).

Morris, Desmond. *The Human Zoo.* New York: Kodansha, 1969/1996.

Morris, Edmund. *Dutch: A Memoir of Ronald Reagan.* New York: Modern Library, 2000.

Mortenson, Chris. "Smith Sends E-mail Detailing Opposition." ESPN. October 12, 2009. sports/espn.go.com/nfl/news/story?id=4551010 (accessed March 14, 2011).

Mouffe, Chantal. *The Return of the Political: Radical Thinkers.* New York: Verso, 2006.

Mumford, Lewis. *The City In History.* New York: MJF Books, 1989.

Newspaper Association of America Business Analysis and Research Department. "Daily Newspaper Readership Trends—Age (1998–2007)." Newspaper Association of America. www.naa.org/Trends-and-Numbers/Readership/~/media/NAACorp/Public%20Files/TrendsAndNumbers/Readership/Age_Daily_National_Top50_98-07.ashx (accessed February 21, 2011).

"Nielsen Television (TV) Ratings: Network Primetime Averages." Zap2it. mserv.zap2it.com/tv/ratings/network/ (accessed November 26, 2011).

Noelle-Neumann, Elisabth. *The Spiral of Silence.* Chicago: University of Chicago, 1993.

Norman, Michael. "TV's Arsenio Hall: Late-Night Cool." *New York Times*, October 1, 1989.

"Obama: The College Years." *Time.* www.time.com/time/photogallery/0,29307,1866765,00.html (accessed January 31, 2011).

"Obama on *60 Minutes*." CBS News. September 13, 2009. www.cbsnews.com/video/watch/?id=5305734n (accessed February 10, 2011).

Ogunnaike, Lola. "Sex, Lawsuits and Celebrities Caught On Tape." *New York Times*, March 19, 2006. query.nytimes.com/gst/fullpage.html?res=9C07E6DB1E31F93AA25750C0A9609C8B63&pagewanted=all (accessed February 7, 2011).

Olbermann, Keith. "Countdown With Keith Olbermann." YouTube. www.youtube.com/watch?v=rdtFWCrCh0s&feature=related (accessed February 21, 2011).

———. "A Veto of the FISA Bill 'Endangers Americans.'" MSNBC. February 14, 2008. www.msnbc.msn.com/id/23173388/ns/msnbc_tv-countdown_with_keith_olbermann/t/veto-fisa-bill-endangers-americans/ (accessed April 22, 2011).

Olson, Lester, and Thomas Goodnight. "Entanglements of Consumption, Cruelty, Privacy, and Fashion: The Social Controversy over Fur" *Quarterly Journal of Speech* 80 (1994): 249–76.

Oney, Steve. "Citizen Breitbart: The Web's New Right-Wing Impresario." *Time*, March 25, 2010. www.time.com/time/magazine/article/0,9171,1975339,00.html (accessed February 21, 2011).

Oppel, Jr., Richard. "Word For Word/Energy Hogs; Enron Traders on Grandma Millie and Making Out Like Bandits." *New York Times*, June 13, 2004.

O'Reilly, Bill. "The O'Reilly Factor." YouTube. www.youtube.com/watch?v=rdtFWCrCh0s&feature=related (accessed February 21, 2011).

Oreskes, Naomi, and Erik Conway. *The Merchants of Doubt: How a Handful of Scientists Obscured the Truth on Issues From Tobacco Smoke to Global Warming.* New York: Bloomsbury Press, 2010.

Osteen, Joel. "Choose to Bless Your Future." Joel Osteen Ministries Notes. January 27, 2009. www.facebook.com/note.php?note_id=46479064421 (accessed August 11, 2009).

Pareene, Alex. "Karl Rove Spending Millions Lying About Everyone." Salon. November 16, 2011. www.salon.com/topic/crossroads_gps/ (accessed December 5, 2011).

"Part 1—Frank Zappa at PMRC Senate Hearing on Rock Lyrics." Video, 1985. YouTube. www.youtube.com/watch?v=lxB-ZePpS7E (accessed November 26, 2011).

Patterson, Thomas. *Out of Order.* New York: Vintage, 1994.

Paul, Ron, interview by Rebecca Diamon. "US Representative." Rep. Ron Paul Is Interviewed on FOX Business Network. FOX Business Network. June 17, 2009.

Pein, Corey. "Blog-Gate." *Columbia Journalism Review* 1 (January/February 2005): 30–35.

Perlow, Leslie. "The Time Famine: Toward a Sociology of Work Time," *Administrative Science Quarterly* 44 (1999): 57–81.

"Pete Stark Won't Pee on Your Leg." Politico. September 15, 2009. www.politico.com/blogs/glennthrush/0909/Pete_Stark_wont_pee_on_your_leg.html (accessed January 31, 2011).

Pew Research Center for the People and the Press. "Growing Number of Americans Say Obama Is a Muslim: Religion, Politics, and the President." Pew Research Center. August 19, 2010. www.people-press.org/2010/08/19/growing-number-of-americans-say-obama-is-a-muslim/ (accessed February 21, 2011).

Phillips, Kendall. "A Rhetoric of Controversy." *Western Journal of Communication* 63 (1999): 488–510.

Piven, Frances Fox. "Crazy Talk and American Politics: Or, My Glenn Beck Story." *Chronicle of Higher Education,* February 10, 2011. chronicle.com/article/Crazy-TalkAmerican/126334/ (accessed February 19, 2012).

Planned Parenthood. "Planned Parenthood At A Glance." Planned Parenthood. www.plannedparenthood.org/about-us/who-we-are/planned-parenthood-glance-5552.htm (accessed April 18, 2011).

Plato. *Plato: Complete Works.* Edited by John M. Cooper. Indianapolis: Hacket Publishing Company, 1997.

———. *Plato Gorgias and Aristotle Rhetoric.* Translated by Joe Sachs. Newburyport, MA: Focus Publishing, 2009.

Pope Paul VI. "Dogmatic Constitution of the Church—Lumen Gentium." Christus Rex at Redemptor Mundi. November 21 1964. www.christusrex.org/www1/CDHN/v3.html (accessed March 26, 2011).

Postman, Neil. *Amusing Ourselves to Death.* New York: Penguin, 1986.

Pritchard, Gregory. *Willow Creek Seeker Services: Evaluating a New Way of Doing Church.* Grand Rapids, MI: Baker, 1996.

Putnam, Robert. *Bowling Alone: The Collapse and Revival of American Community.* New York: Simon & Schuster, 2000.

Rand, Ayn. "A Defense of Ethical Egoism." In *Moral Philosophy,* edited by Louis Pojman. Indianapolis: Hacket Publishing Company, 2003.

———*Atlas Shrugged.* New York: Plume, 1999.

———. *Letters of Ayn Rand.* Edited by Michael Berliner. New York: Plume, 1995.

———. "The Only Path To Tomorrow." *Readers Digest,* January (1944): 88–90.

———. *The Virtue of Selfishness.* New York: Signet, 1964.

Raymond, Allen. *How to Rig An Election: Confessions of a Republican Operative.* New York: Simon & Schuster, 2008.

Reagan, Ron. *My Father at 100.* New York: Viking Adult, 2011.

Reagan, Ronald. "Executive Order 12294—Suspension of Litigation Against Iran." The American Presidency Project. February 24, 1981. www.presidency.ucsb.edu/ws/index.php?pid=43455&st=12294&st1=#axzz1mlQhoVeq (accessed March 14, 2011).

———. *This American Life.* New York: Simon & Schuster, 1990.

Reed, Travis. "Study: NFL Has Slightly More Latino, Asian Players." *USA Today,* August 27, 2008.

Rendall, Steve. "An Aggressive Conservative vs. a 'Liberal To Be Determined.'" FAIR. November/December 2003. www.fair.org/index.php?page=1158 (accessed March 14, 2011).

Rich, Frank. "Closet Clout." *New York Times*, February 2, 1995.

"Robert A. Iger." *Forbes*. people.forbes.com/profile/robert-a-iger/79382 (accessed April 22, 2011).

Rocchio, Christopher, and Steve Rogers. "MTV to Debut New 'Tila Tequila' Bisexual Reality Dating Show October 9." Reality TV World. September 7, 2007. www.realitytvworld.com/news/mtv-debut-new-tila-tequila-bisexual-reality-dating-show-october-9-5753.php (accessed March 11, 2011).

Rodda, Chris. *Liars for Jesus: The Religious Right's Alternate Version of American History*, vol. 1. Charleston, SC: BookSurge, 2006.

Rollins, Ed. *Bare Knuckles and Back Rooms: My Life in American Politics*. New York: Broadway/Doubleday, 1997.

Romney, Mitt. "Transcript: Mitt Romney's Faith Speech." National Public Radio. December 6, 2007. www.npr.org/templates/story/story.php?storyId=16969460 (accessed November 30, 2011).

Rose, Charlie. *An Hour with Jeff Zucker*. Televised interview, recorded December 2, 2010.
———. *An Hour with Mel Karmazin*. Televised interview, recorded October 10, 2007.

Rose, Lacey. "Glenn Beck Inc." *Forbes*. April 26, 2010. www.forbes.com/forbes/2010/0426/entertainment-fox-news-simon-schuster-glenn-beck-inc_print.html (accessed August 8, 2010).

Rousseau, Jean-Jacques. *Discourse on Inequality*. Translated by G. D. H. Cole. Whitefish, MT: Kessinger Publishing, 2004.
———. *The Social Contract and Discourses by Jean-Jacques Rousseau*. Translated by G. D. H. Cole. Toronto: J. M. Dent and Sons, 1923.

Russakoff, Dale. "He Knew What He Wanted:Gingrich Turned Disparate Lessons into a Single-Minded Goal." *Washington Post*, December 18, 1994.

Russell, James. "Evangelical Audiences and 'Hollywood' Film: Promoting Fireproof." *Journal of American Studies* 44 (2010): 391–407.

"Savings and Loan Association." *New York Times*. topics.nytimes.com/top/reference/timestopics/subjects/s/savings_and_loan_associations/index.html (accessed March 13, 2011).

Sayre, Nora. "Assaulting Hollywood." *World Policy Journal* 12 (December 1995): 51.

Schlesinger, Robert. "Poll: Birthers Now Make Up a Majority of Republican Primary Voters." *USNews*, February 16, 2011. www.usnews.com/opinion/blogs/robert-schlesinger/2011/02/16/poll-birthers-now-make-up-a-majority-of-gop-primary-voters (accessed February 21, 2011).

Schudson, Michael. "The Concept of Politics in Contemporary US Journalism." *Political Communication* 24 (2007): 131–42.

Schwarz, Gabriella. 'Cheney, Rumsfeld Face Jeers and Cheers." CNN. February 10, 2011. politicalticker.blogs.cnn.com/2011/02/10/cheney-rumsfeld-face-jeers-and-cheers/ (accessed April 22, 2011).

Searle, Adrian. "Painted Screams." *Guardian*, September 9, 2009. www.guardian.co.uk/artand-design/2008/sep/09/bacon.art

Seidman, Robert. *Monday Cable*. Zap2it. August 16, 2011. tvbythenumbers.zap2it.com/ (accessed November 25, 2011).

Selcraig, Bruce. "The Worst Newspaper in America." *Columbia Journalism Review* 37 (January/February 1999): 46–51.

Shahid, Aliyah. "Tea Party Candidates, Joe Miller, Clint Didier, Jane Norton Try to Knock Off Republicans Across the US." *NY Daily News*, July 3, 2010. articles.nydailynews.com/2010-07-03/news/27068993_1_tea-party-express-candidates-gop-senate (accessed February 16, 2011).

Shaxson, Nicholas. *Treasure Island*. London: Bodley Head, 2011.

Sidoti, Liz. "CPAC Speeches & Fiery Attacks Suggest 2012 Campaign Has Begun." *Huffington Post*. February 13, 2011. www.huffingtonpost.com/2011/02/13/cpac-speeches-fiery-attac_n_822677.html (accessed February 14, 2011).

Siler, Wes. "Obama's New Cadillac Limo Officially Unveiled," Jalopnik. January 14, 2009. jalopnik.com/5131380/obamas-new-cadillac-limo-officially-unveiled (accessed November 30, 2011).

Slansky, Paul. *The Clothes Have No Emperor.* Riverside, NJ: Simon & Schuster, 1989.

Sloterdijk, Peter. *Critique of Cynical Reason.* Minneapolis: University of Minnesota Press, 2001.

Smith, Adam. *The Wealth of Nations.* New York: Penguin, 1999.

"Smothers Feels 'A Lot of Pain' Over FCC Skirmish." *Chattanooga Times Free Press*, April 24, 2004.

Sombart, Werner. "Medieval and Modern Commercial Enterprise." In *Enterprise and Secular Change: Readings in Economic History*, edited by Frederick Lane and Jelle Riemnersma. New York: R. D. Irwin, 1953.

Sonmez, Felicia. "Who Is 'Americans for Prosperity?'" *Washington Post*, August 26, 2011. voices.washingtonpost.com/thefix/senate/who-is-americans-for-prosperit.html (accessed February 16, 2011).

Specter, Arlen. "Full Text of Arlen Specter's Farewell Speech." New Mexico Central. December 22, 2010. nm-central.com/blog/?p=1657 (accessed March 4, 2011).

Spitz, David. "Preface." In *On Liberty*, by John Stuart Mill. New York: Norton, 1975.

Stecklow, Steve. "WSJ Editor's Resignation Is Criticized by Committee." *Wall Street Journal*, April 30, 2008.

Steptoe, Sonja. "The Man with the Purpose." *Time*, March 29, 2004.

Stern, Christopher. "Court Ends 'Fairness Doctrine.'" *Washington Post*, October 12, 2000.

Stockman, David. *The Triumph of Politics—The Crisis in American Government and How It Affects the World.* New York: Bodley Head, 1981.

Stonebraker, Robert. "Optimal Church Size: The Bigger the Better," *Journal for the Scientific Study of Religion* 32 (1993): 231–41.

Sunstein, Cass. *Republic.com.* Princeton, NJ: Princeton University Press, 2009.

Szalai, Georg. "Analyst: Howard Stern-Sirius XM Contract Worth $400 Million." *Hollywood Reporter*, December 9, 2010. www.hollywoodreporter.com/news/analyst-howard-stern-sirius-xm-58336 (accessed January 31, 2011).

Tapper, Jake. "Coming out Shooting." Salon. May 2, 1999. www.salon.com/1999/05/02/nra/ (accessed February 7, 2011).

Task Force on Inequality and American Democracy. "American Democracy in an Age of Rising Inequality." *American Political Science Association.* 2004. www.apsanet.org/img-test/taskforcereport.pdf (accessed February 17, 2012).

Thomas, Clarence. *My Grandfather's Son.* New York: HarperCollins, 2007.

Thompson, E. P. *The Making of the English Working Class.* New York: Penguin, 1980.

Thomas, Devon. "Kendra Wilkinson Sex Tape Video: 'People Are Going to Judge Me and Stuff.'" CBS News. June 1, 2010. www.cbsnews.com/8301-31749_162-20006408-10391698.html&usg=AFQjCNEgNUSWiwSls03yCFkjvkF6tLK0CA (accessed February 7, 2011).

Thoreau, Henry David. *Walden: A Fully Annotated Edition.* New Haven, CT: Yale University Press, 2004.

Thornton, Emily. "Roads to Riches." *Businessweek*, May 7, 2007. www.businessweek.com/magazine/content/07_19/b4033001.htm (accessed April 18, 2011).

Thumma, Scott. "Exploring the Megachurch Phenomena." Hartford Institute for Religion Research. hirr.hartsem.edu/bookshelf/thumma_article2.html (accessed March 25, 2011).

Thumma, Scott, and Warren Bird. "Changes in American Megachurches: Tracing Eight Years of Growth and Innovation in the Nation's Largest-Attendance Congregations," Hartford Institute for Religion Research, accessed March 25, 2011, hirr.hartsem.edu/megachurch/Changes%20in%20American%20Megachurches%20Sept%2012%202008.pdf.

Thumma, Scott, Dave Travis, and Warren Bird, "Megachurches Today 2005: Summary of Research Findings." Hartford Institute for Religion Research. hirr.hartsem.edu/megachurch/megastoday2005summaryreport.pdf (accessed March 26, 2011).

"Tim Bishop Protest, Setauket, NY." YouTube. www.youtube.com/watch?v=UOLs7Cybnqw (accessed February 21, 2011).

Time Warner Corporation. "Jeffrey L. Bewkes." TimeWarner. www.timewarner.com/our-company/management/senior-corporate-executives/jeffrey-l-bewkes/ (accessed April 22, 2011).

"Timeline: Ronald Reagan's Life." PBS. www.pbs.org/wgbh/americanexperience/features/timeline/reagan/ (accessed March 14, 2011).

Tolchin, Martin. "Federal Grand Jury Indicts Ex-Chairman of Silverado." *New York Times*, September 11, 1992. www.nytimes.com/1992/09/11/business/federal-grand-jury-indicts-ex-chairman-of-silverado.html?ref=neilbush (accessed March 13, 2011).

Trent, Judith. "Presidential Surfacing: The Ritualistic and Crucial First Act." *Communication Monographs* 45 (1978): 281–92.

"Trump Fortune Revealed." CNN. September 22, 2010. edition.cnn.com/TRANSCRIPTS/1009/22/sitroom.02.html (accessed February 21, 2011).

Tuccille, Jerome. *Alan Shrugged: Alan Greenspan, The World's Most Powerful Banker.* Hoboken, NJ: Wiley, 2002.

Tucker, Neely. "Limbaugh Spins Reid's Letter into Charity Gold." *Washington Post*, October 20, 2007.

Twitchell, James. *Branded Nation: The Marketing of Megachurch.* New York: Simon & Schuster, 2004.

———. *Lead Us into Temptation: The Triumph of American Capitalism.* New York: Columbia University Press, 2000.

US Census Bureau. "Educational Attainment in the United States: 2008." US Census Bureau. September 22, 2010. www.census.gov/hhes/socdemo/education/data/cps/2008/tables.html (accessed March 11, 2011).

"US Slipping in Education Rankings." UPI. November 19, 2008. www.upi.com/Top_News/2008/11/19/US-slipping-in-education-rankings/UPI-90221227104776/ (accessed April 2, 2011).

"Van Jones 'Is an Avowed, Self-avowed Radical Revolutionary Communist.'" *Tampa Bay Times* (PolitiFact). September 8, 2009. www.politifact.com/truth-o-meter/statements/2009/sep/08/glenn-beck/glenn-beck-says-van-jones-avowed-communist/ (accessed February 21, 2011).

Vanderberg, Marcus. "Controversy Haunts Cam Newton's Heisman Quest." The Grio. December 10, 2010. www.thegrio.com/sports/controversy-haunts-cam-newtons-heisman-quest.php (accessed March 11, 2011).

Varadarajan, Tunku. "In Defense of Tea Parties." *Daily Beast*, January 10, 2010. www.thedailybeast.com/articles/2010/01/11/in-defense-of-tea-parties.html (accessed February 5, 2011).

Vega, Tanzina. "Be Wary of the Gold Rush." *New York Times*, May 22, 2010.

Von Drehle, David, and Howard Schneider. "Foster's Death a Suicide." *Washington Post*, July 1, 1994.

Walsh, Lawrence. *Firewall: The Iran-Contra Conspiracy and Cover-Up.* New York: Norton, 1998.

Watts, Thomas, and Richard Whittle. "Rumors about Foster Attacked at Whitewater Hearing; Senate Panel Opens Sessions With Focus on Death of Aide." *Dallas Morning News*, July 30, 1994.

Weber, Max. *The Protestant Ethic and the Spirit of Capitalism.* Mineola, NY: Dover, 2003.

"William Buckley on Ayn Rand & Atlas Shrugged." YouTube. www.youtube.com/watch?v=5KmPLkiqnO8 (accessed November 30, 2011).

Weigel, David. "Rand Paul Telling the Truth." *Washington Post*, May 20, 2010. voices.washingtonpost.com/right-now/2010/05/rand_paul_telling_the_truth.html (accessed February 7, 2011).

Weinberger, David. *Everything Is Miscellaneous.* New York: Times Books, 2007.

Weinstein, Adam. "Tea Party Leader Plans to Infiltrate Union Goons." *Mother Jones*, February 20, 2011. motherjones.com/mojo/2011/02/tea-party-leader-plan-infiltrate-wisconsin-seiu-wiunion (accessed February 21, 2011).

Weiss, Joana. "With Fewer Limits, Will Stern Still Have a Shtick?" *Boston Globe*, December 11, 2005.

Williams, Lee. "DIY Self-Defense is Teen's Goal." *Oregonian*, August 8, 2006. www.oregonlive.com/living/oregonian/index.ssf?   /base/living/115499853367770.xml& coll=7 (accessed October 9, 2009).

Wolfe, Alan. "Hobbled From the Start." Salon. December 15, 2000. www.salon.com/2000/12/15/trust_4/ (accessed February 2, 2011).

Wolfensberger, Don. "Civility, Society and Politics: Is There a Problem?" Woodrow Wilson International Center for Scholars. September 19, 2007. www.wilsoncenter.org/sites/default/files/Civility-rmks-drw-9-19-07.pdf (accessed February 18, 2012).

Wood, Ellen. *Democracy Against Capitalism*. Cambridge: Cambridge University Press, 1995
———. *The Origin of Capitalism*. New York: Verso, 2002.

Zaitchick, Alexander. "Common Sense: Glenn Beck and the Triumph of Ignorance." Salon. September 21, 2009. www.salon.com/news/feature/2009/09/21/glenn_beck/print.html (accessed March 14, 2011).

Zaller, John. *The Nature and Origins of Mass Opinion*. Cambridge, MA: Cambridge University Press, 1992.

Zinn, Howard. *A People's History of the United States: 1492–Present*. New York: Harper Perennial Modern Classics, 2005.

Zucco, Tom. "Rush's Drug Use Has Palm Beach in Tizzy." *St. Petersburg Times*, December 14, 2003.

Index

About the Authors

Philip Dalton, PhD, assistant professor and chair of speech communication, rhetoric, and performance studies, teaches courses in political communication, argumentation and debate, qualitative research methods, and intercultural communication. His research has examined national political strategy and political semiotics. He is the author of two books, including a study of swing voting in the United States (*Swing Voting: Understanding Late Deciders in Late Modernity*) and an edited volume examining communication and culture. Other works have appeared in the *Western Journal of Communication*, the *Atlantic Journal of Communication*, and *The American Journal of Semiotics*.

Eric Mark Kramer, PhD, is full professor of communication at the University of Oklahoma. He is also affiliate faculty in the College of International Studies as well as Film and Media Studies. He is editor of the book series Communication and Comparative Cultures, associate editor of *Journal of Intercultural Communication Research* and founding editor of the *Journal of Intercultural Communication*. He is author of seven books including a best-selling and award-winning intercultural textbook in Japan, and several articles and book chapters. He has chaired over forty doctoral dissertations and is a coordinator in the University of Oklahoma's international relations interdisciplinary master's degree. He has been a Fulbright Scholar.